THE RAILWAY THROUGH THE CENTRAL HIGHLANDS

DAVID PRICE

AMBERLEY

Front Cover: Class 5 No. 44871 works through the passing loop at Slochd Summit with the Great Britain tour on 30 April 2016.

Back Cover: Class 66 No. 66432 has just crossed Culloden viaduct with the Inverness to Mossend Tesco working on 2 May 2016.

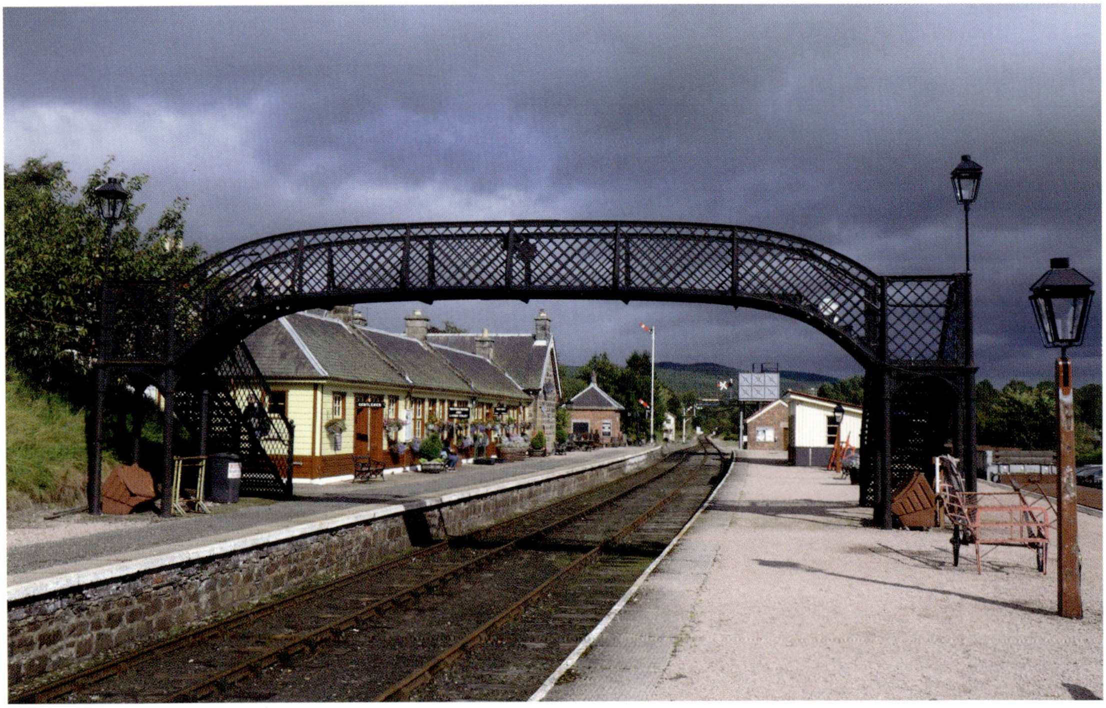

The restored Highland Railway station at Boat of Garten on the preserved Strathspey line on 11 September 2019.

First published 2022

Amberley Publishing
The Hill, Stroud
Gloucestershire, GL5 4EP

www.amberley-books.com

ISBN 978 1 3981 0229 3 (print)
ISBN 978 1 3981 0230 9 (ebook)

British Library Cataloguing in Publication Data.
A catalogue record for this book is available from the British Library.

Typesetting by SJmagic DESIGN SERVICES, India.
Printed in the UK.

Introduction

Situated at a crossing point of the River Tay, Perth has long been one of the most important cities in Scotland. Its position at the ends of Strathtay and Strathearn made it a useful transport route, with roads converging there from several directions, so it became a natural meeting point as railways were constructed in the 1840s. The Scottish Central Railway reached Perth in 1848 with a line from Glasgow, and within a short period of time routes from Dundee, Fife and Forfar were using Perth General station, the latter entering from the north.

With its location at the head of the Great Glen, alongside the Moray Firth, Inverness became the main town of the Highlands as routes from all directions met there. Its strategic position led to a fairly turbulent history, but a period of prosperity ensued when the Caledonian Canal opened in 1822, providing a safe inland link between the North Sea and the Atlantic Ocean, and by the 1840s the town was looking to establish railway connections to the south.

The Monadliath and Grampian mountains presented a formidable barrier to communication through the Central Highlands but there was an easier route available by going east to Aberdeen and south from there, although this was noticeably further. In 1845, the Great North of Scotland Railway was floated to build a line from Aberdeen to Inverness, but a direct line through the mountain was then proposed by a group including Joseph Mitchell, a civil engineer who had worked on road building in the Highlands. When the Bills were presented to Parliament only the Great North of Scotland's was approved. However, that company had already incurred major debts so work was not started until November 1852 and it became obvious that it would be some time before the line would be completed. In 1854, separate powers were obtained to build the Inverness & Nairn Railway, and this was opened on 6 November 1855 with later extensions to Elgin and Keith, where it eventually met the G.N.S. In the meantime, the Perth & Dunkeld Railway had obtained powers for a line between those places, and this was opened on 7 April 1856, sharing the section to Stanley Junction with the Scottish Midland line to Forfar.

Relations between the Highland and Great North of Scotland railways were always difficult and there remained inconvenience at Aberdeen with separate stations for onward travel. A new company, the Inverness & Perth Junction Railway, made another attempt to establish a more direct route by heading south from Forres and an Act was passed on 22 July 1861. This company agreed to take over the Perth & Dunkeld and the through line was opened in stages, the final section from Aviemore to Pitlochry being completed in September 1863. It was mainly single track with passing loops, although the difficult section from Blair Atholl to Dalwhinnie was double-track and a branch from Ballanluig to Aberfeldy was added in 1865. Mergers of the Inverness-based companies resulted in the formation of the Highland Railway in June 1865.

There followed a period of consolidation on this line and expansion to the north and west, but the Highland realised that their domination of Inverness was under threat when an independent company, backed by the North British Railway, proposed a route from Glasgow to Crianlarich and on to Fort William via Glencoe. Their plans also included an extension through the Great Glen to Inverness. The mileage from Glasgow to Inverness via this route was 160 miles, whereas the distance using the Highland and its connecting company, the Caledonian, was around 210.

The Highland decided to build a more direct line from Inverness to Aviemore, joining the existing route there and saving about 25 miles compared to the original distance. This was opened on 1 November 1898. Substantial engineering work was required with two very large viaducts over the rivers Findhorn and Nairn and other major viaducts at Carrbridge, Slochd and Tomatin, with difficult climbs up to 1 in 60 in places. This was established as the main line, with the original section reduced to secondary status.

A line from Glasgow to Fort William via Rannoch Moor was built by the West Highland Railway, opening in 1894. Both the Highland and North British companies put forward various plans to link to Inverness but in the event the only line built in the Great Glen was a local branch from Spean Bridge to Fort Augustus, which was closed to passengers as early as 1933. Thus the Highland had Inverness to itself.

The First World War saw much additional traffic on the line, with naval and military equipment and personnel to Inverness and beyond. The company struggled to cope, having to borrow additional locomotives and rolling stock, and was in a very rundown state at the end of the war. It was incorporated into the London, Midland & Scottish Railway at the Grouping in 1923 but managed to retain much of its individuality over the period until nationalisation in 1948. Despite the increased competition from road traffic, services continue with little change until the 1960s, when diesel traction replaced steam. The Aberfeldy branch was closed completely in May 1965 and the original line from Aviemore to Forres followed in October. Express trains to Aberdeen were diverted away from the Forfar line, it was reduced to freight only and finally closed completely from Stanley Junction onwards in May 1982. Fortunately a section of the original route from Aviemore has been reopened by the Strathspey Railway, initially to Boat of Garten in 1978 and later extended to Broomhill, with plans in place to reach Grantown. Here preserved steam and diesel locomotives operate for much of the year.

The line currently sees a busy service of units operating between Inverness and Glasgow or Edinburgh, with a daily service to and from London King's Cross and a sleeper service to and from Euston. There are also freight workings and occasional visits from the luxurious Royal Scotsman touring train as well as some diesel-hauled and steam charters. The line offers a superb journey through ever-changing landscapes. Hopefully this selection of the author's photographs, taken over the last four decades, will encourage the reader to travel the line and enjoy the beauty of the Central Highlands.

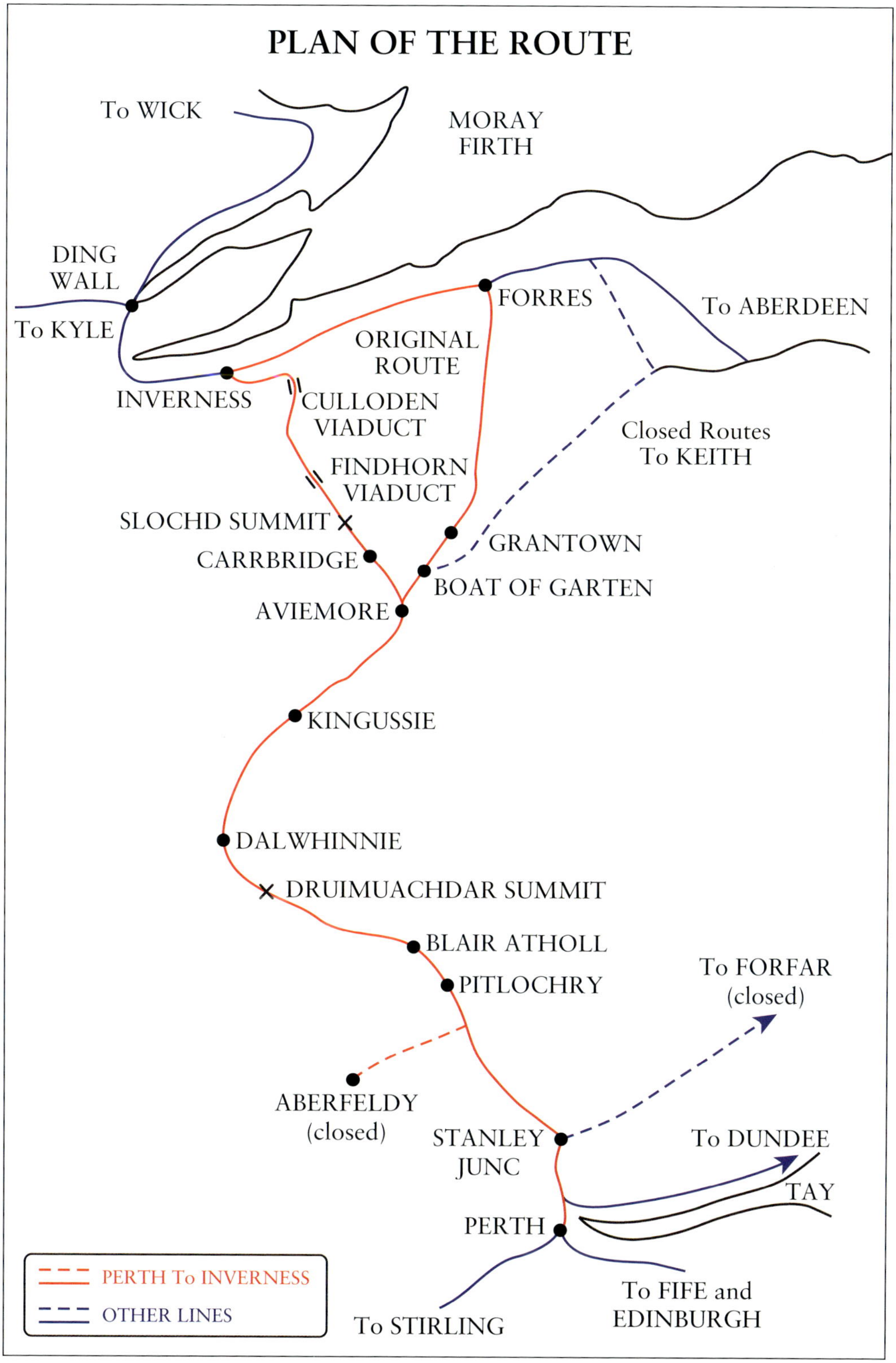
PLAN OF THE ROUTE
To WICK
MORAY FIRTH
DING WALL
To KYLE
FORRES
To ABERDEEN
ORIGINAL ROUTE
INVERNESS
CULLODEN VIADUCT
Closed Routes To KEITH
FINDHORN VIADUCT
SLOCHD SUMMIT
GRANTOWN
CARRBRIDGE
BOAT OF GARTEN
AVIEMORE
KINGUSSIE
DALWHINNIE
DRUIMUACHDAR SUMMIT
BLAIR ATHOLL
PITLOCHRY
To FORFAR (closed)
ABERFELDY (closed)
STANLEY JUNC
To DUNDEE
TAY
PERTH
PERTH To INVERNESS
OTHER LINES
To FIFE and EDINBURGH
To STIRLING

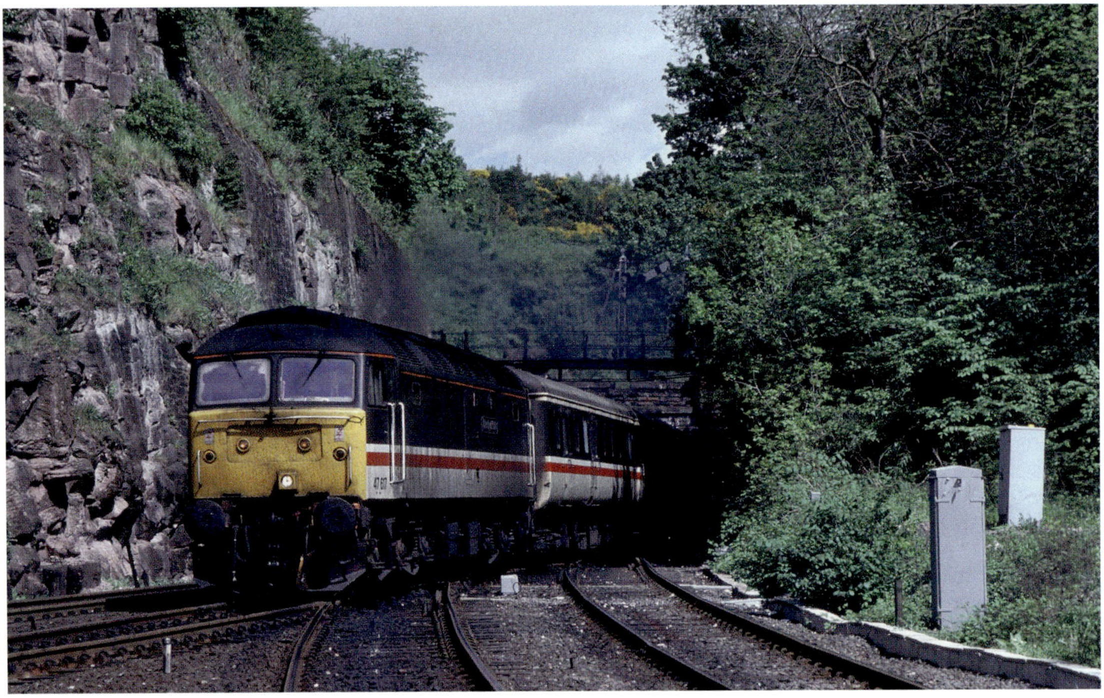

Class 47 No. 47617 leaves Hilton Tunnel and takes the line to Stirling on 23 May 1991.

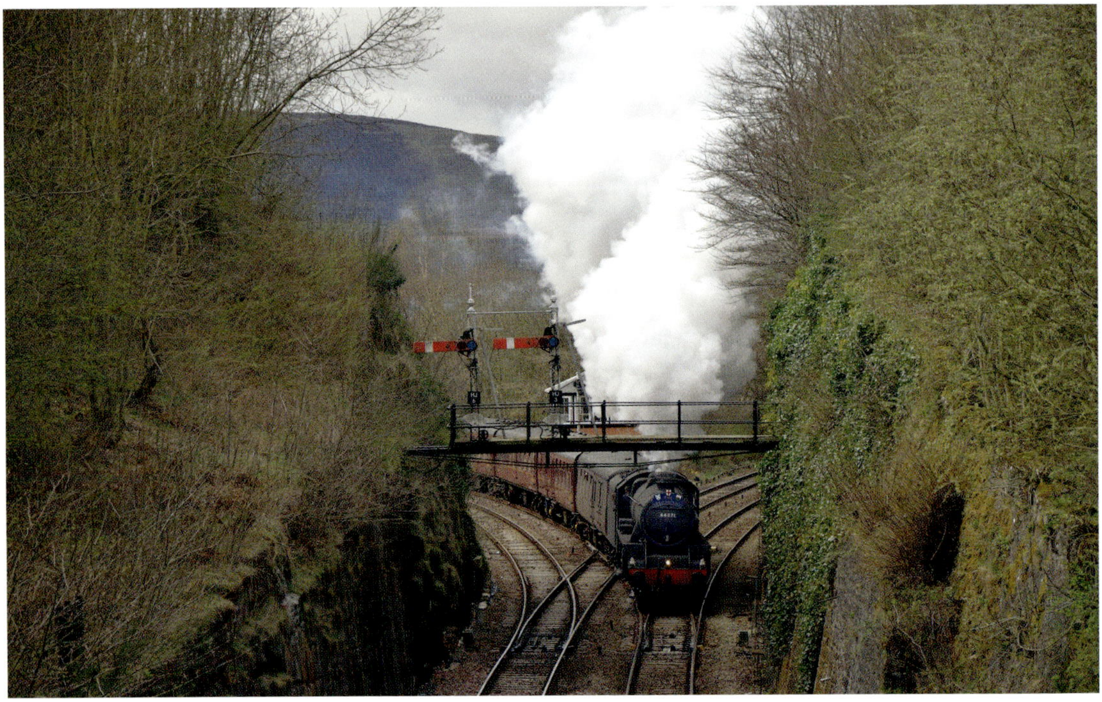

Class 5 No. 44871 comes off the line from Ladybank at Hilton Junction with the Edinburgh to Inverness leg of the Great Britain VI tour on 25 April 2013.

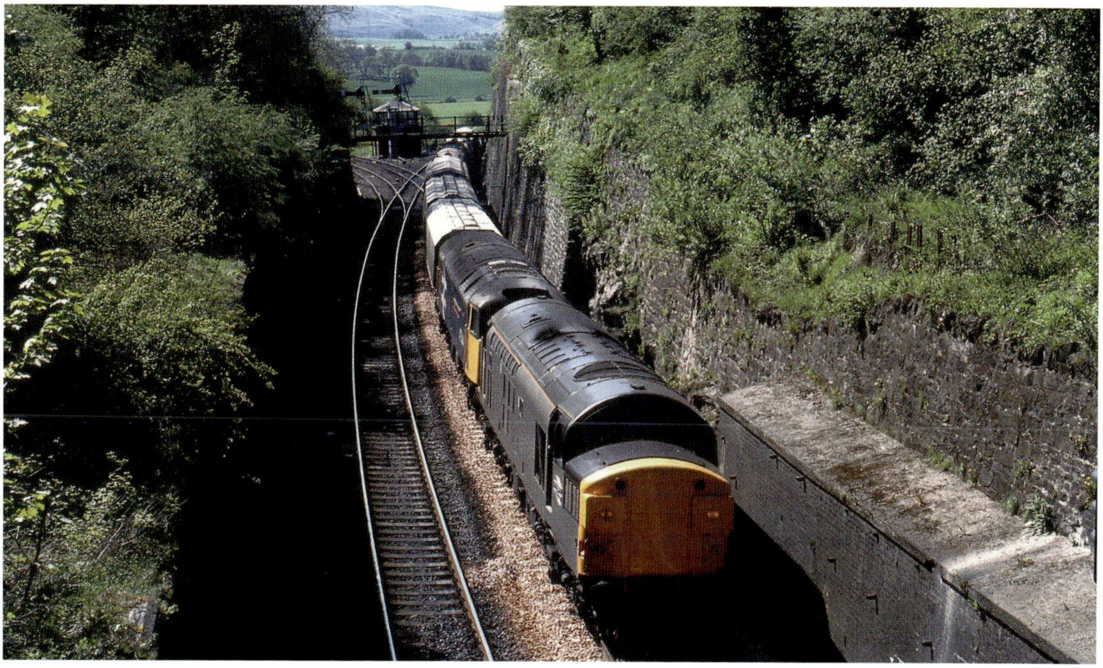

A northbound freight, double-headed by Class 37 and 47 locomotives, approaches Hilton Tunnel on 5 May 1990.

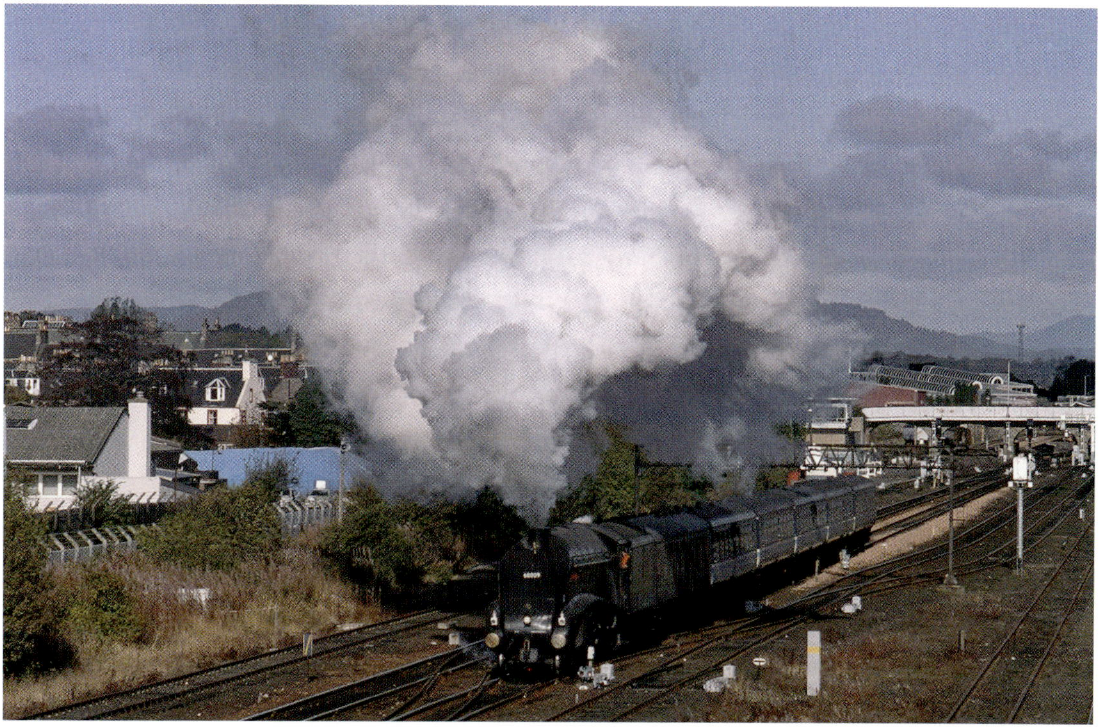

A4 Pacific 60009 *Union of South Africa* leaves Perth with a crew training trip on 15 October 1993.

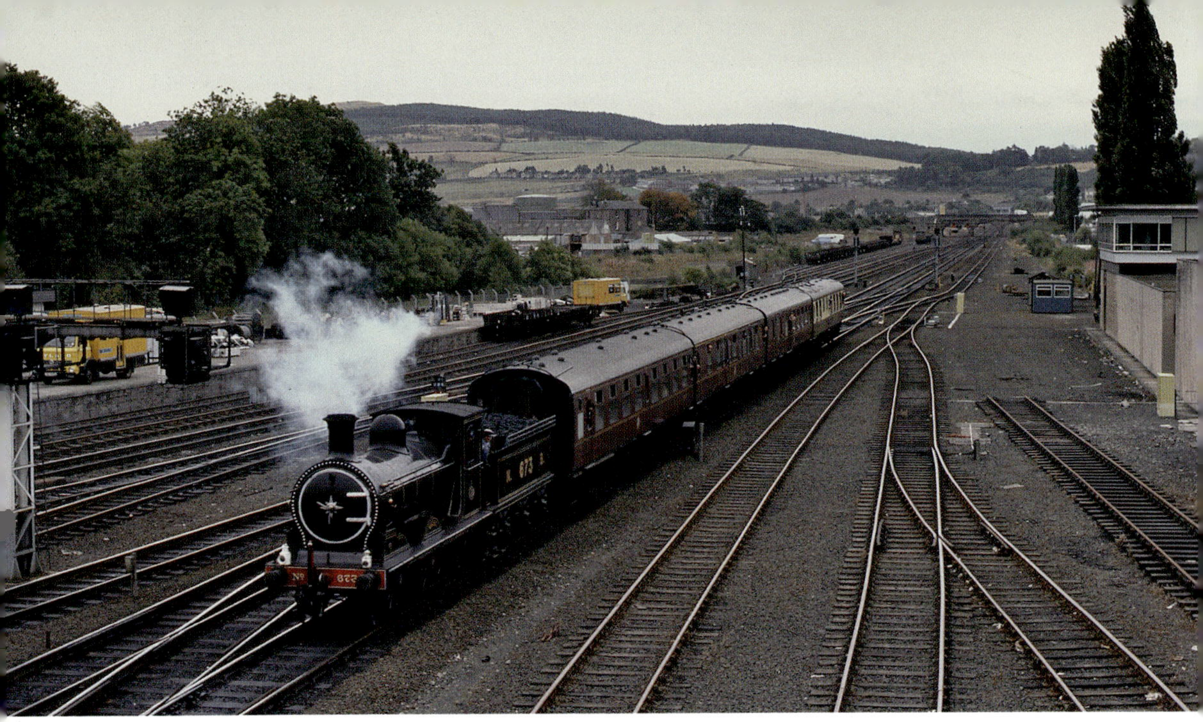

North British Railway Class C No. 673 *Maude* approaches Perth station with a northbound SRPS tour on 20 September 1986.

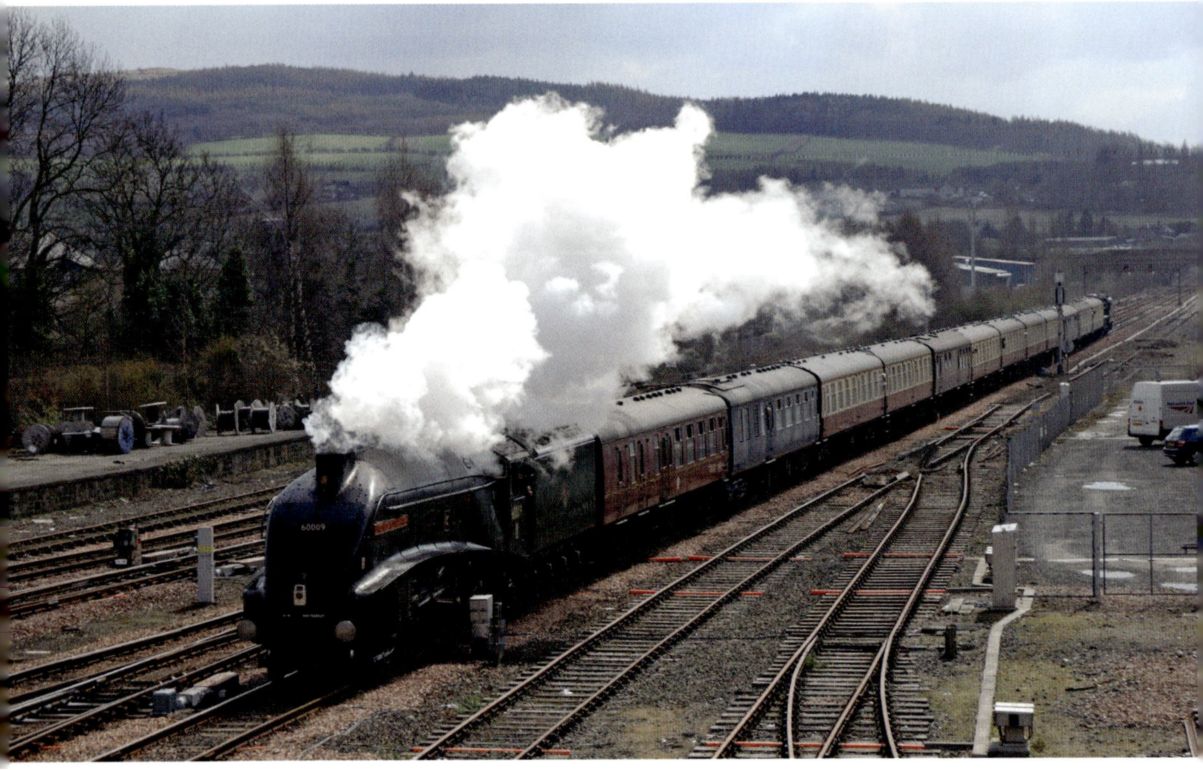

A4 60009 takes the North Briton tour back into Perth station on 13 April 2008. The train had been hauled from Dundee to Perth by Class 5 No. 45407, running tender-first.

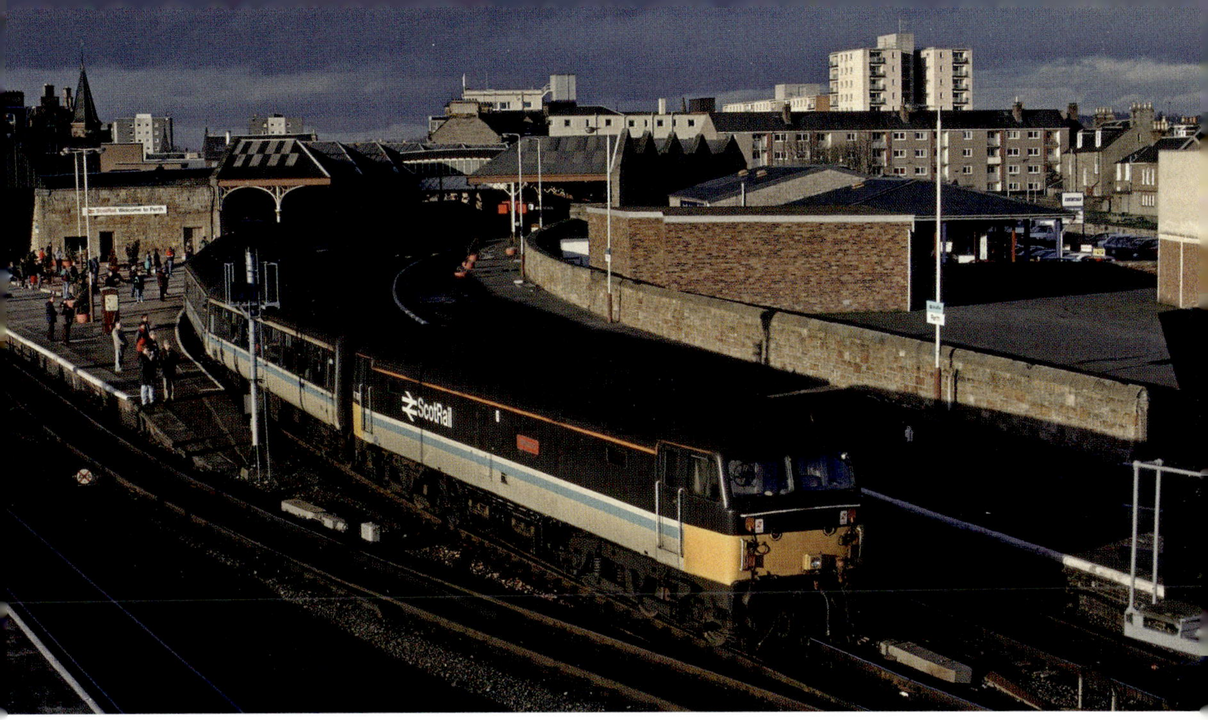

Class 47 No. 47707 waits in the Dundee platforms at Perth station with a train to Glasgow on 4 March 1990.

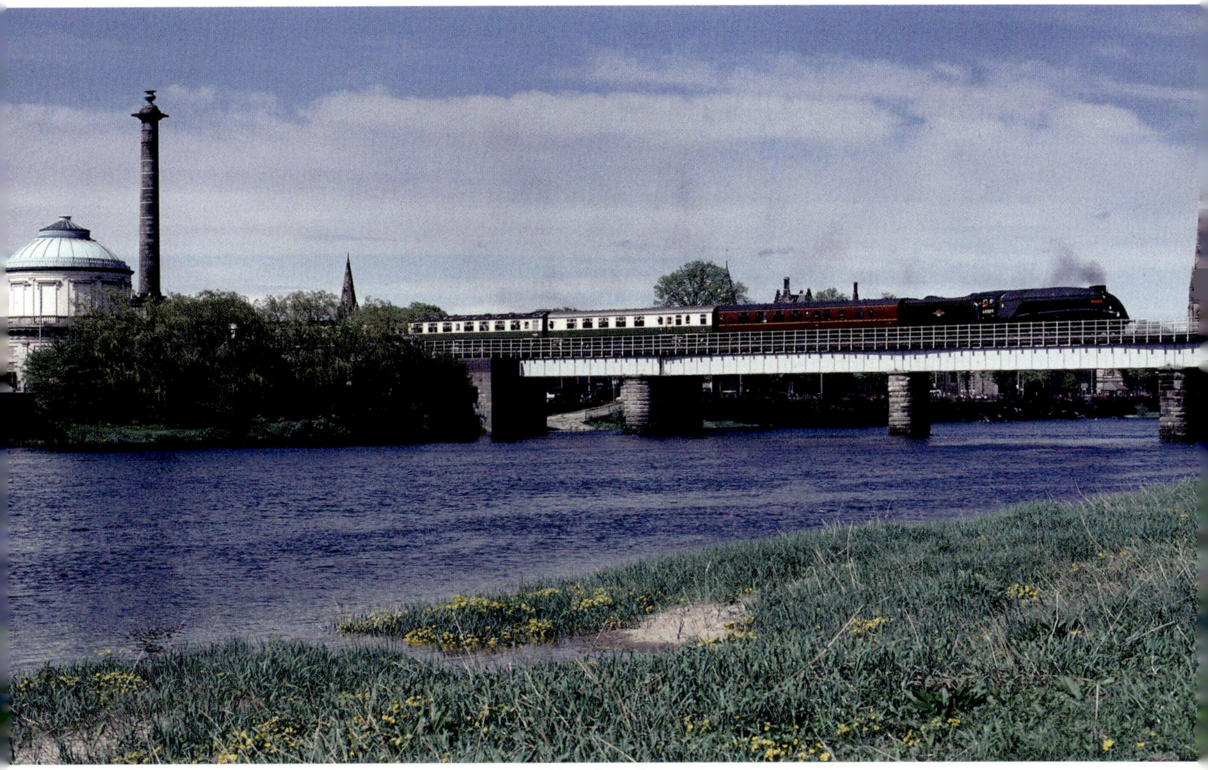

A4 60009 crosses the River Tay with a tour to Aberdeen on 5 May 1990. At that time it had been renamed *Osprey*.

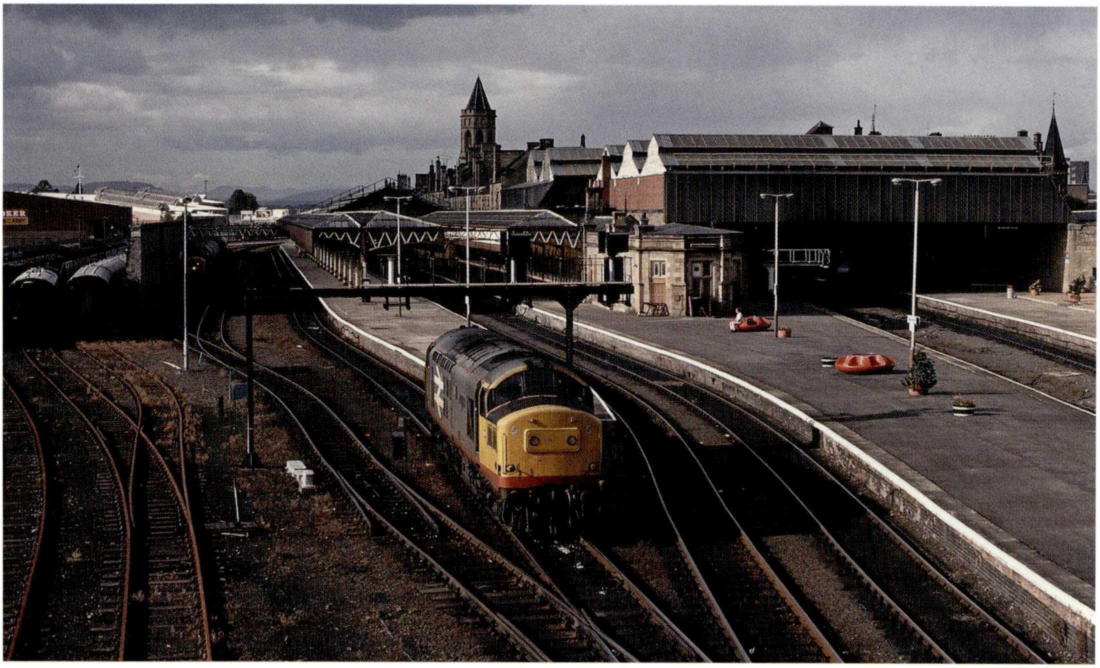

A view of Perth station from the south on 8 September 1989. Class 37 No. 37196 is in the foreground with a classmate just visible further back.

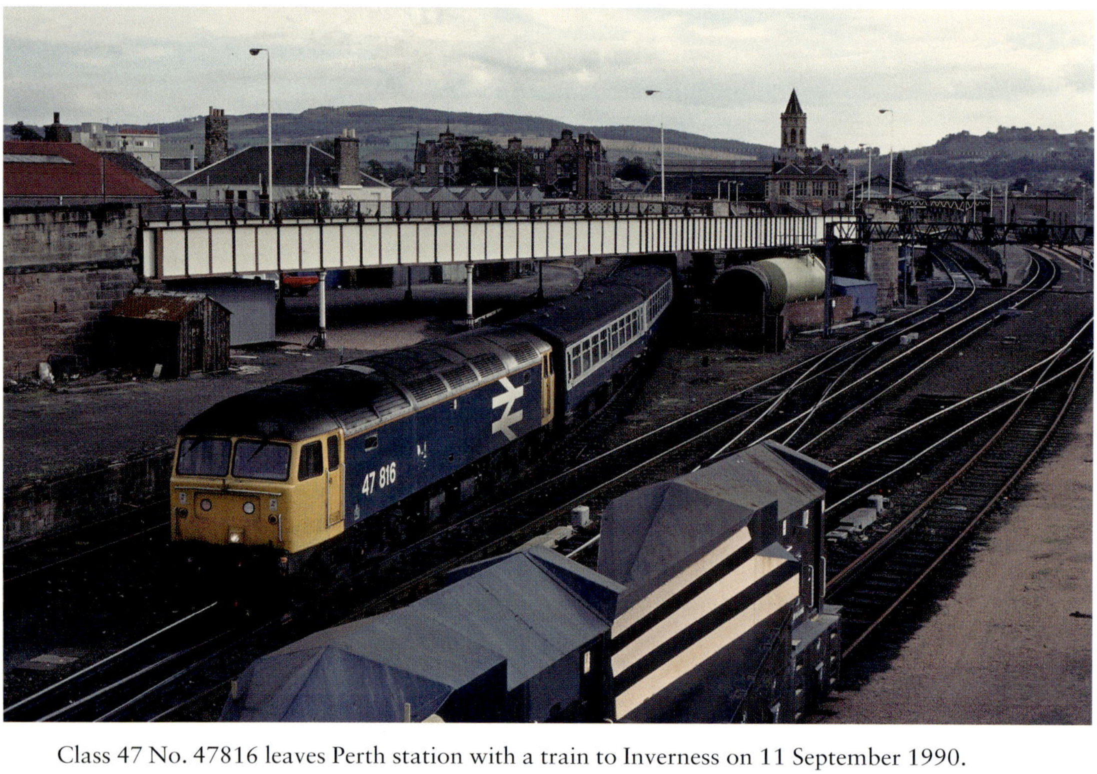

Class 47 No. 47816 leaves Perth station with a train to Inverness on 11 September 1990.

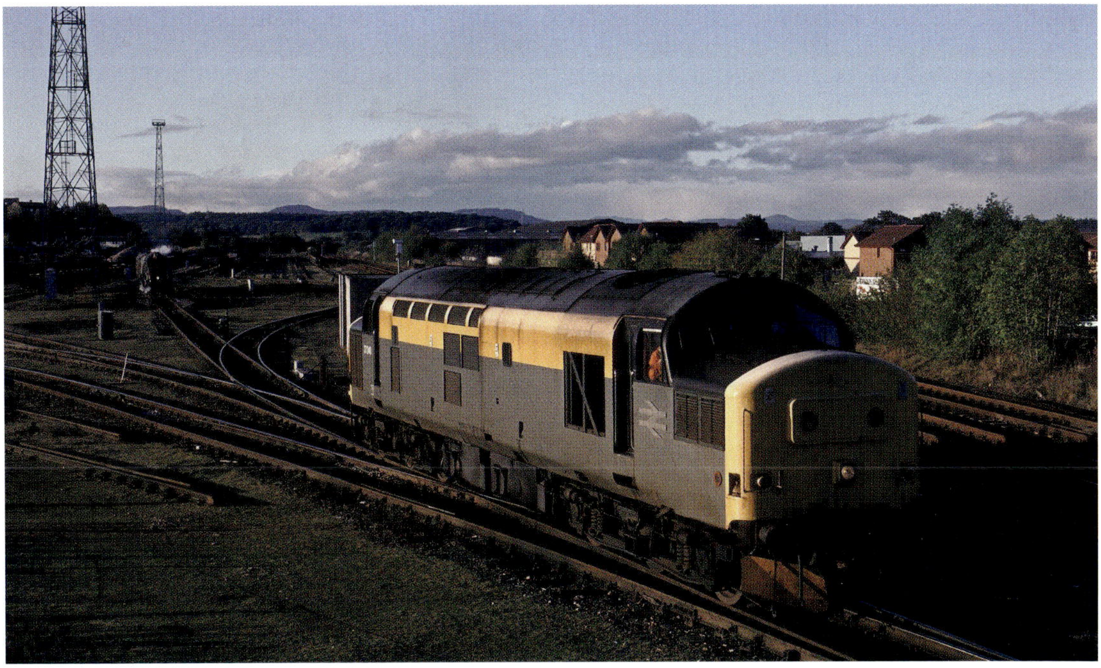

A view of Perth new yard at Muirtown on 15 October 1993 with No. 37240 shunting and A4 60009 in the background. The yard was opened in 1962 but closed in 2008.

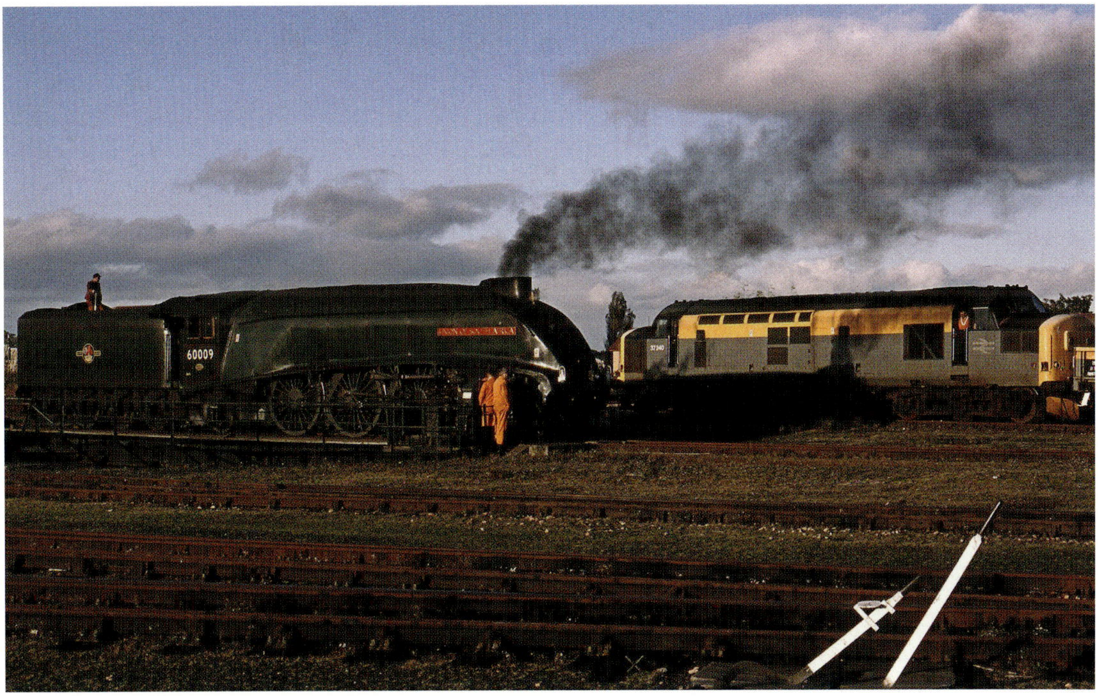

No. 60009 is on the turntable in the yard as No. 37240 passes on 15 October 1993. The turntable was reportedly broken up by error when the yard was cleared.

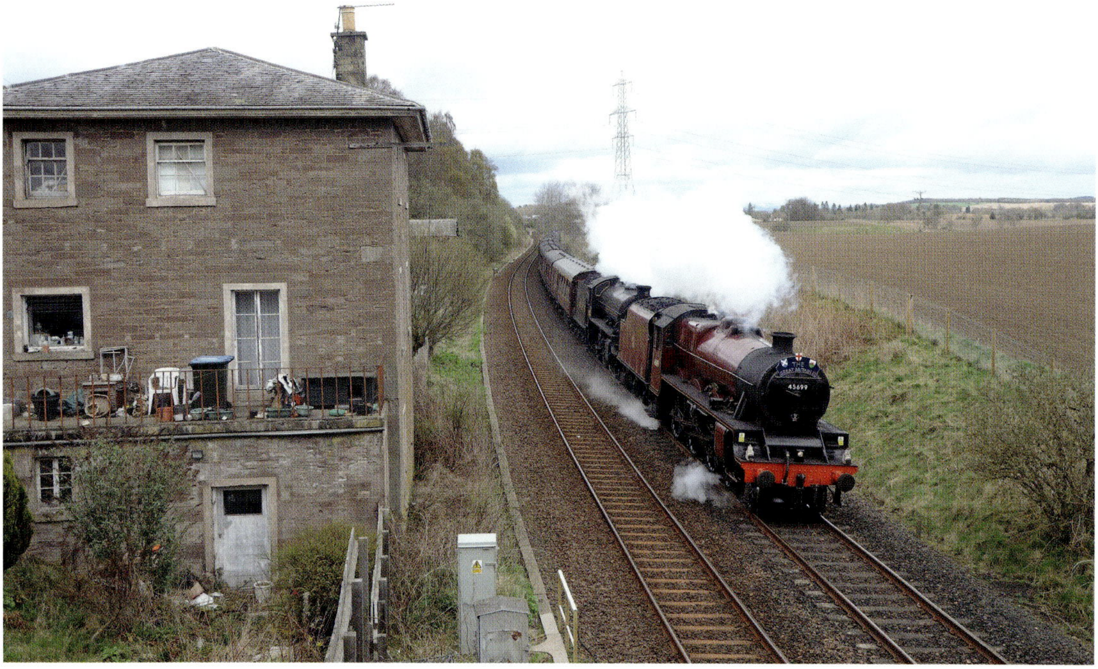

Jubilee Class No. 45699 *Galatea* leads B1 1264 with the Inverness to Perth leg of GB XI near Luncarty on 23 April 2018.

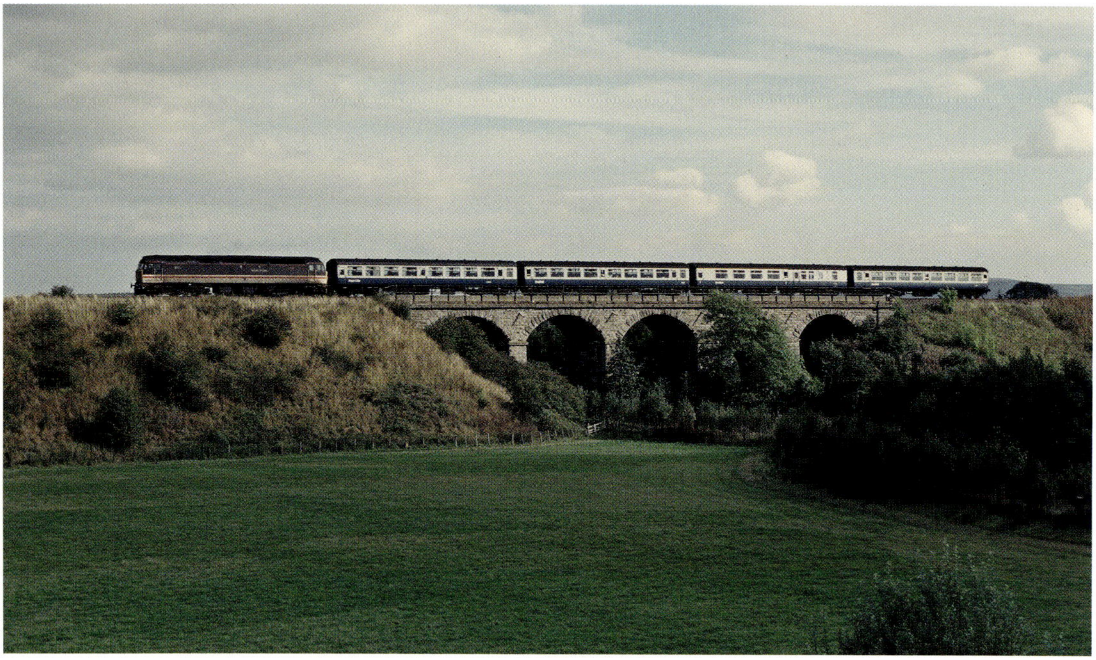

Class 47 No. 47617 crosses a viaduct near Luncarty with a service to Inverness on 11 September 1990.

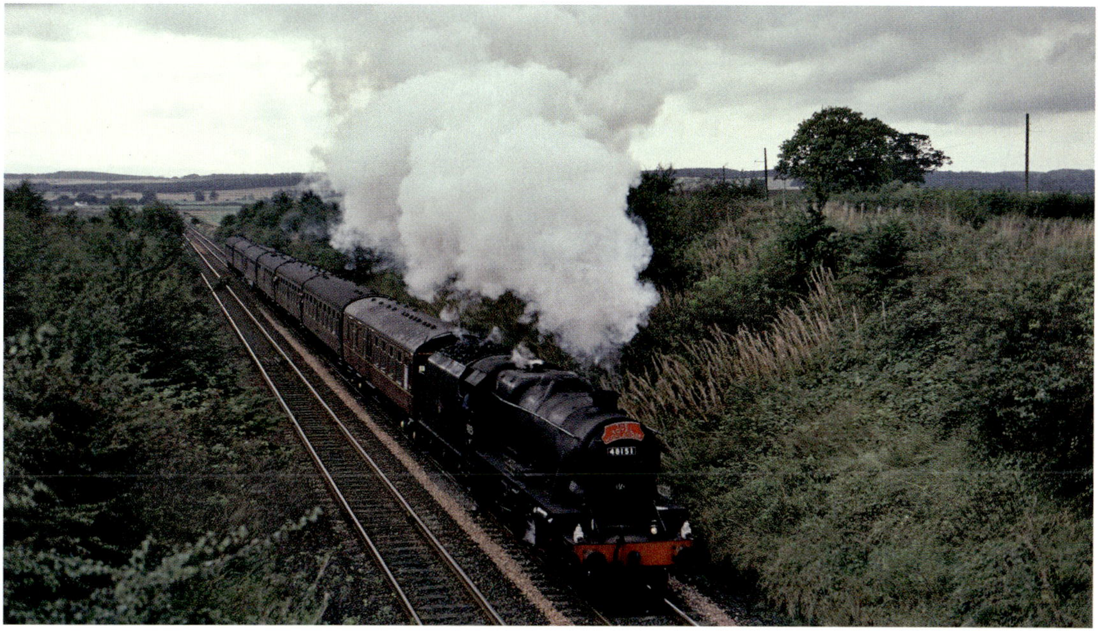

LMS 8F No. 48151 passes Stanley with a Highland Railway Heritage trip from Edinburgh to Inverness on 3 October 1998.

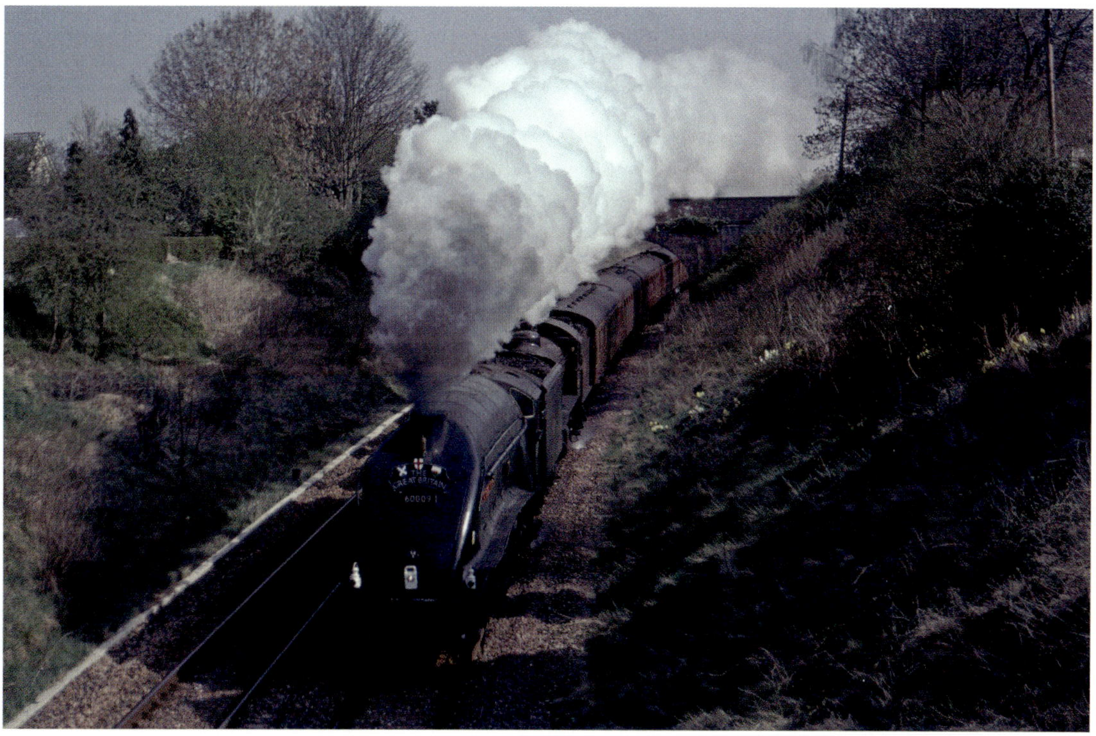

A4 60009 and K4 61994 *The Great Marquess* at Stanley with the southbound Great Britain on 14 April 2007.

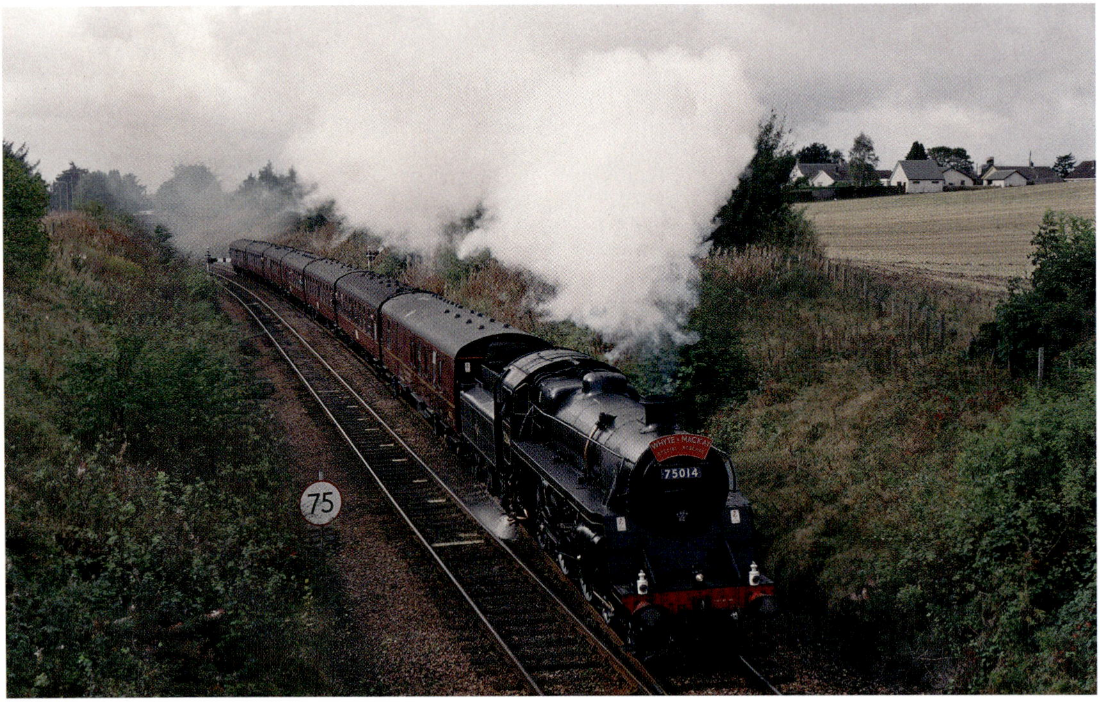

Standard Class 4 No. 75014 enters the single line section at Stanley Junction on the way to Inverness on 4 October 1997.

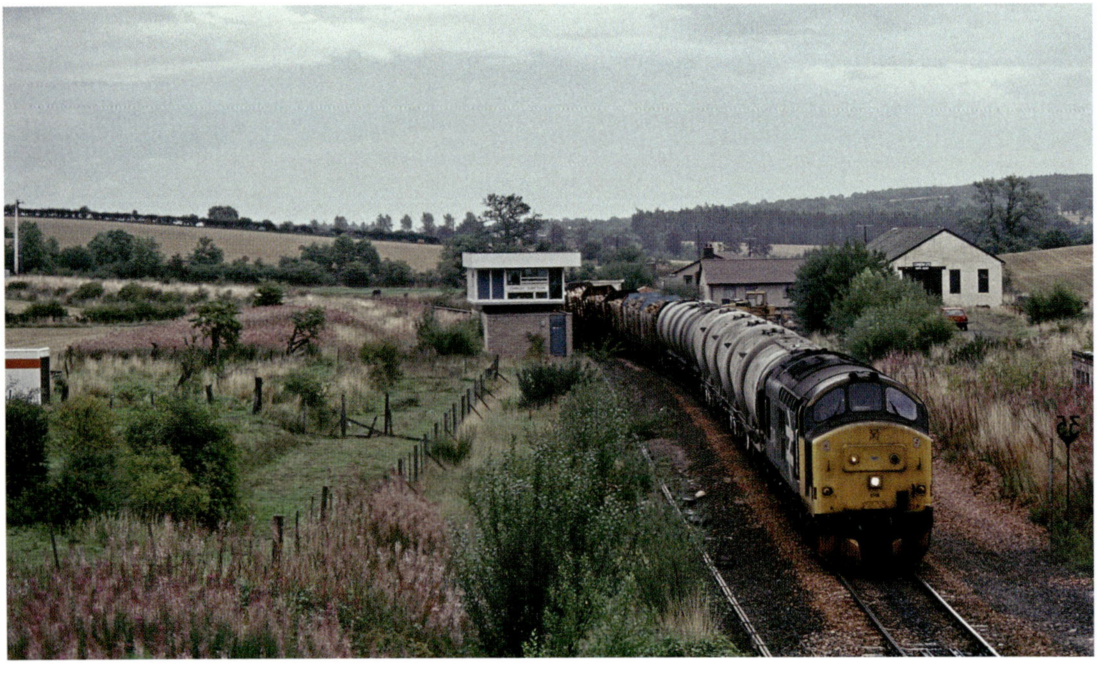

Class 37 No. 37419 passes the signal cabin at Stanley Junction with a mixed freight from Inverness on 5 September 1989. The line to Forfar went straight ahead past the buildings.

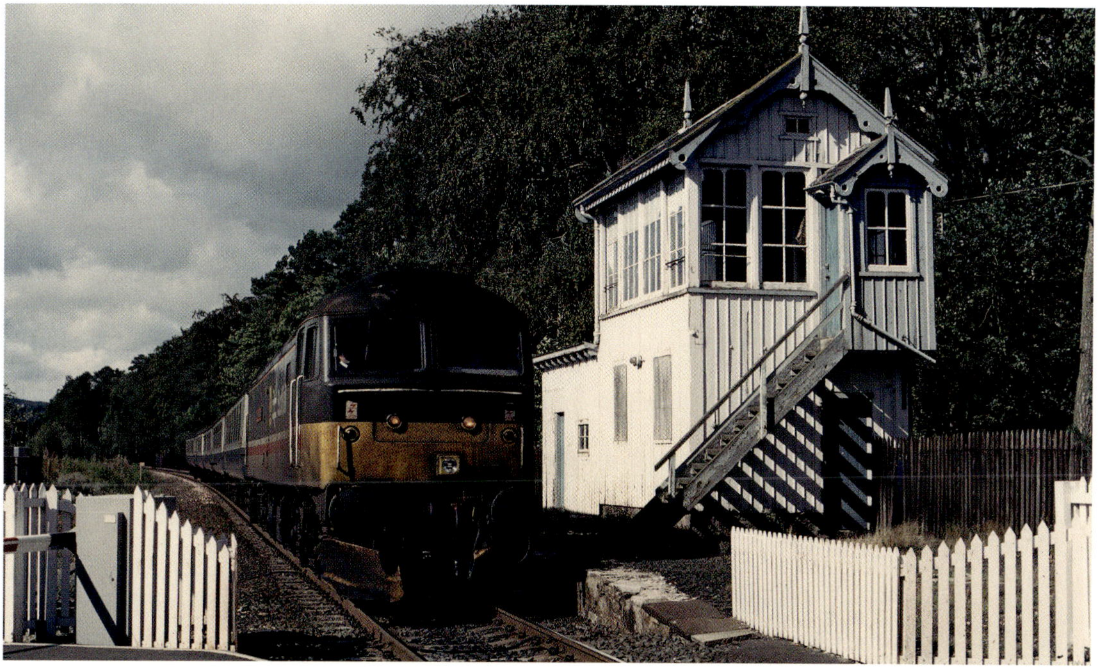

A Class 47 passes the disused but listed signal cabin at Murthly with a southbound working on 6 September 1990.

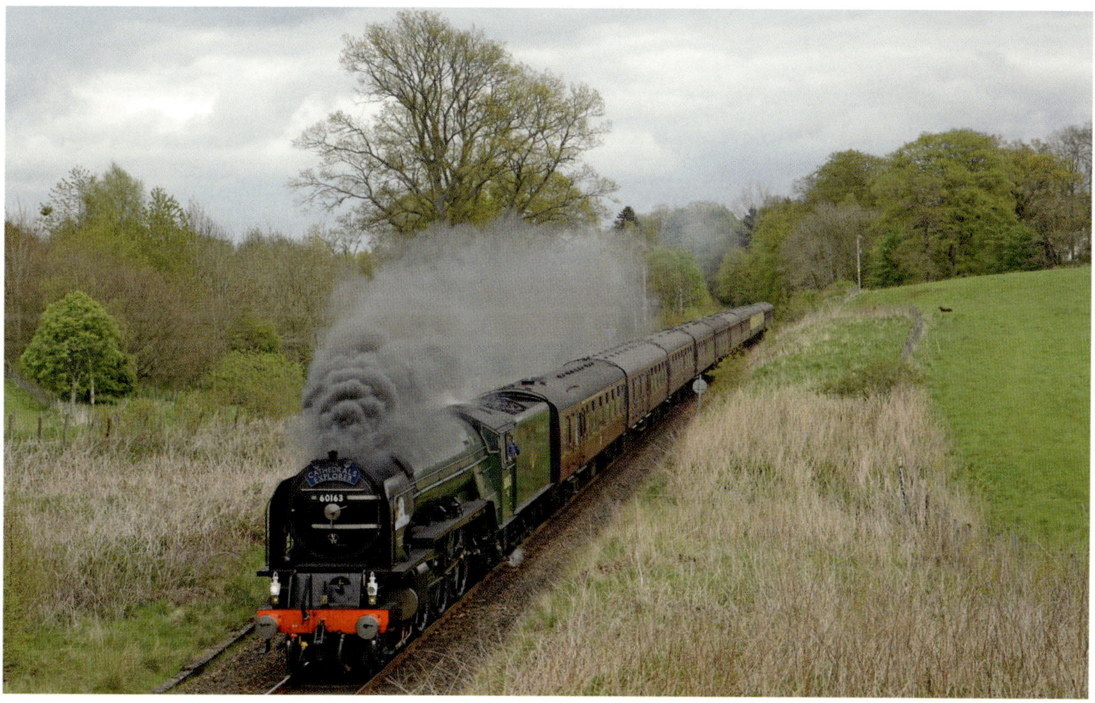

A1 Pacific No. 60163 *Tornado* passes Kingswood with the Cathedrals Explorer to Inverness on 19 May 2012. The engine was built as recently as 2008.

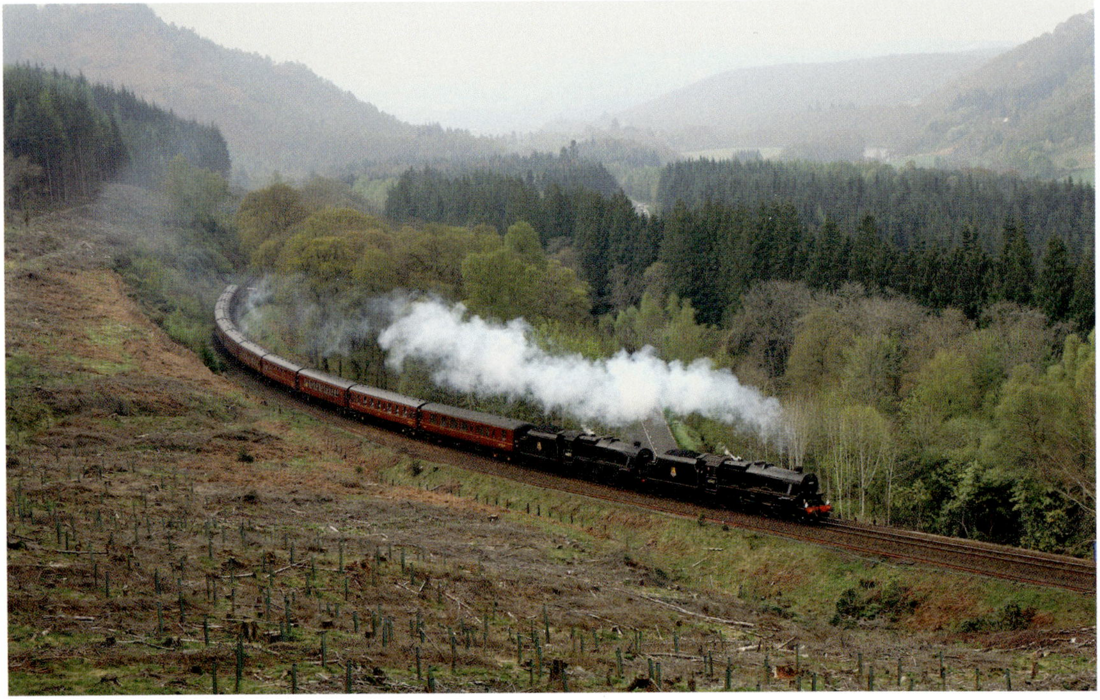

Class 5s Nos 45407 and 44871 pass cleared forestry land south of Dunkeld with GBIV from Inverness to Glasgow on 20 April 2011.

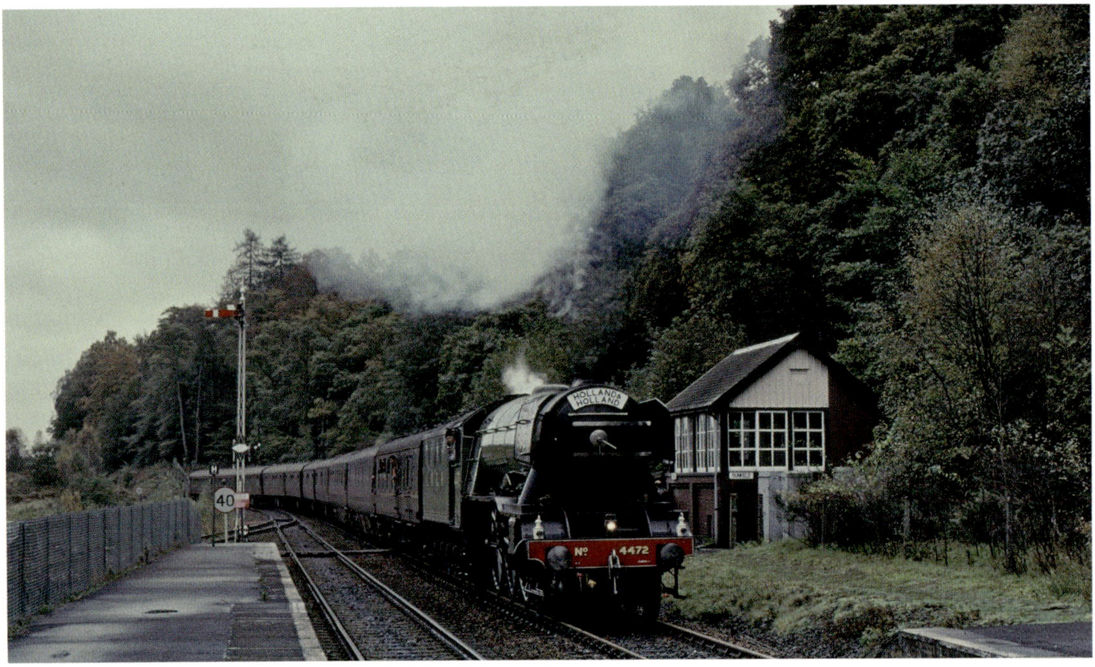

LNER A3 Pacific No. 4472 *Flying Scotsman* approaches Dunkeld station on its way north on 19 October 2000. The headboard shows the train's sponsor.

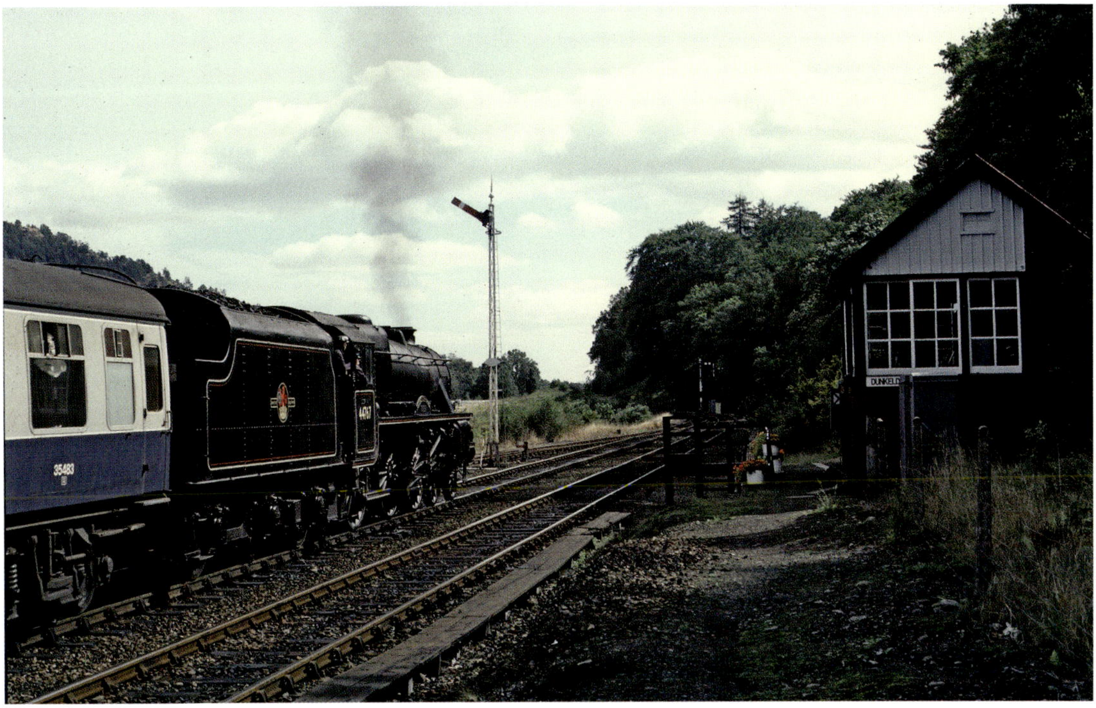

Class 5 No. 44767 gets the road south from Dunkeld on 1 September 1986. It had been used on a special to Helmsdale on the Far North line to test radio signalling equipment for use on steam engines.

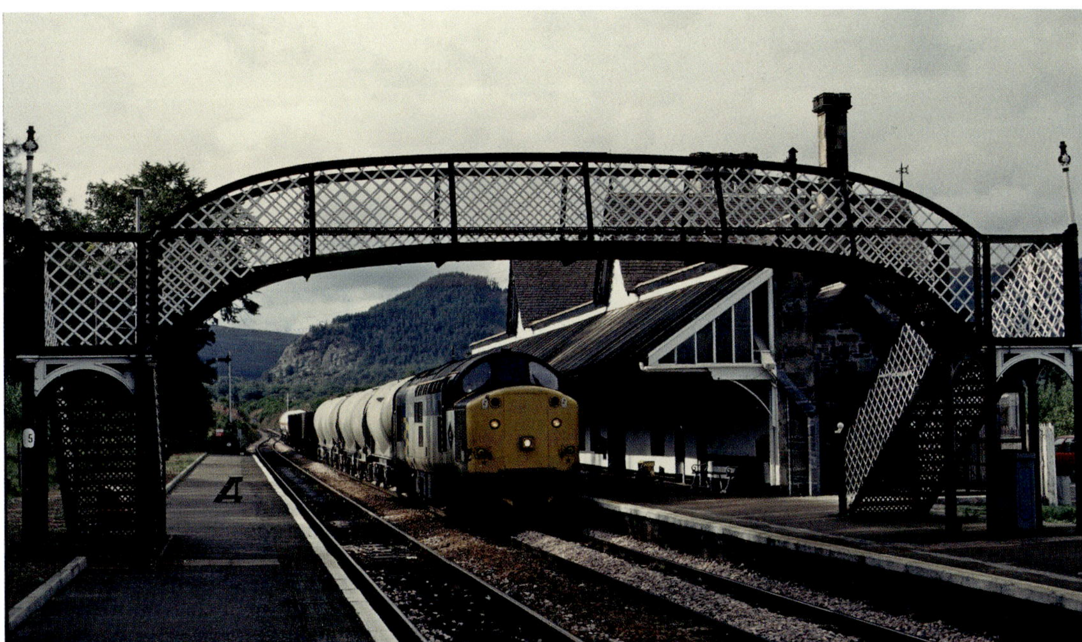

No. 37708 passes Dunkeld station with a southbound freight on 6 September 1990.

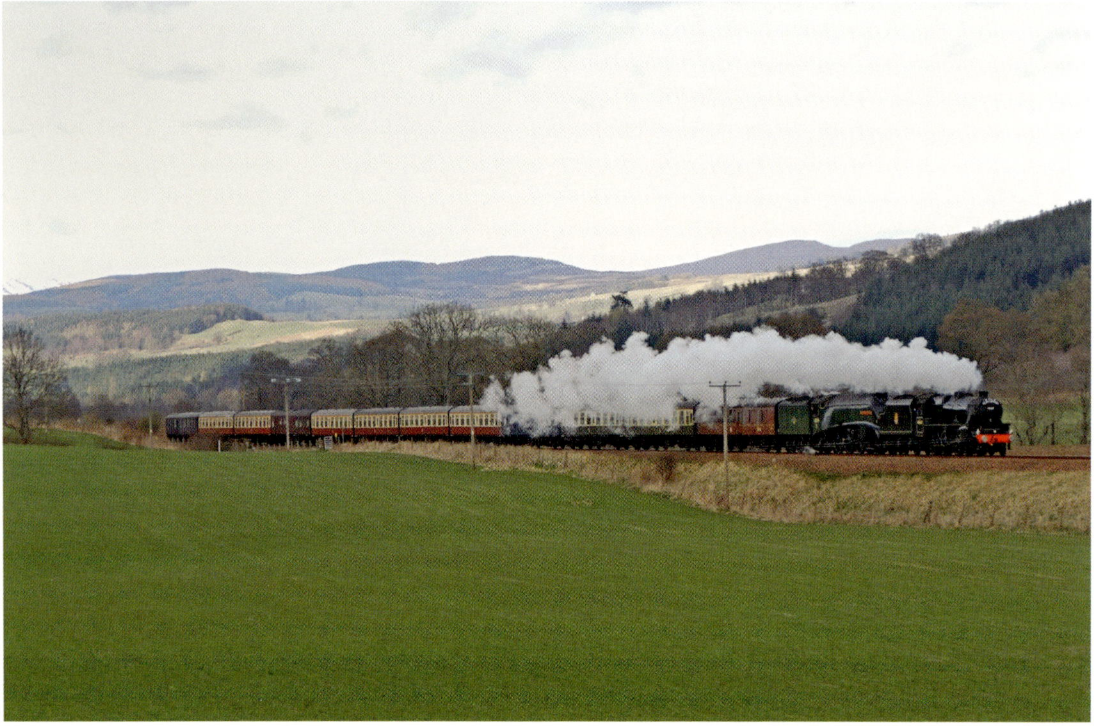

Nos 45407 and 60009 take the North Briton tour south through Strathtay on 15 April 2008.

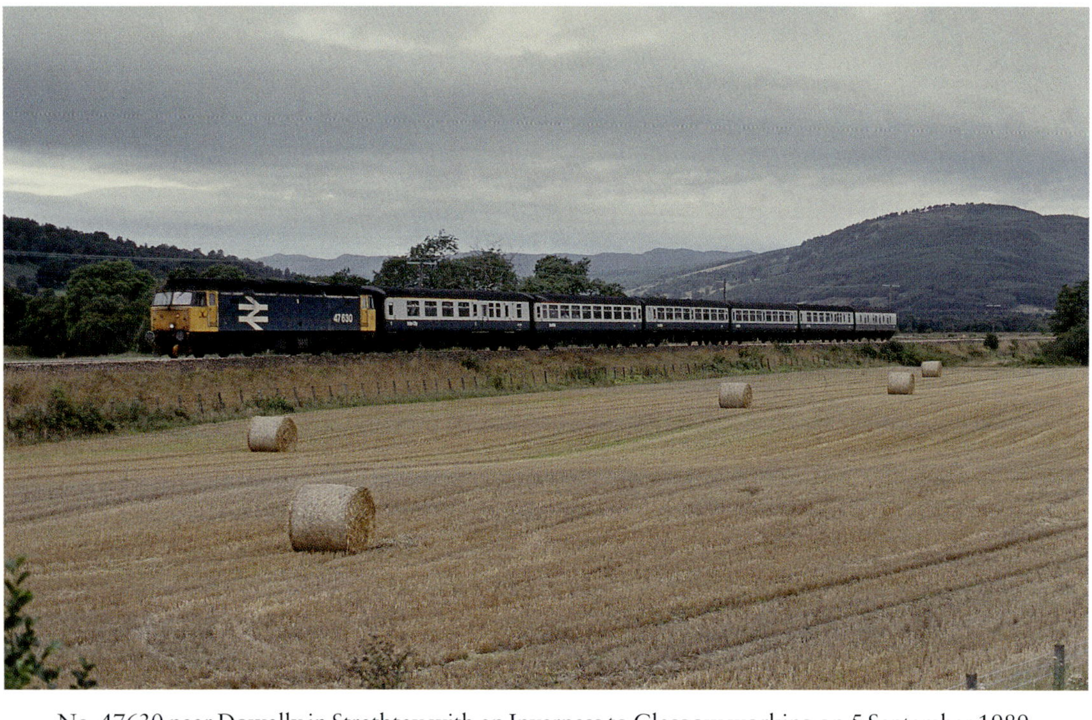

No. 47630 near Dowally in Strathtay with an Inverness to Glasgow working on 5 September 1989.

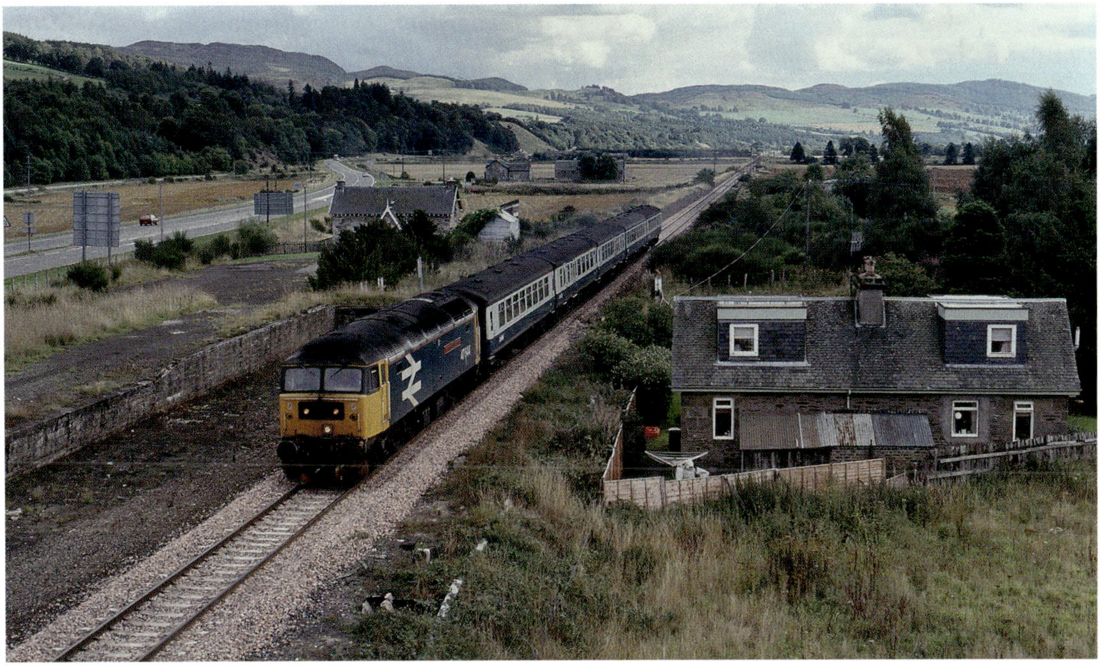

No. 47644 passes the site of Ballanluig station on the way north on 8 September 1989. This was the junction for the branch to Aberfeldy, closed in 1965.

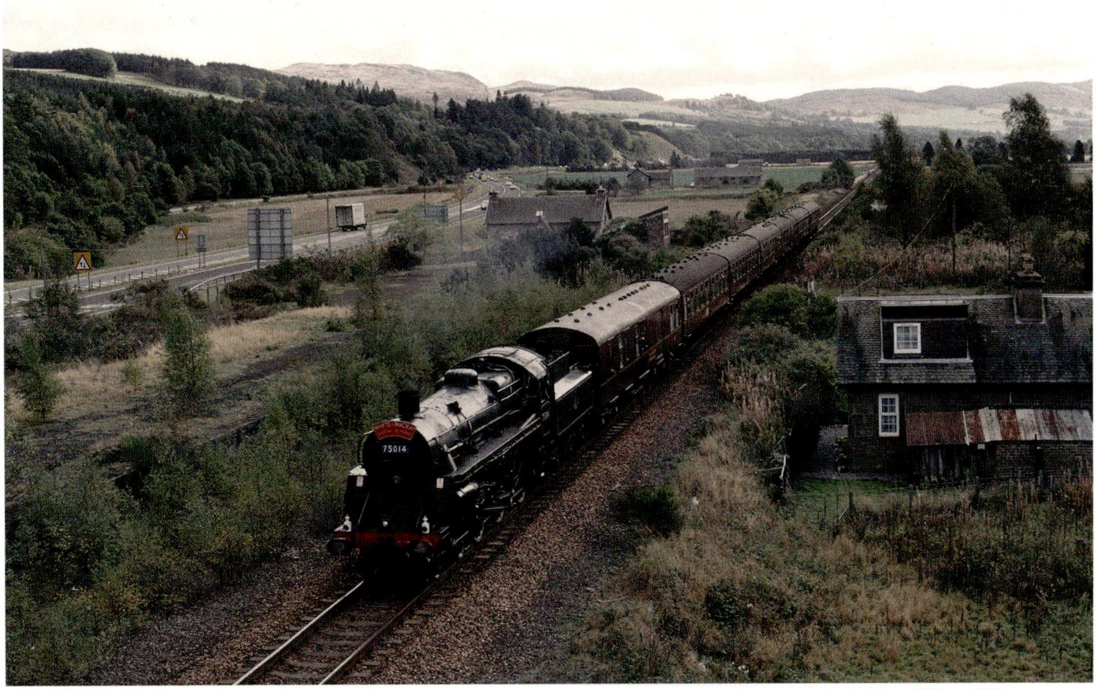

No. 75014 at Ballanluig with the Highland Railway Heritage tour from Edinburgh to Inverness on 4 October 1997.

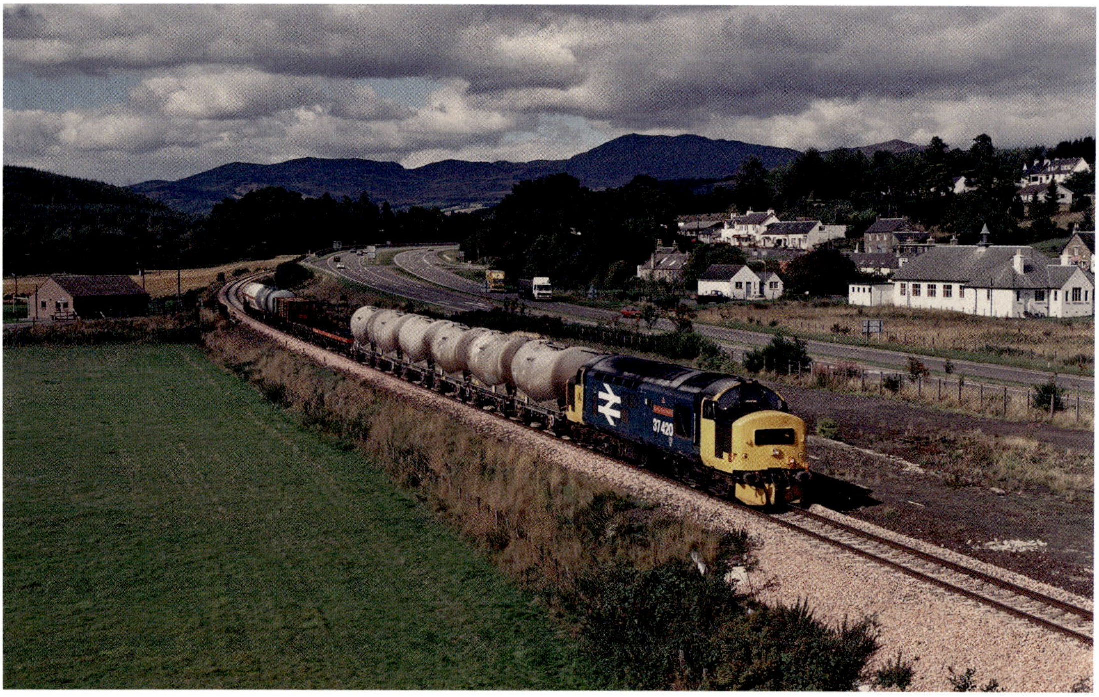

No. 37420 passes Ballanluig with a southbound freight on 8 September 1989.

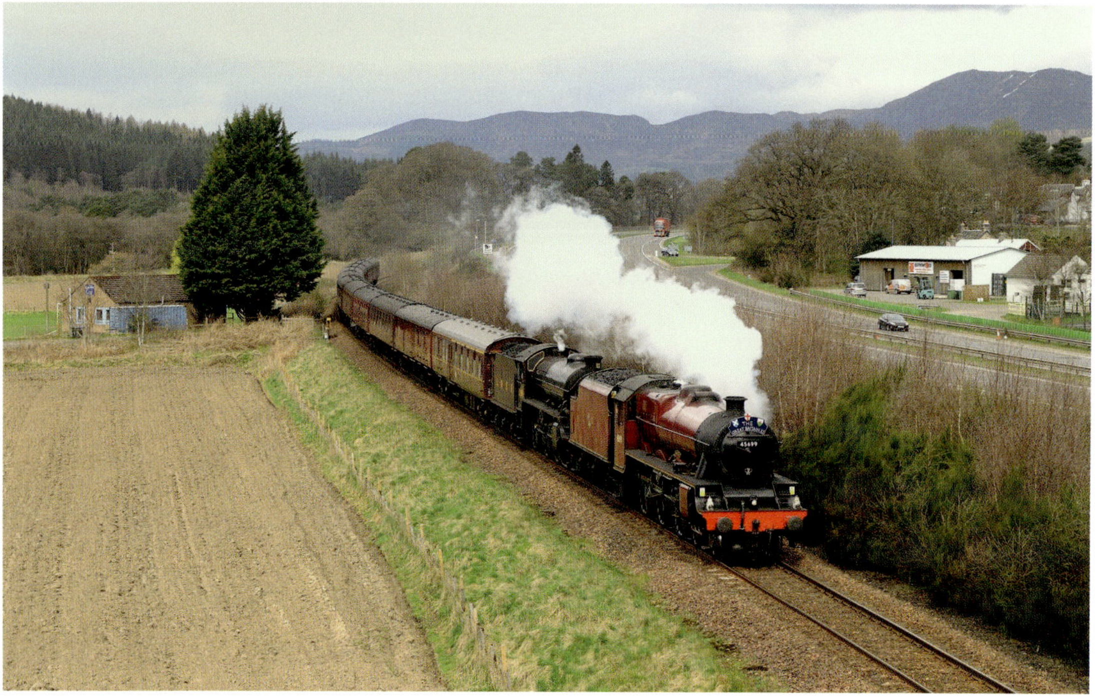

The lineside vegetation has grown considerably as No. 45699 *Galatea* and No. 1264 pass Ballanluig with GBXI on 23 April 2018.

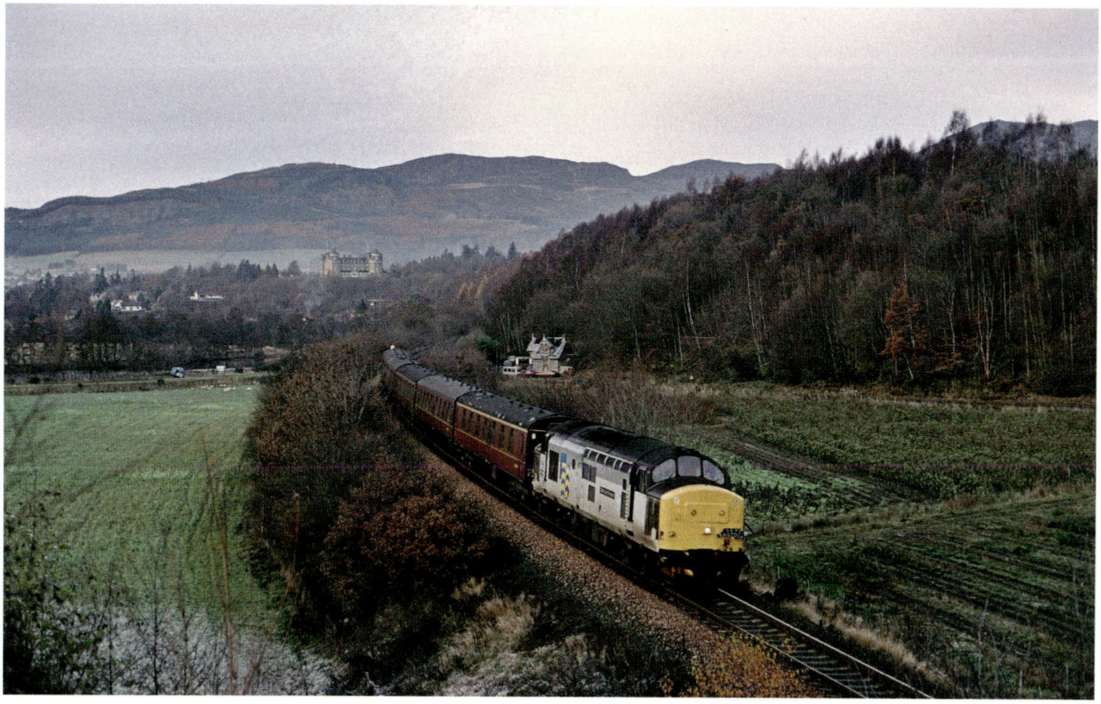

Standing in for a failed steam engine, No. 37428 hauls a SRPS special away from Pitlochry on 13 November 1993.

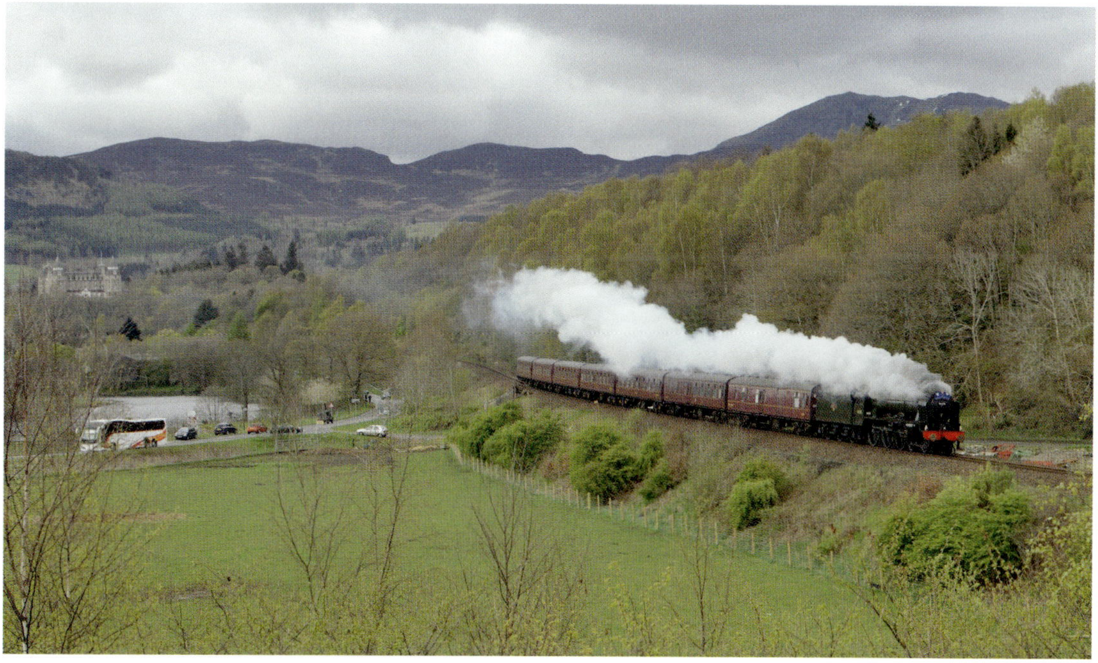

LMS No. 46115 *Scots Guardsman* leaves Pitlochry with the Inverness to Glasgow leg of GB V on 24 April 2012.

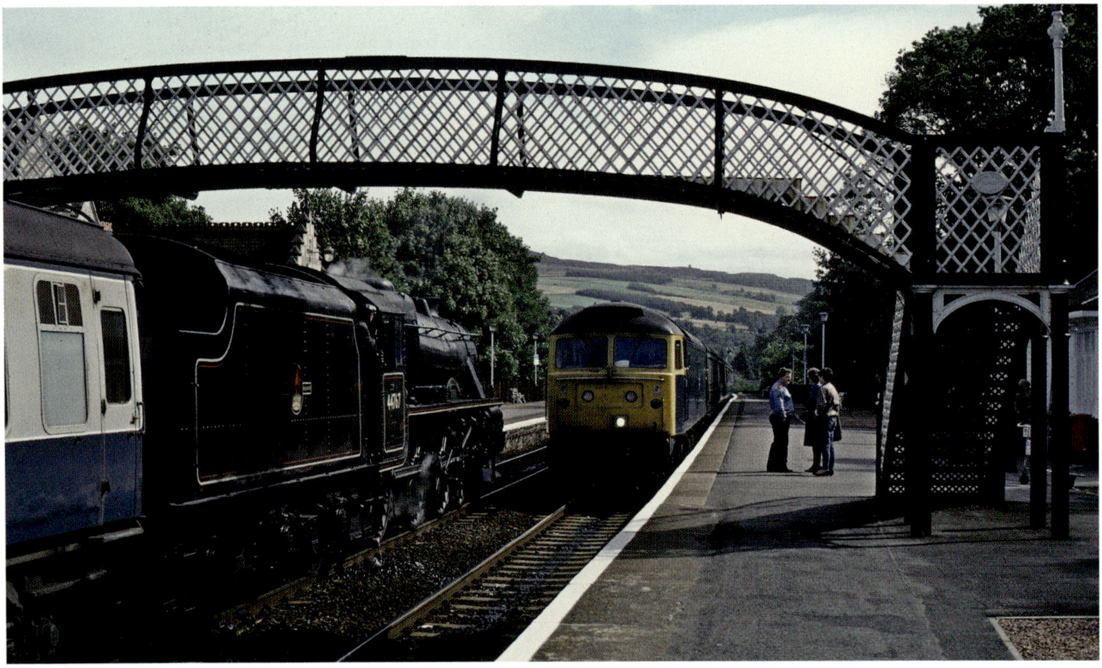

Class 5 No. 44767, heading south, meets a northbound Class 47-hauled service train at Pitlochry on 1 September 1986.

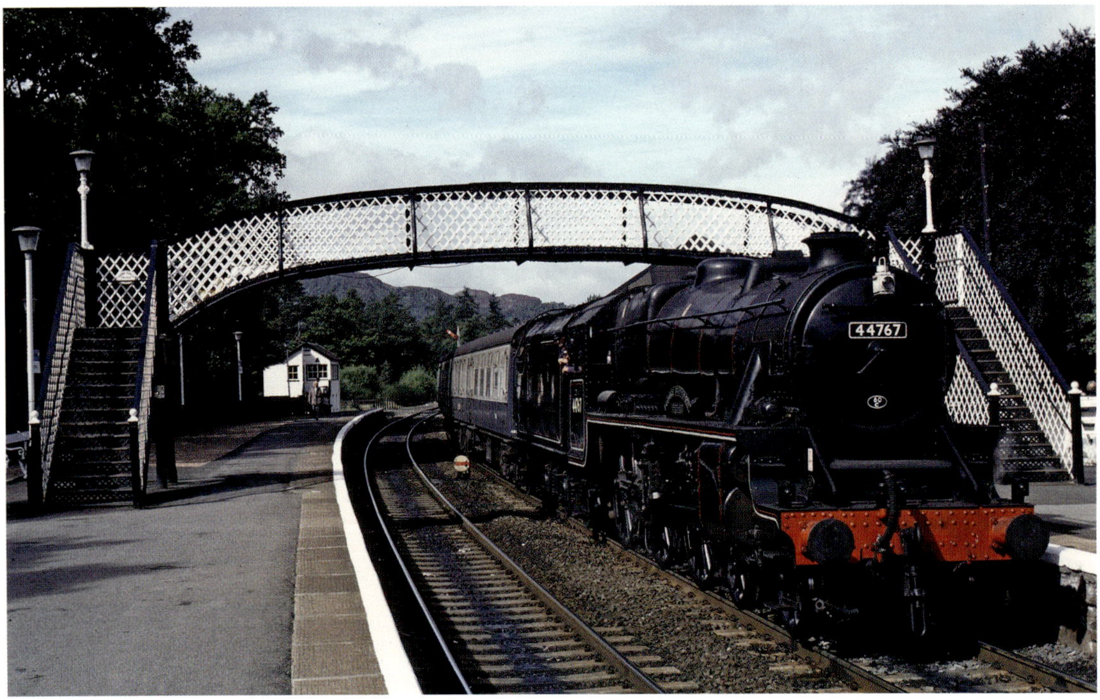

No. 44767 sits under the footbridge at Pitlochry on 1 September while it waits to cross the service train shown in the previous picture.

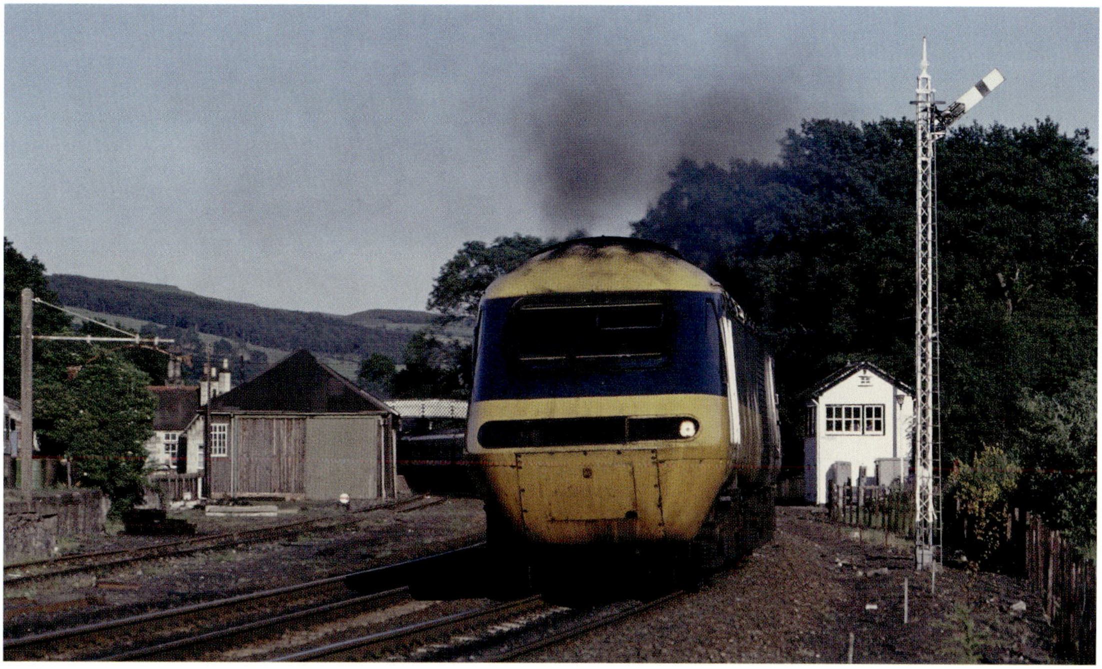

Plenty of Highland Railway infrastructure still on display as a HST set heads north from Pitlochry on 29 June 1986.

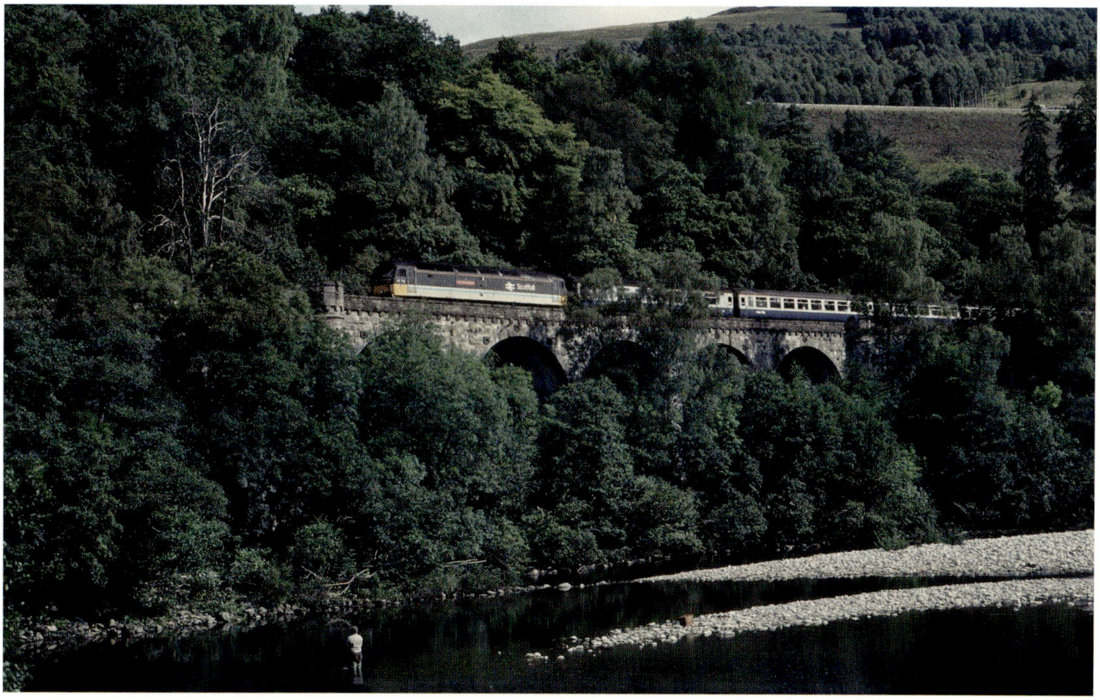

A fisherman is busy in the river at Killiecrankie as No. 47712 *Lady Diana Spencer* crosses the viaduct with a working north on 11 September 1990.

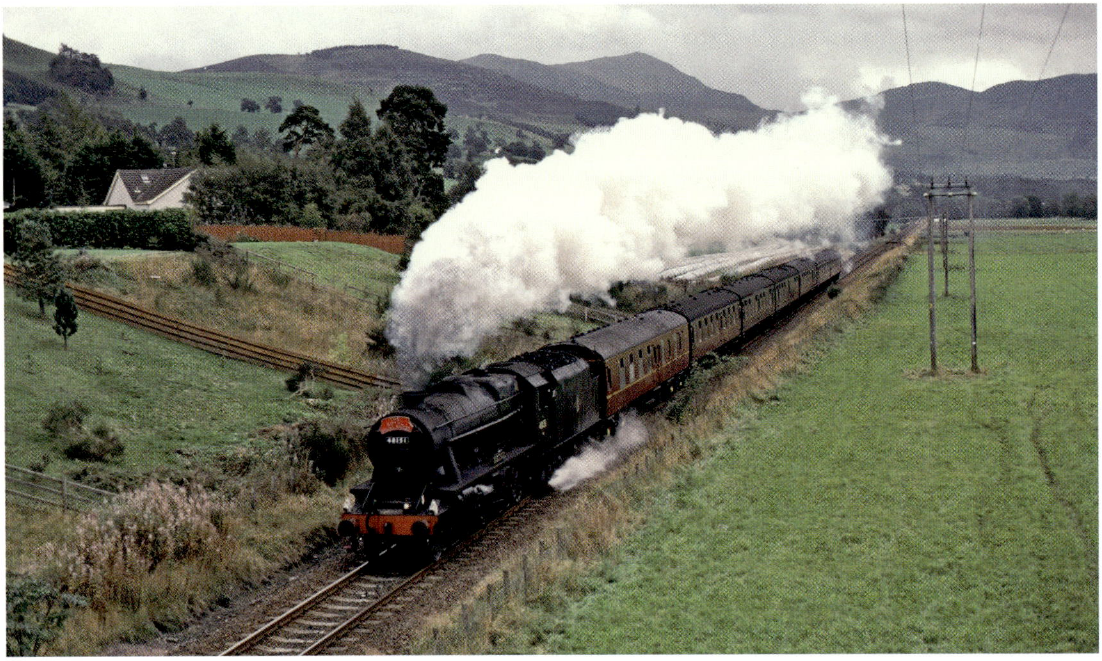

8F No. 48151 nears Blair Atholl on the way north on 3 October 1998.

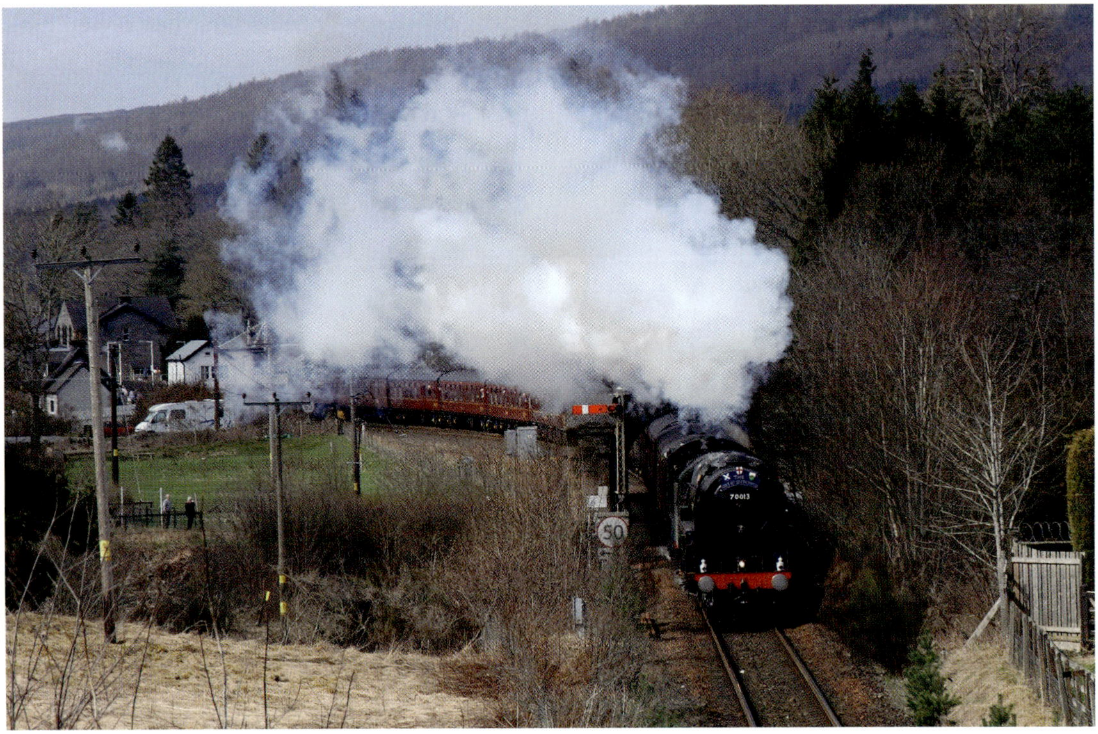

Britannia Class No. 70013 *Oliver Cromwell* and K4 61994 leave Blair Atholl with GB II on 13 April 2010.

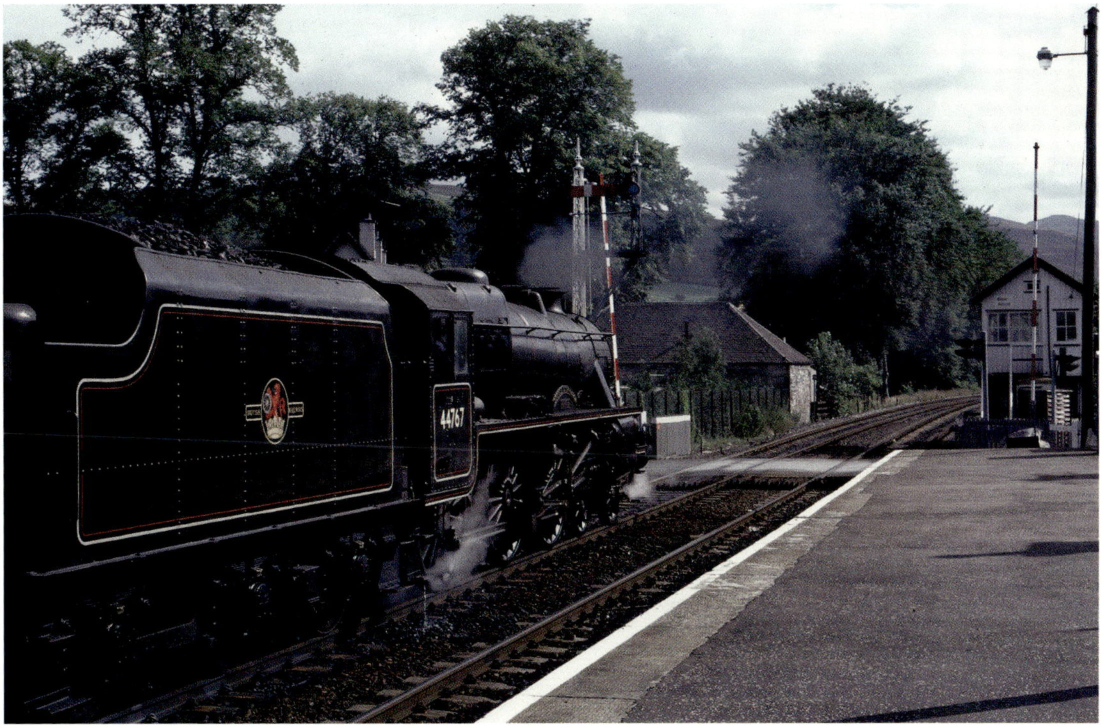

Class 5 No. 44767 and the signal cabin at Blair Atholl on 1 September 1986.

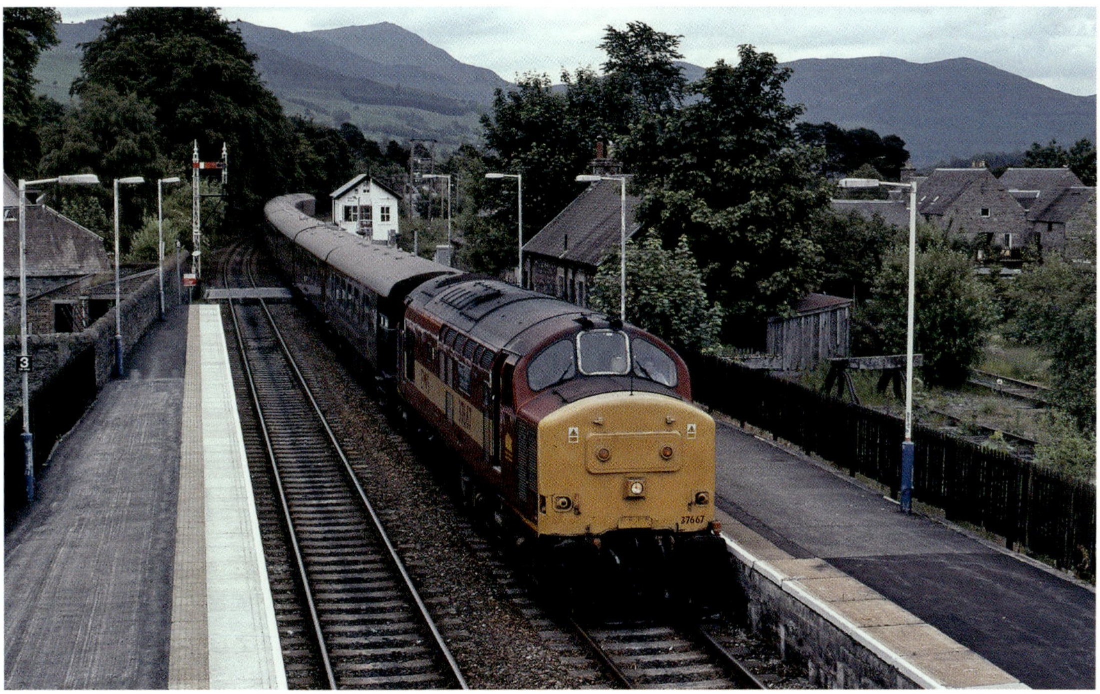

No. 37667 northbound at Blair Atholl with the Royal Scotsman luxury touring train on 27 June 2000.

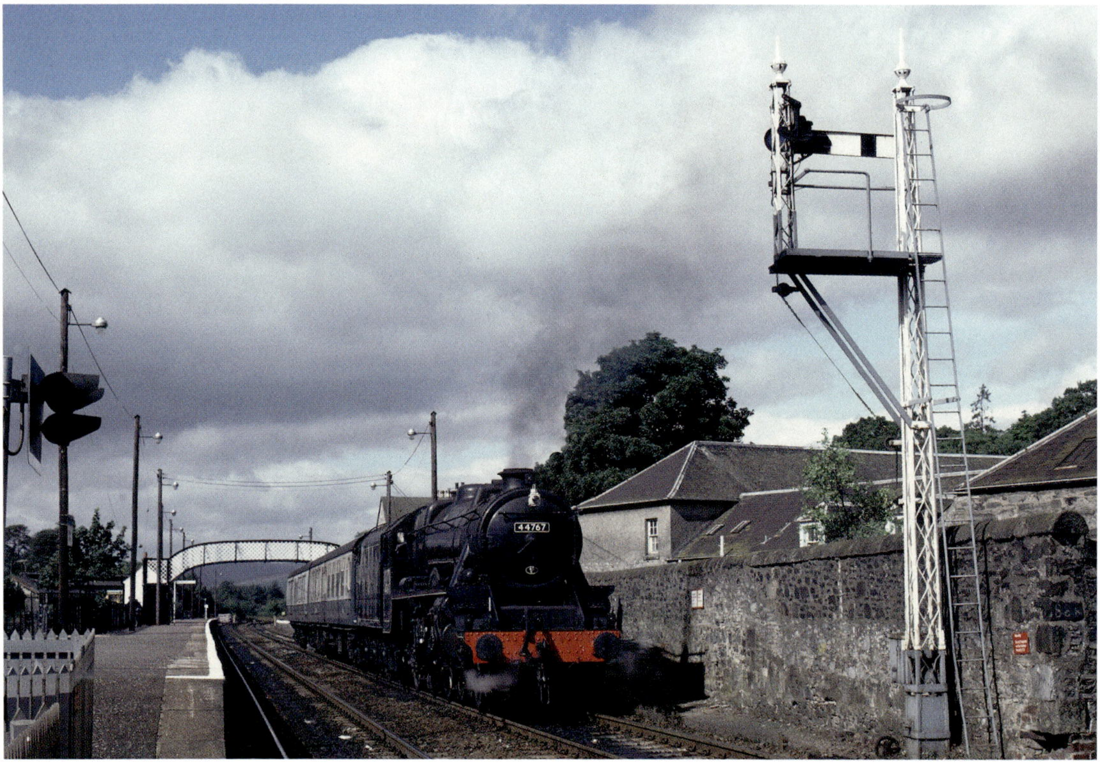

No. 44767 waits by the signal to cross a northbound service at Blair Atholl on 1 September 1986.

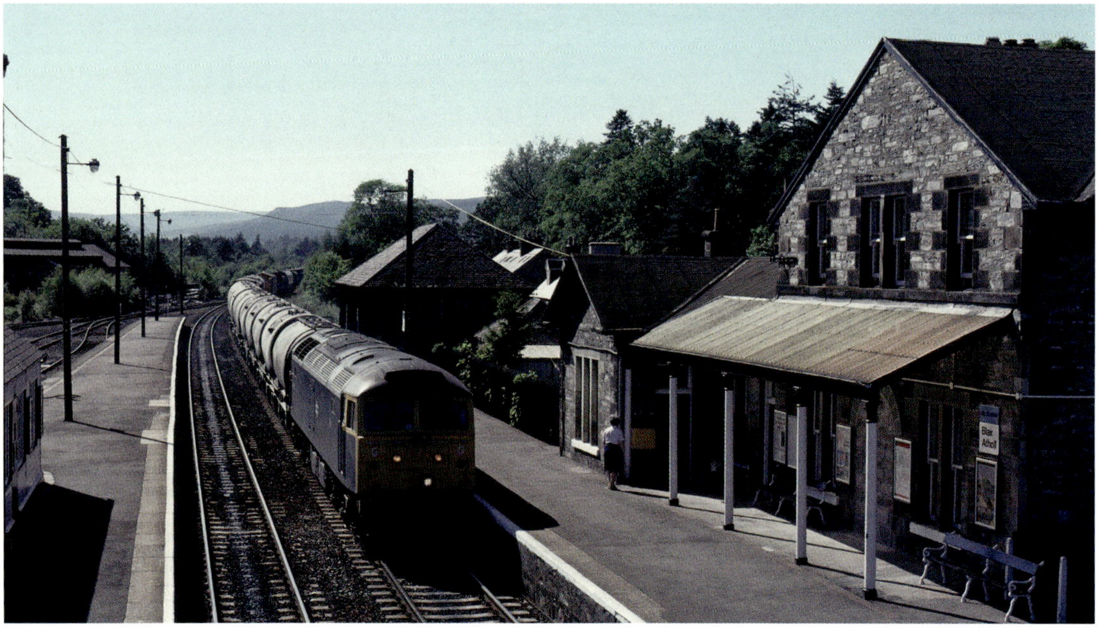

A Class 47 with a southbound freight working passes Blair Atholl station. on 30 June 1986. In steam days, banking engines for the climb to the summit were stabled in the sidings to the left.

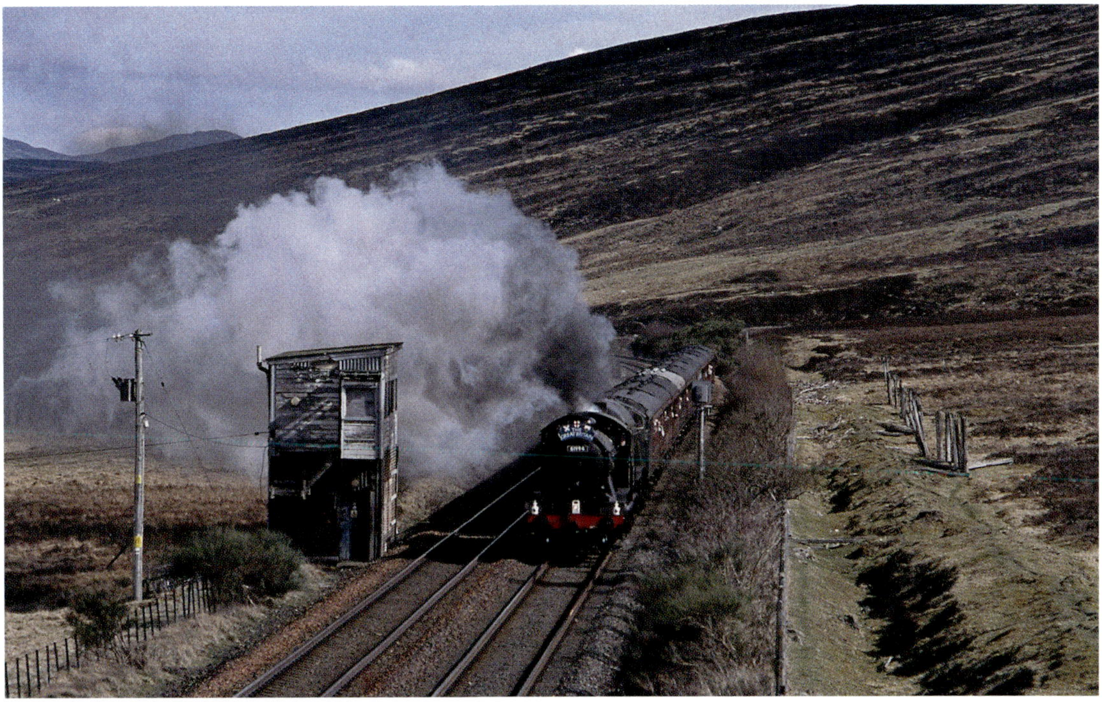

The former signal cabin at Dalnacardoch looks in poor condition as No. 61994 and No. 60009 work north with the inaugural Great Britain tour on 10 April 2007.

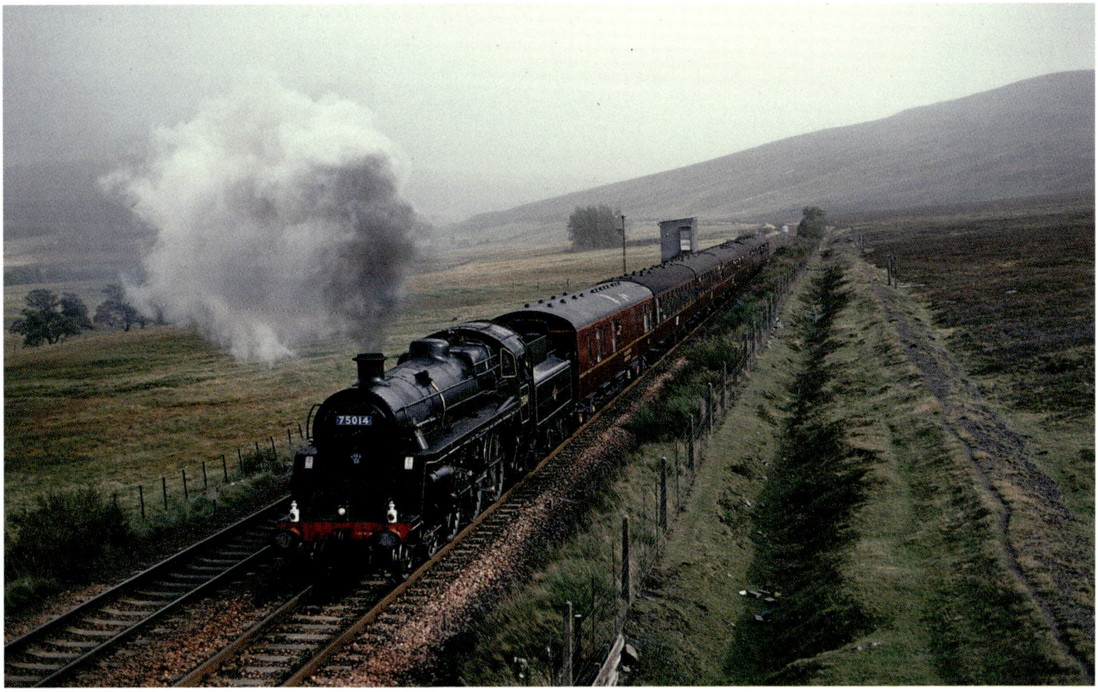

Standard Class 4 No. 75014 at Dalnacardoch on 4 October 1997.

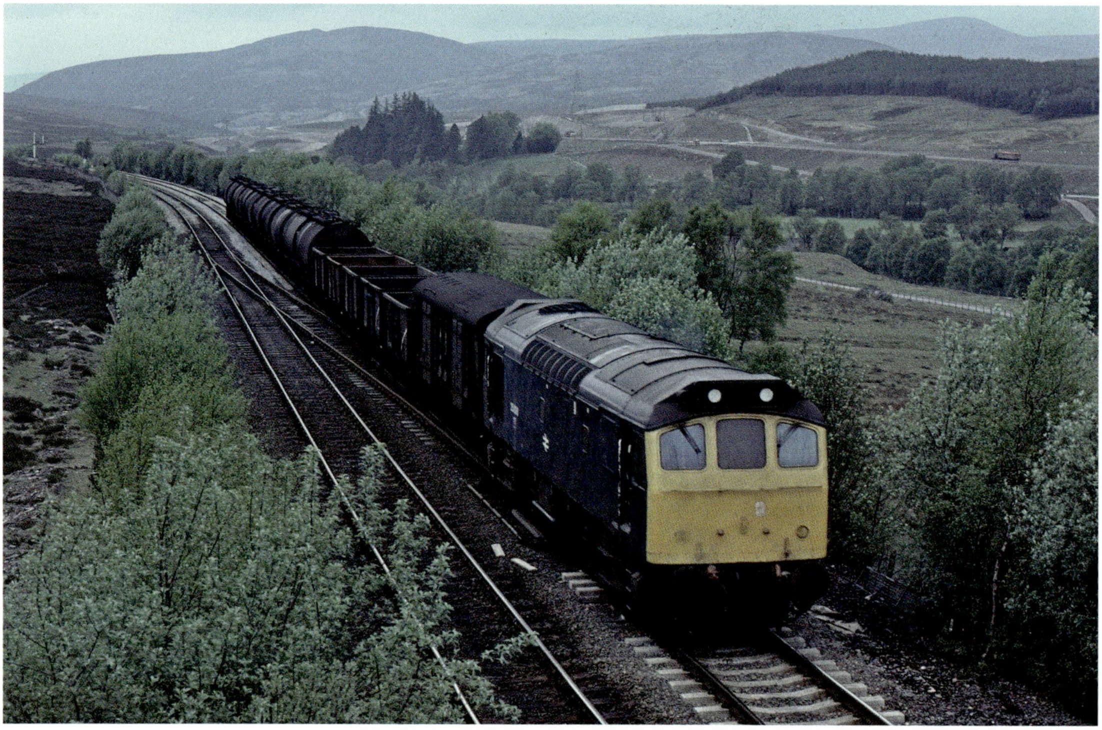

A Class 25 heads a southbound freight at Dalnacardoch in May 1980.

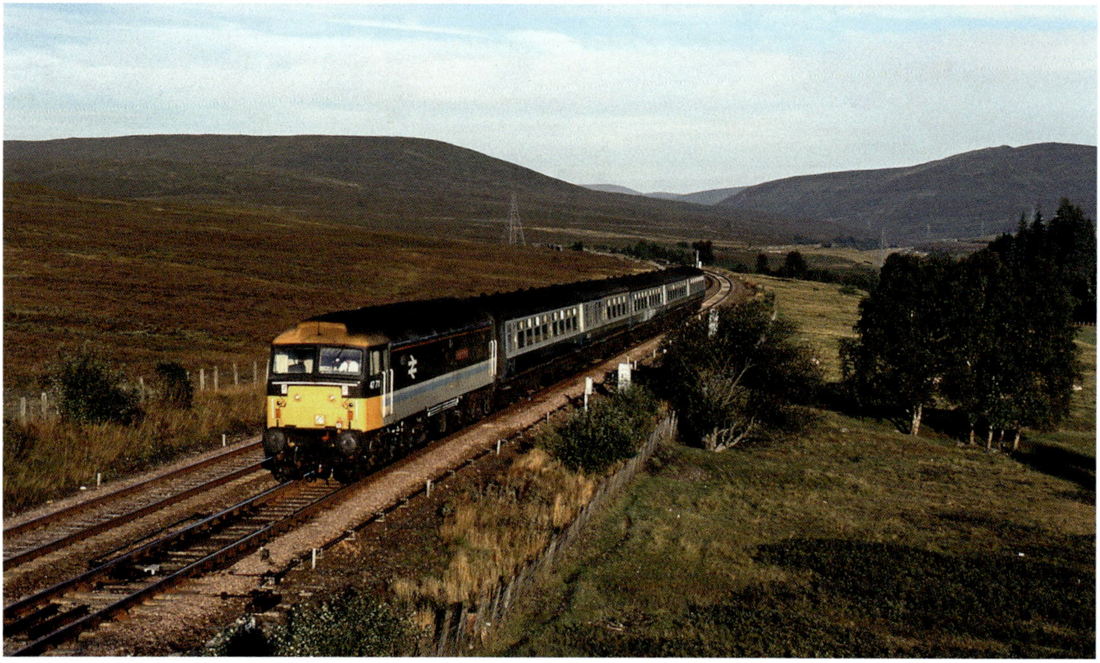

No. 47711 approaches Dalnacardoch with an Inverness to Glasgow service early on 11 September 1990.

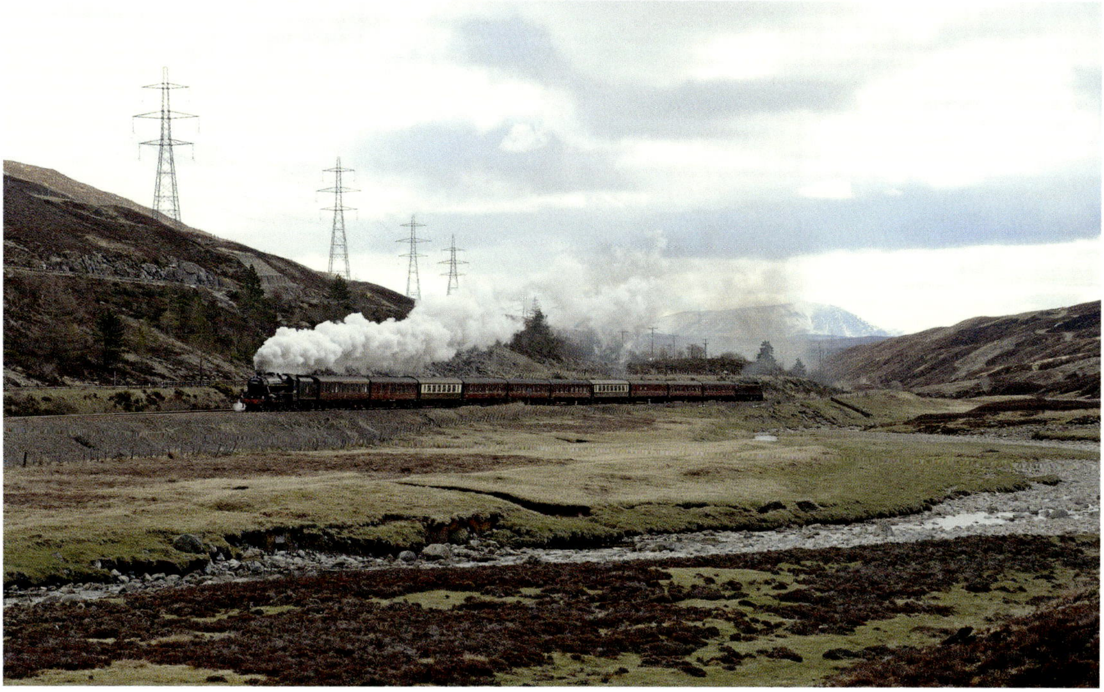

Class 5 No. 44871 in Glen Garry with GB IX to Inverness on 30 April 2016.

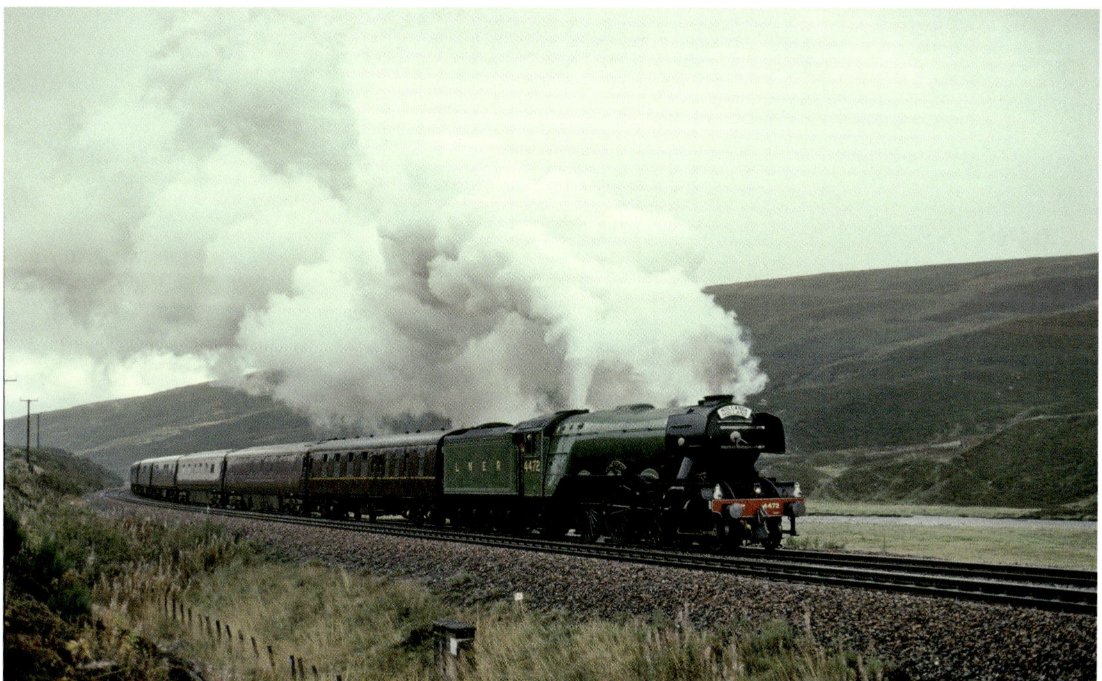

Reduced to walking pace on the wet rail, No. 4472 *Flying Scotsman* struggles through Glen Garry on 19 October 2000.

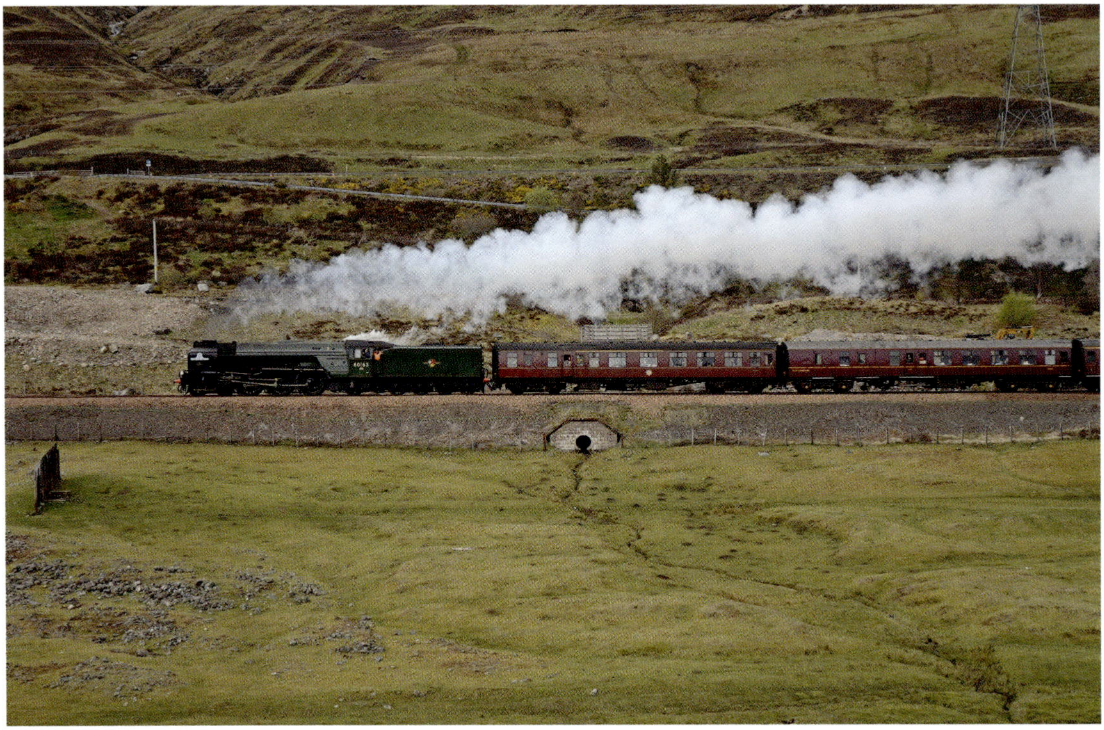

A broadside view of No. 60163 *Tornado* in Glen Garry on 19 May 2012.

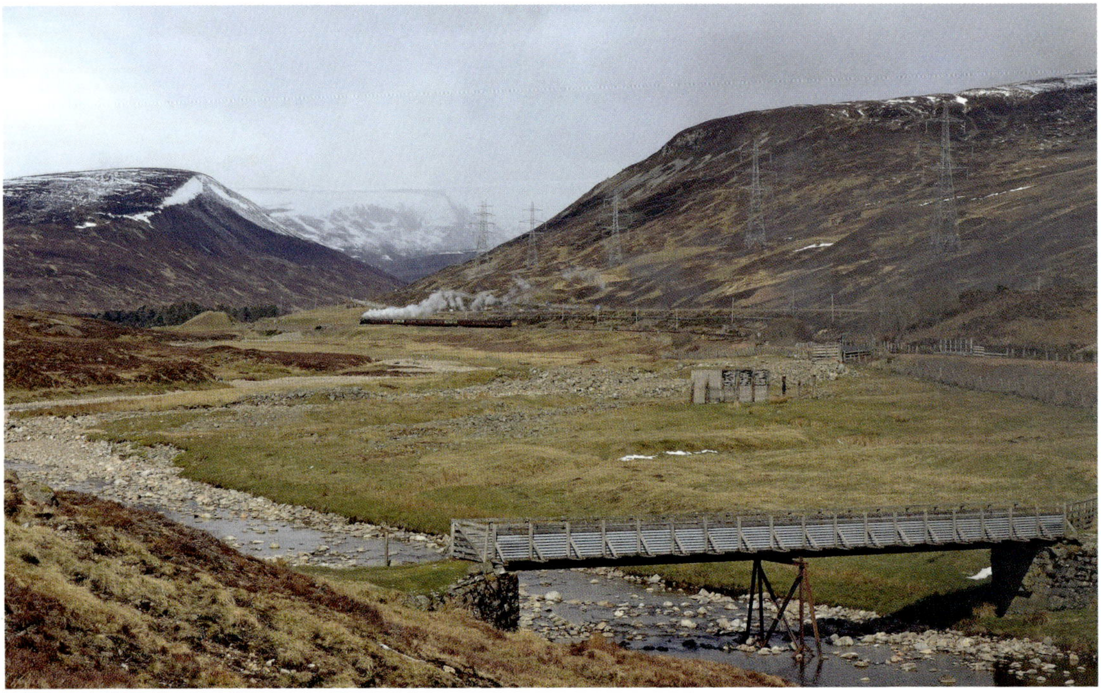

No. 44871 northbound near Dalnaspidal on 30 April 2016.

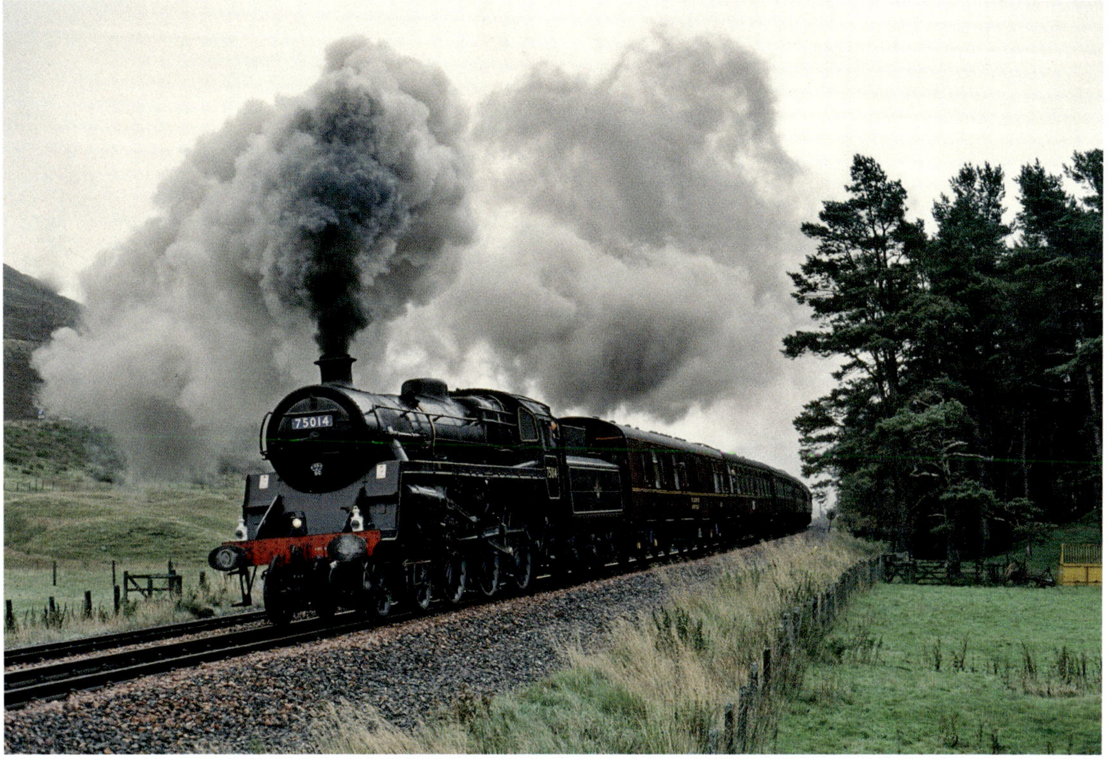

No. 75014 approaches Dalnaspidal with the Highland Heritage trip to Inverness on 4 October 1997.

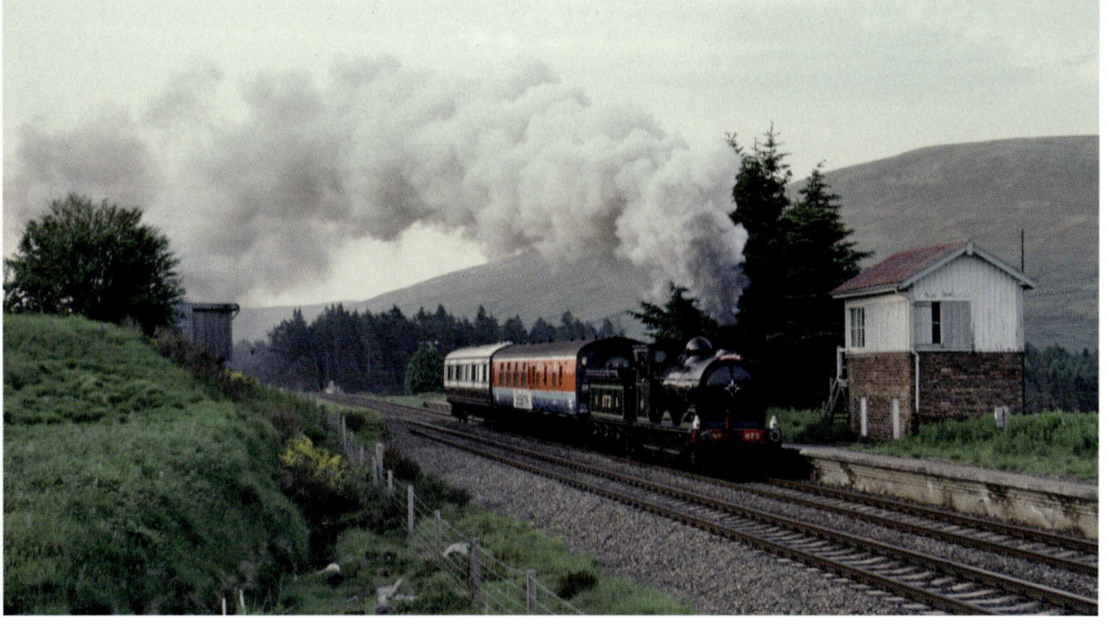

No. 673 *Maude*, owned by the SRPS, passes the closed station and signal cabin at Dalnaspidal on 27 June 1986. It was on the way to a Railfair at Inverness.

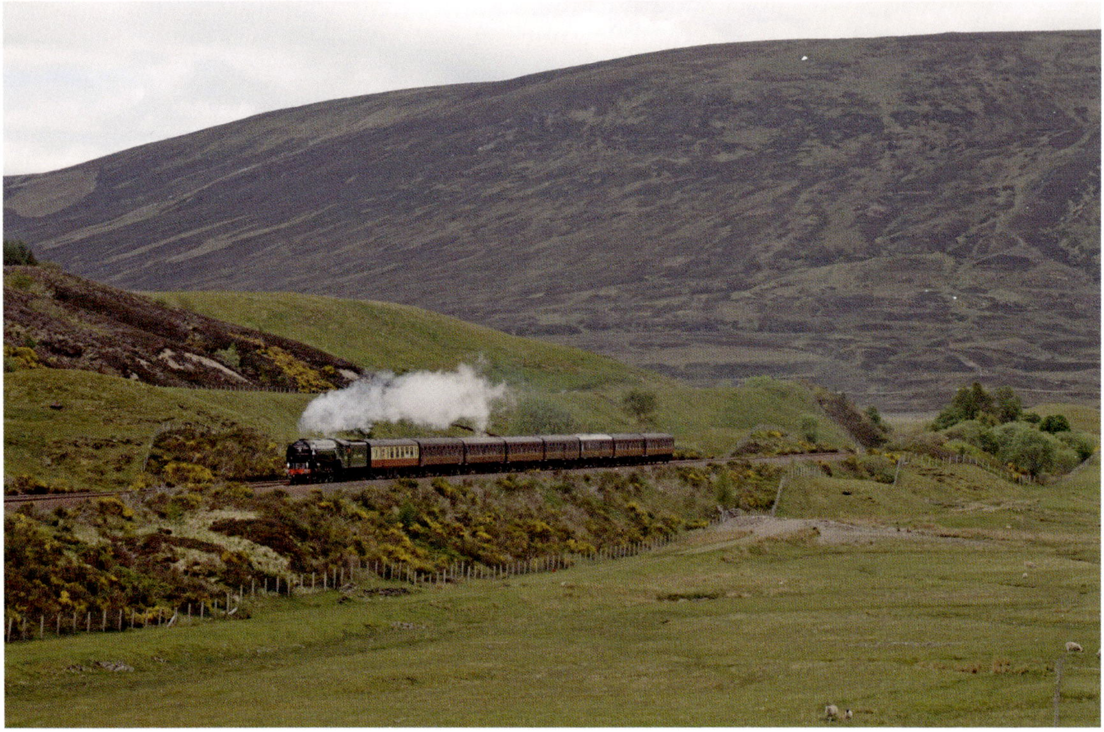

A1 Pacific No. 60163 *Tornado* tackles the northbound climb to Druimuachdair (otherwise known as Drumochter) Summit on 20 June 2015.

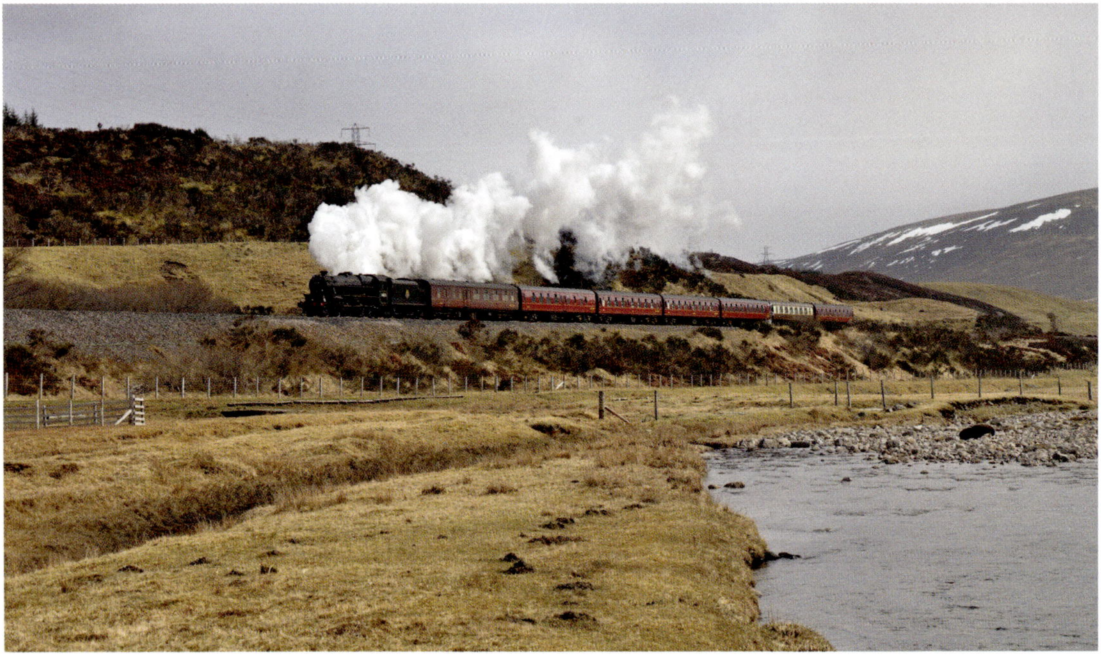

No. 44871 heads north on the climb with GB VI tour on 25 April 2013.

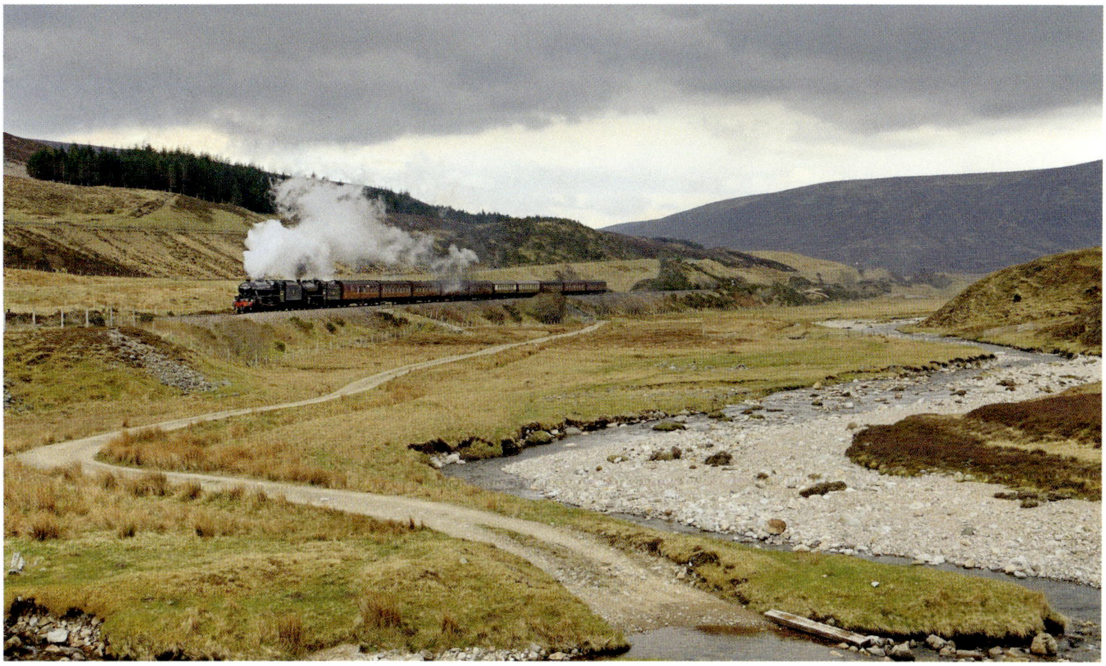

Class 5 No. 45212 and K1 No. 62005 alongside the River Dubhaig with the GB X leg from Perth on 30 April 2017.

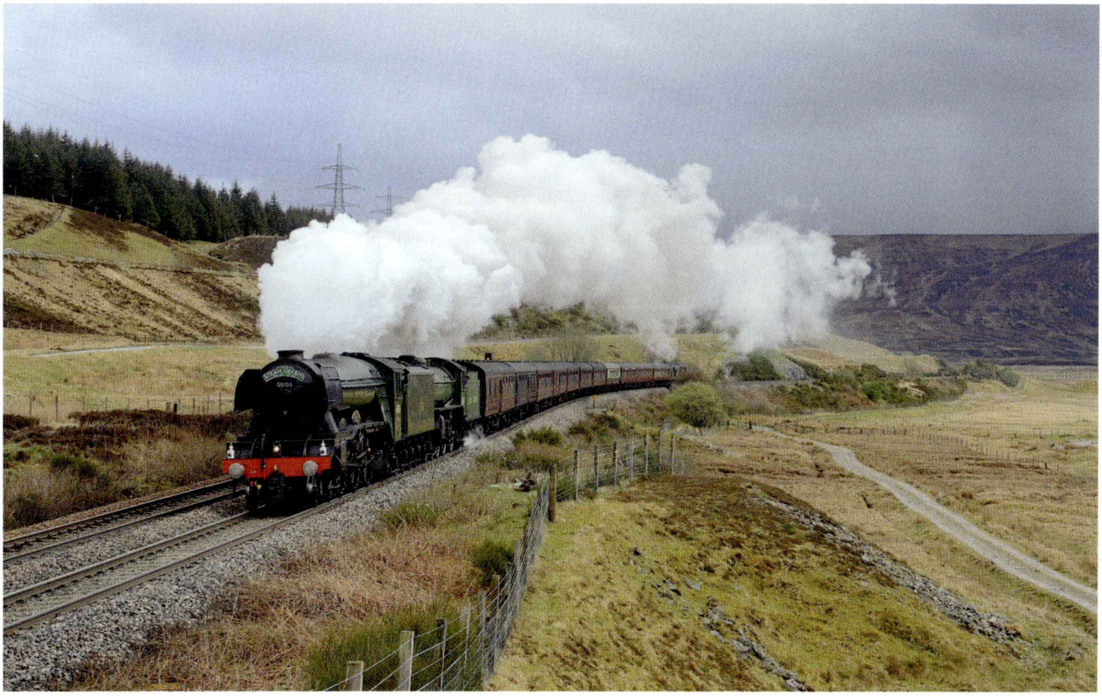

Ex-LNER engines Nos 60103 *Flying Scotsman* and 61306 *Mayflower* approach the summit from the south with a Steam Dreams tour on 10 May 2019.

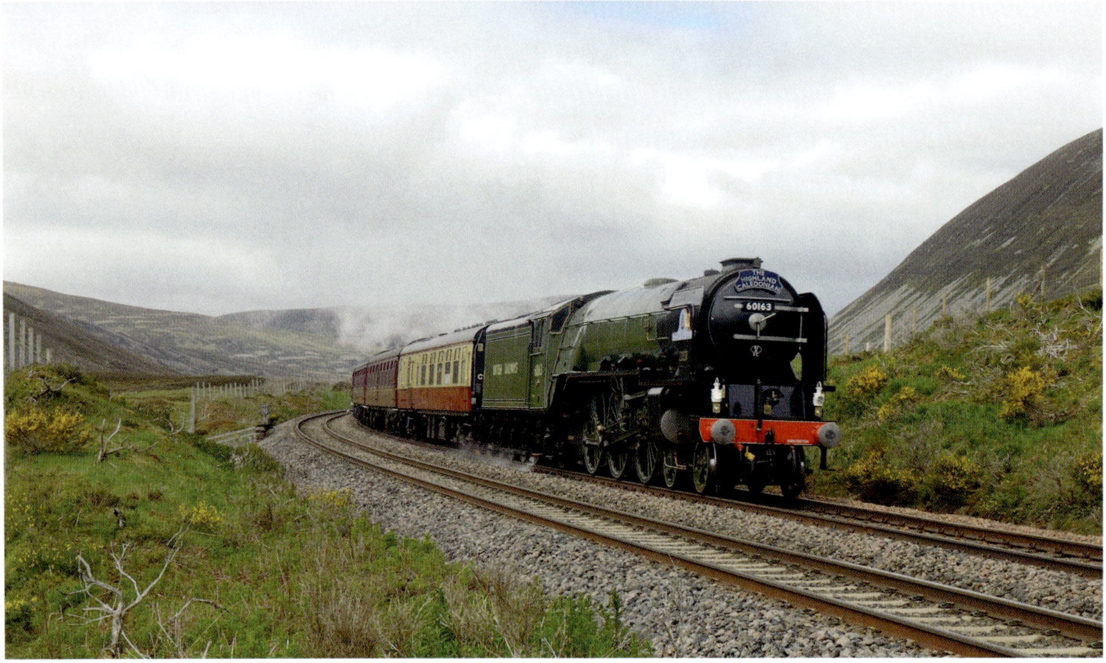

No. 60163 *Tornado* has just passed the summit with a ScotRail sponsored trip from Inverness on 22 June 2015.

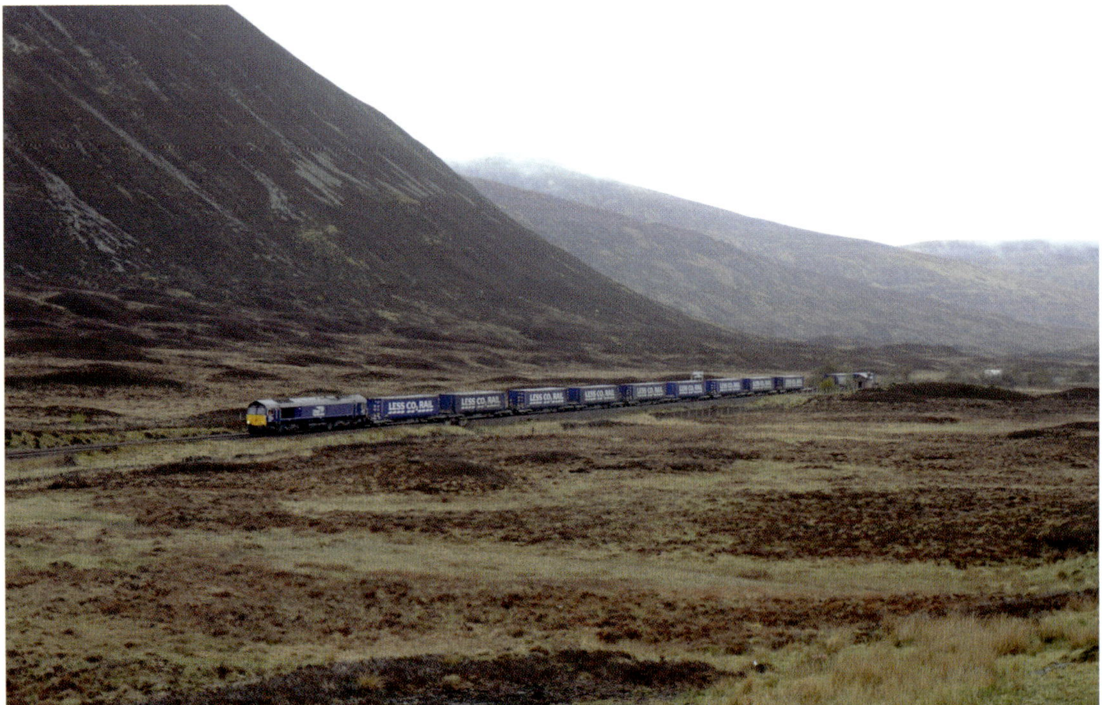

A Class 66 passes the summit nameboard with the Inverness to Mossend freight on 10 May 2019.

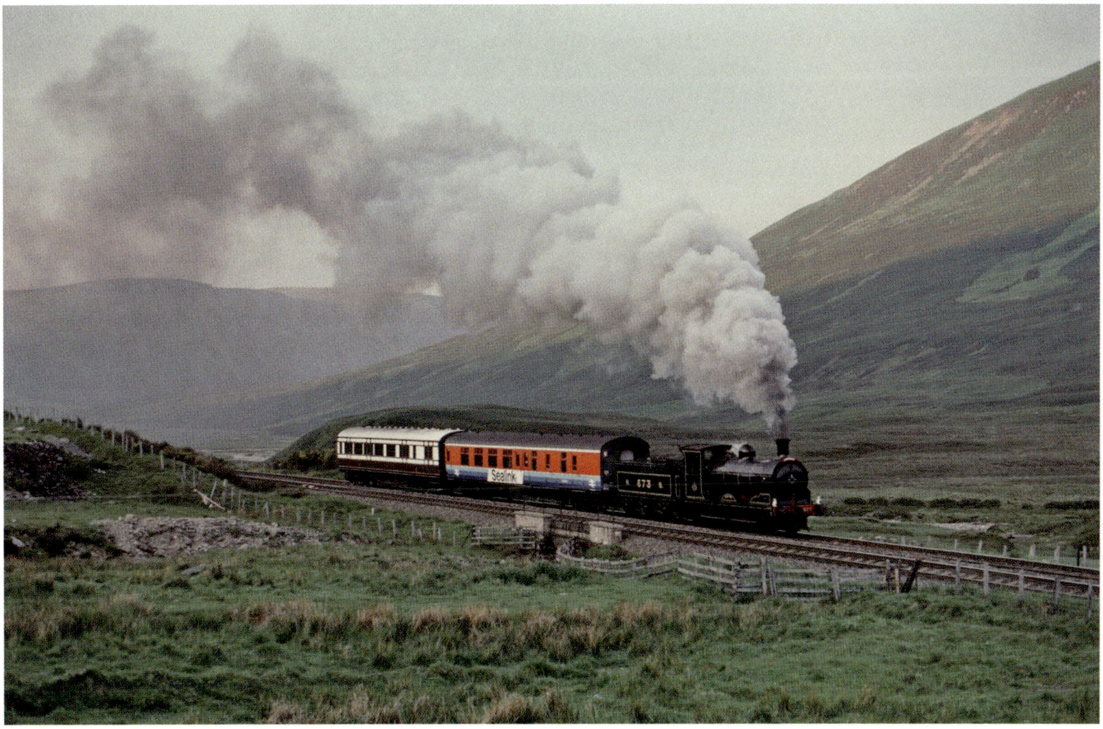

No. 673 *Maude* nears the summit in the early hours of 27 June 1986, on the way to Inverness Railfair.

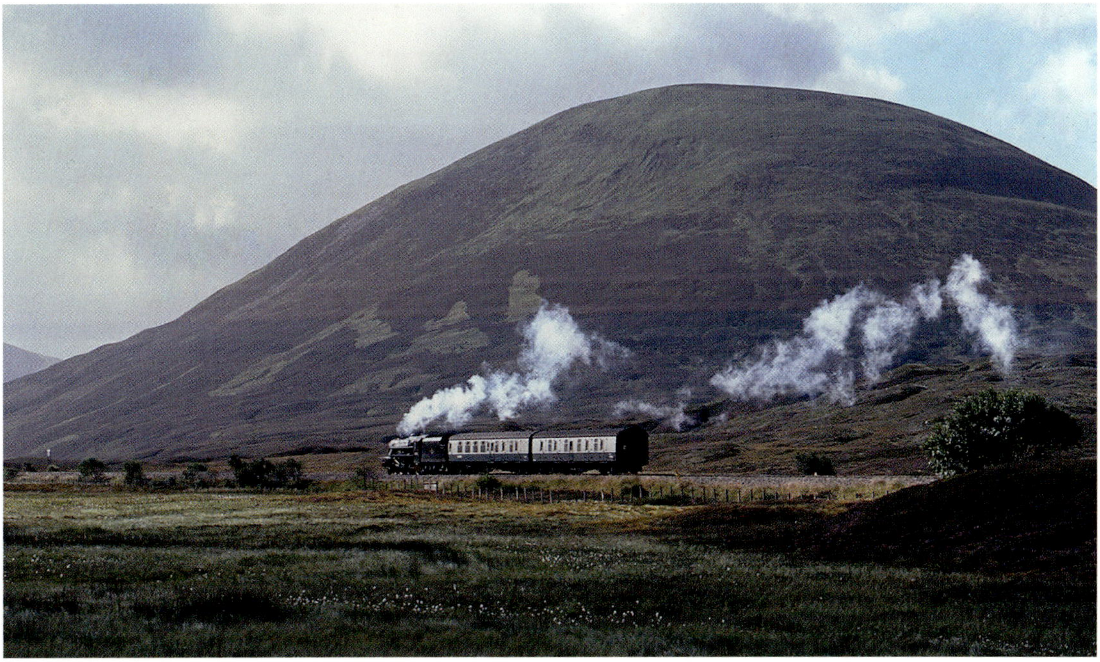

The Boar of Badenoch dominates the background as No. 44767 works south towards the summit with a short train on 1 September 1986.

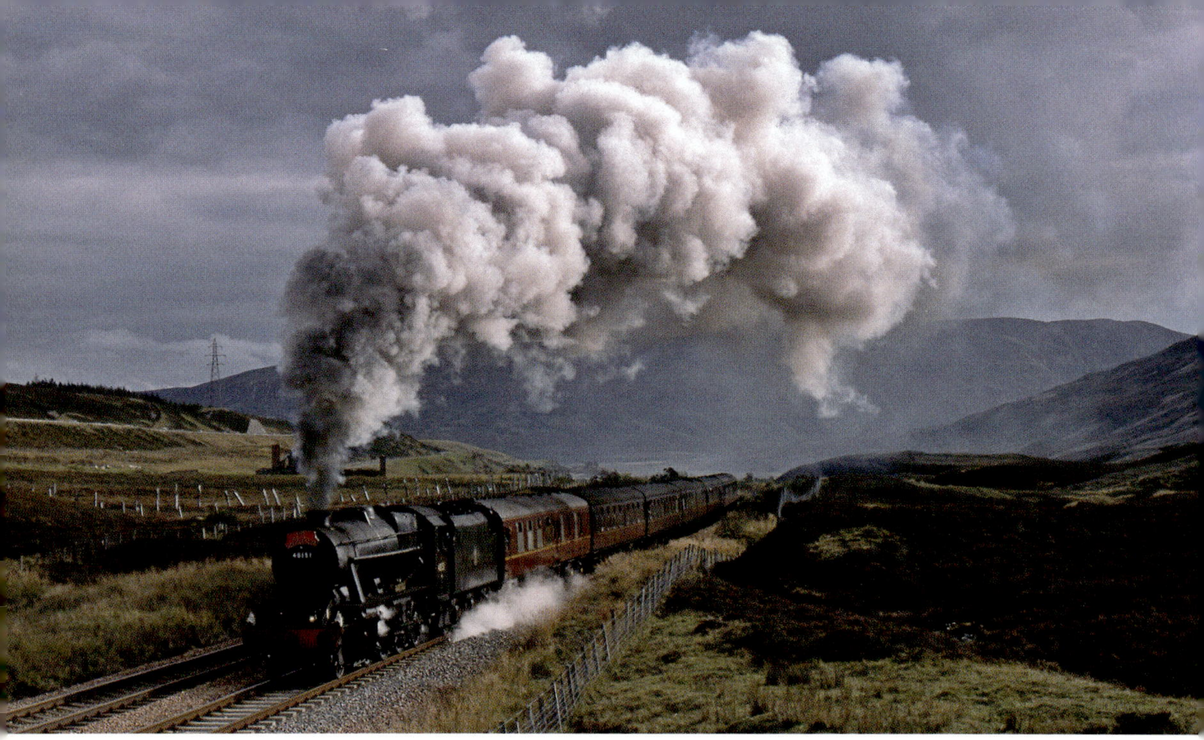

8F No. 48151 tops the climb in fine style on the way north on 3 October 1998.

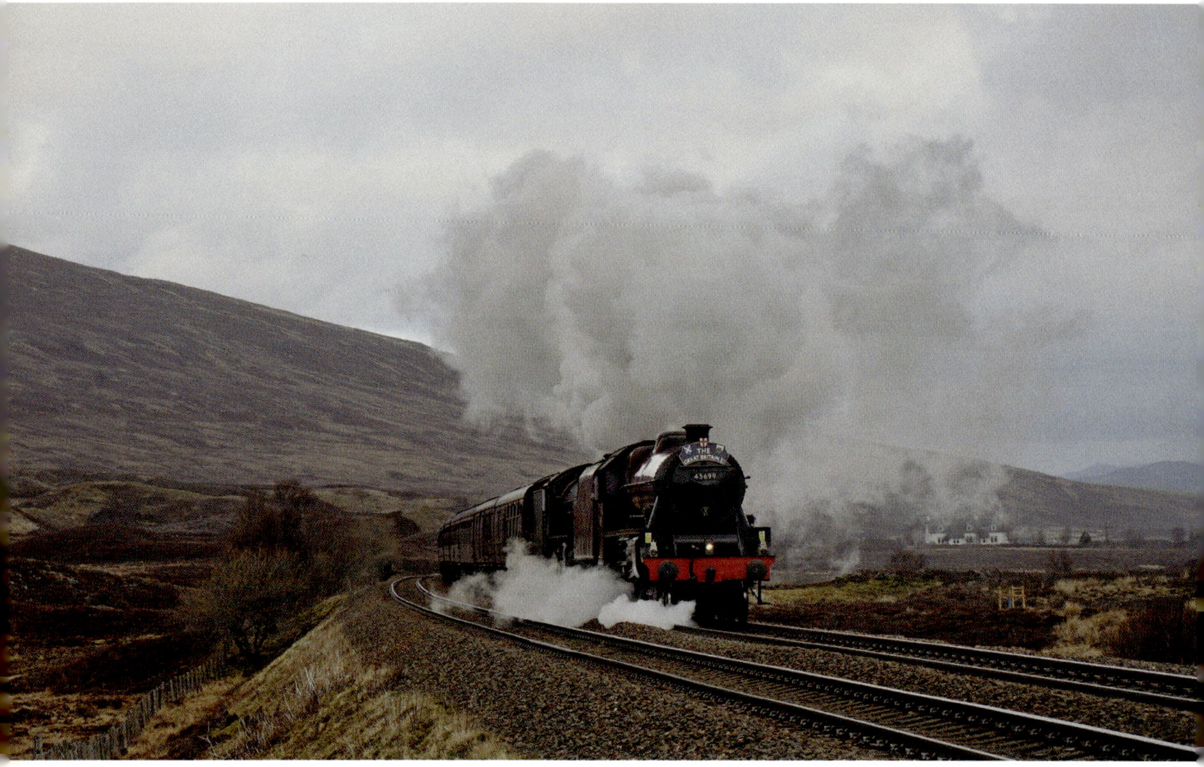

Balsporran cottages are visible in the background as No. 45699 *Galatea* and No. 1264 near the summit from the north on 23 April 2018.

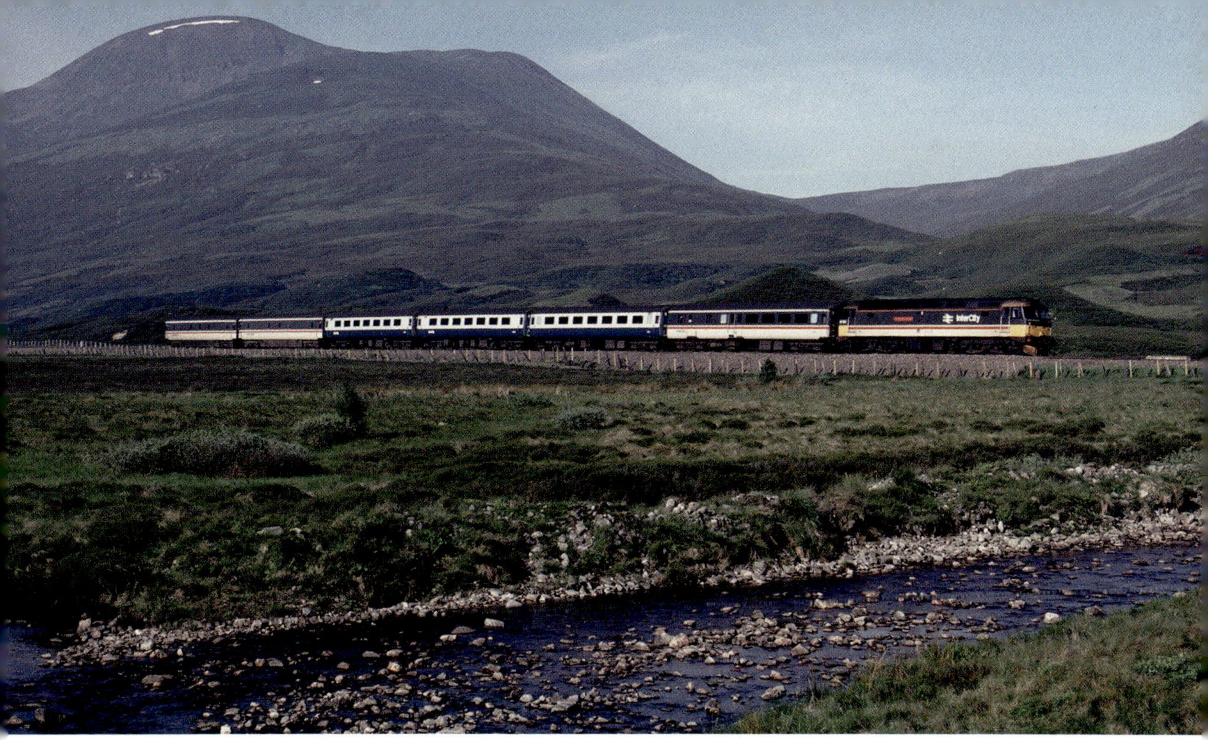

Class 47 No. 47583 near Balsporran cottages with a Glasgow to Inverness train on 19 June 1989.

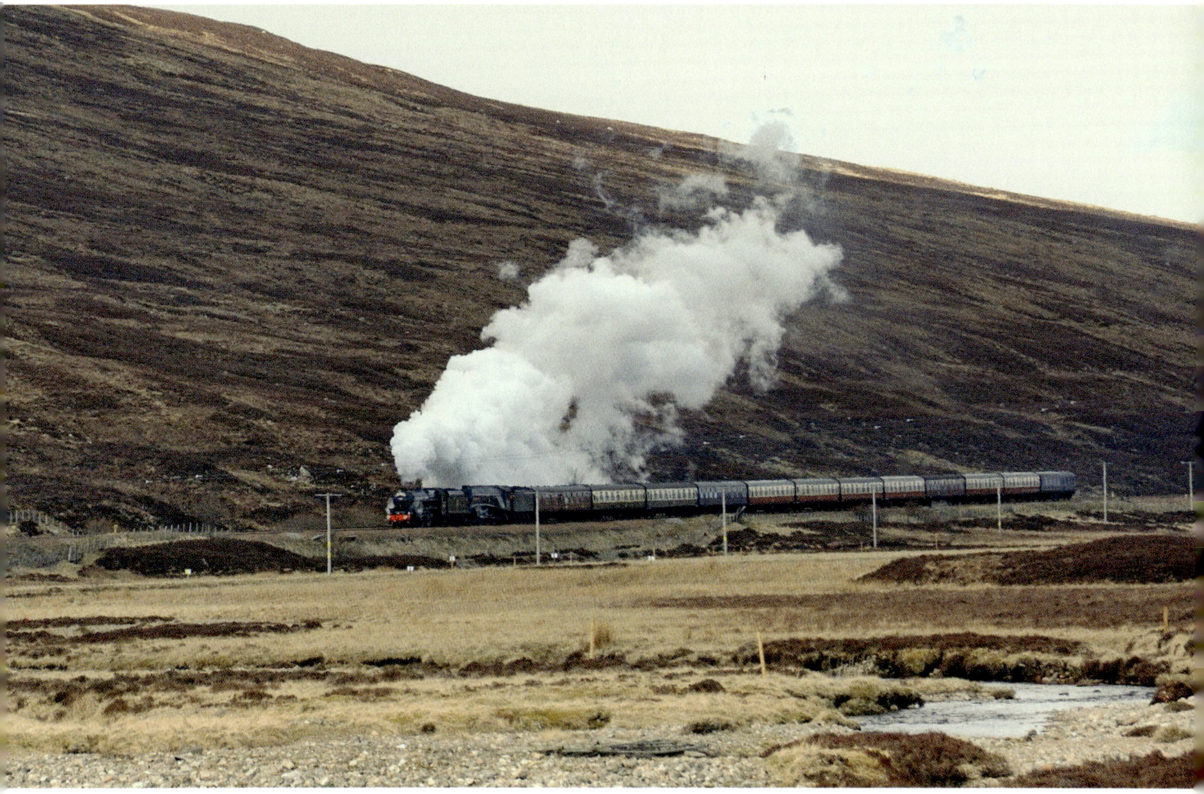

Nos 45407 and 60009 near Balsporran with the North Briton leg to Perth on 15 April 2008.

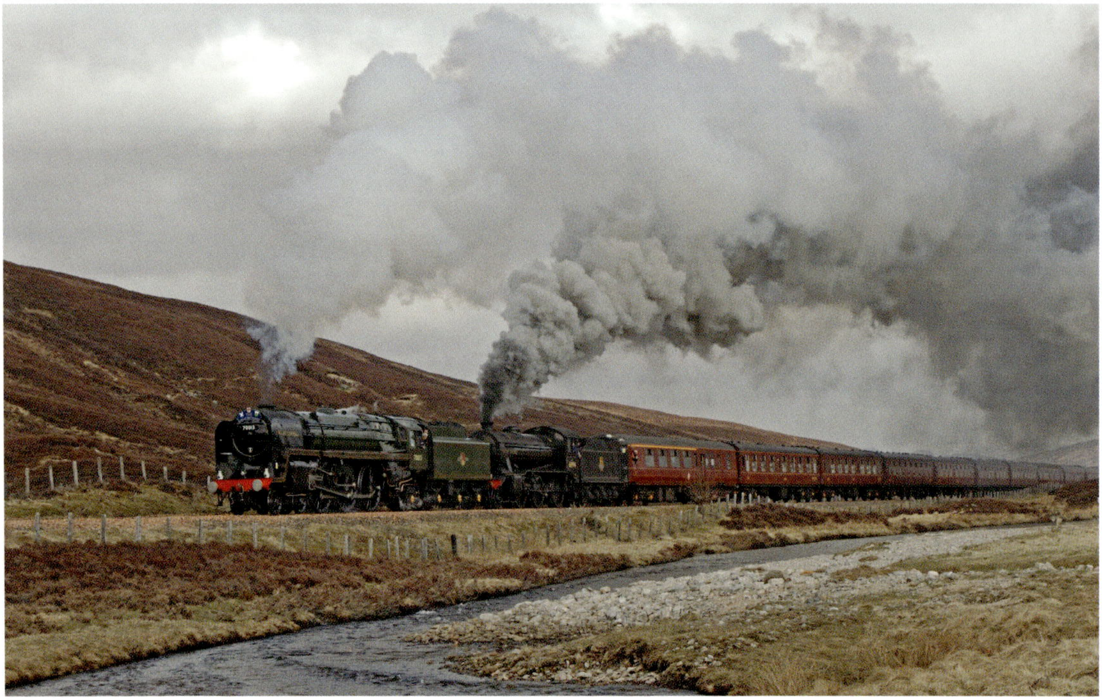

Nos 70013 *Oliver Cromwell* and 61994 *The Great Marquess* work hard on the southbound climb on 13 April 2010.

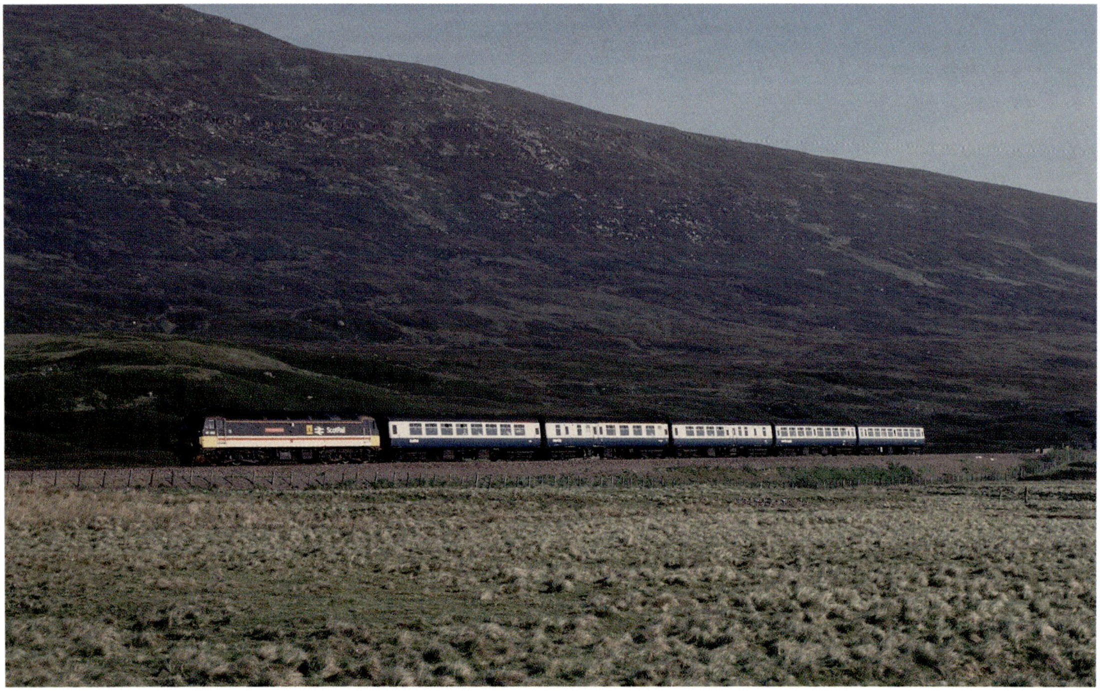

Class 47 No. 47492 on the climb south from Dalwhinnie on 19 June 1989.

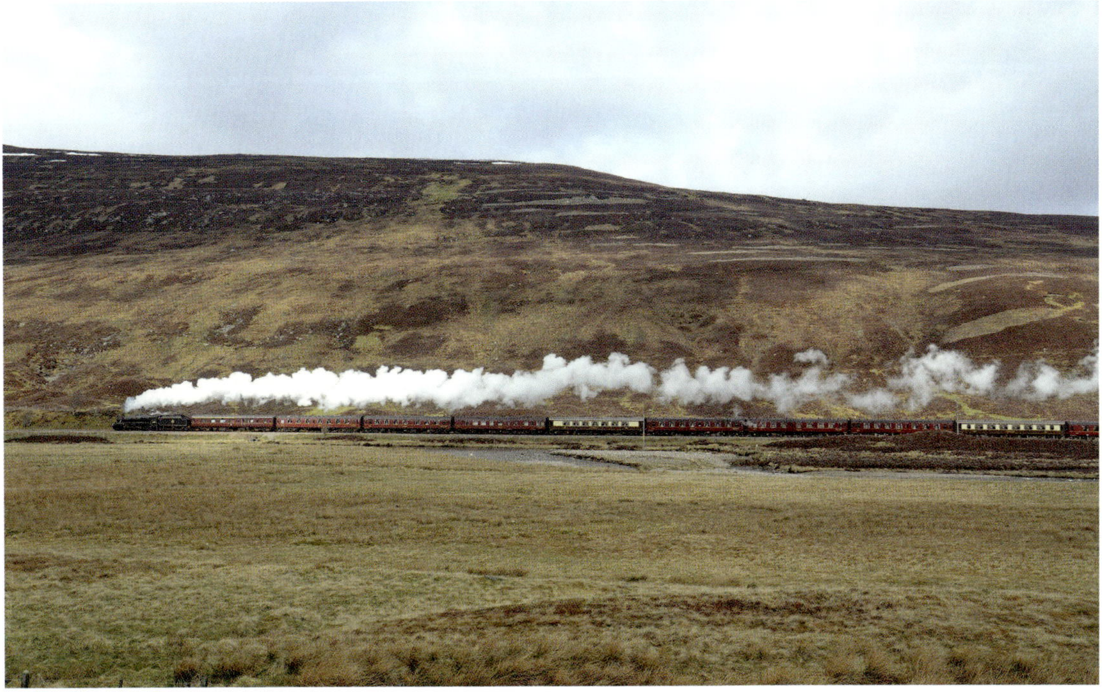

The pass widens somewhat closer to Dalwhinnie as No. 44871 takes GB IX south on 3 May 2016.

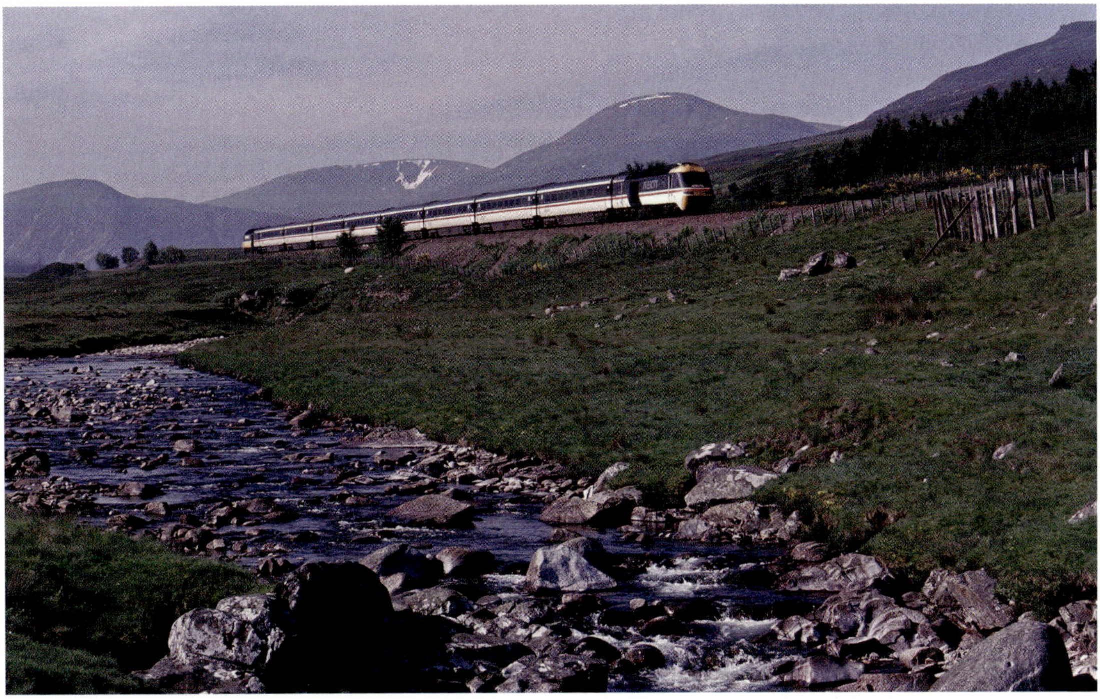

Heading away from the camera near Dalwhinnie, a HST set works the Inverness to Kings Cross service on 19 June 1989.

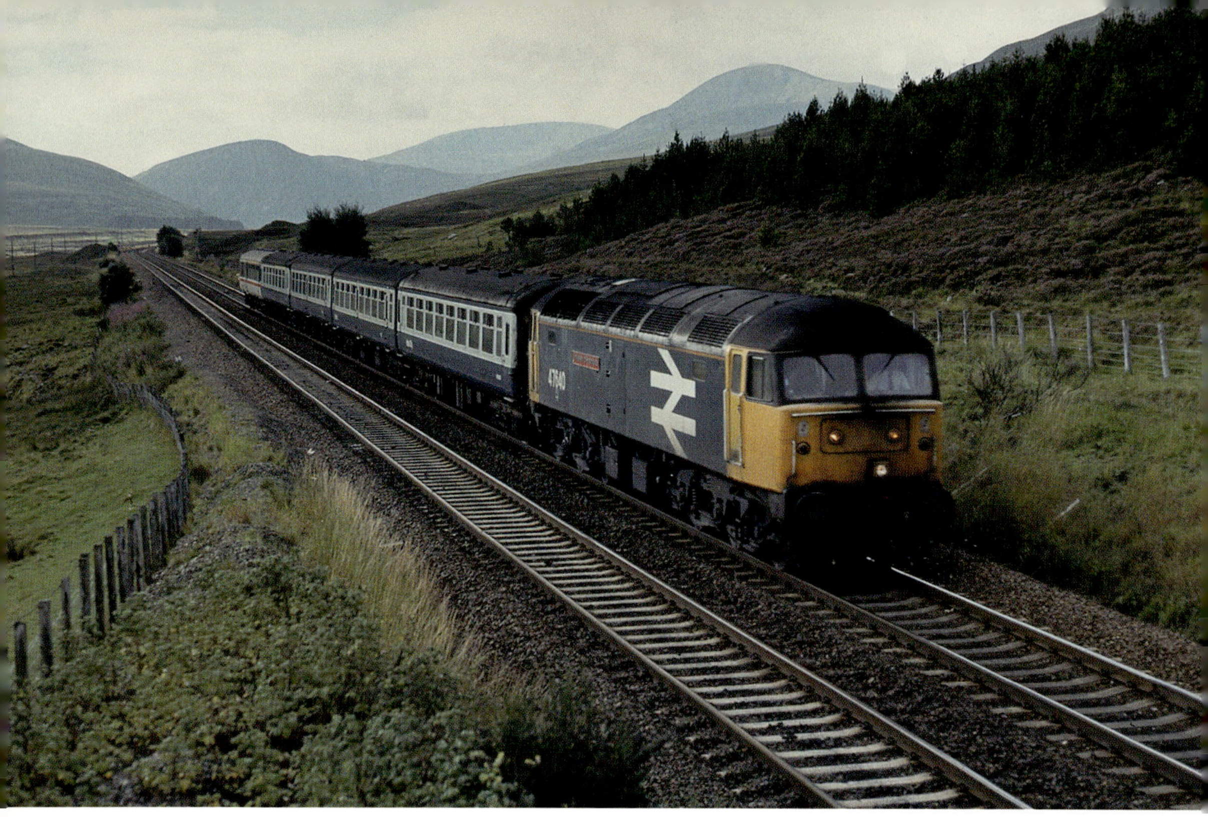

Seen from an overbridge near Dalwhinnie, No. 47640 heads to Inverness on 11 September 1990.

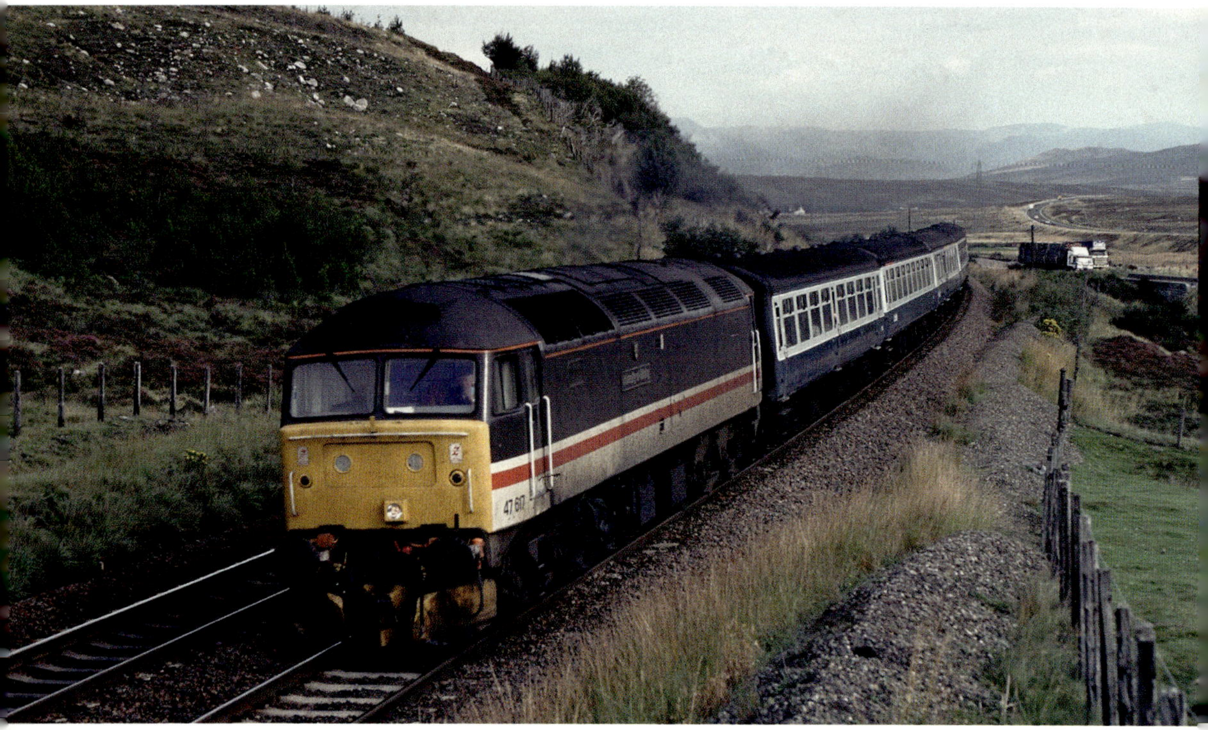

The view north from the bridge as No. 47617 works to Glasgow on the same day.

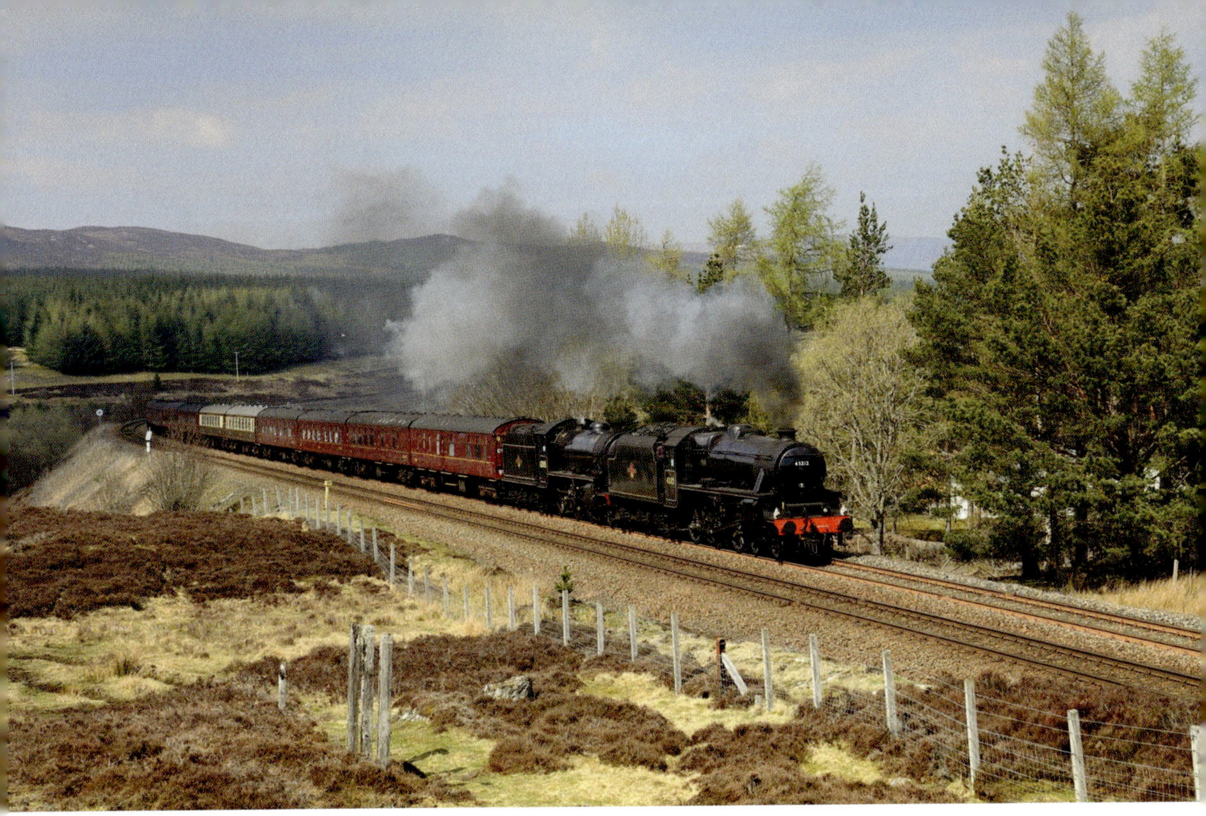

Nos 45212 and 62005 work away from Dalwhinnie with the southbound GB X on 2 May 2017.

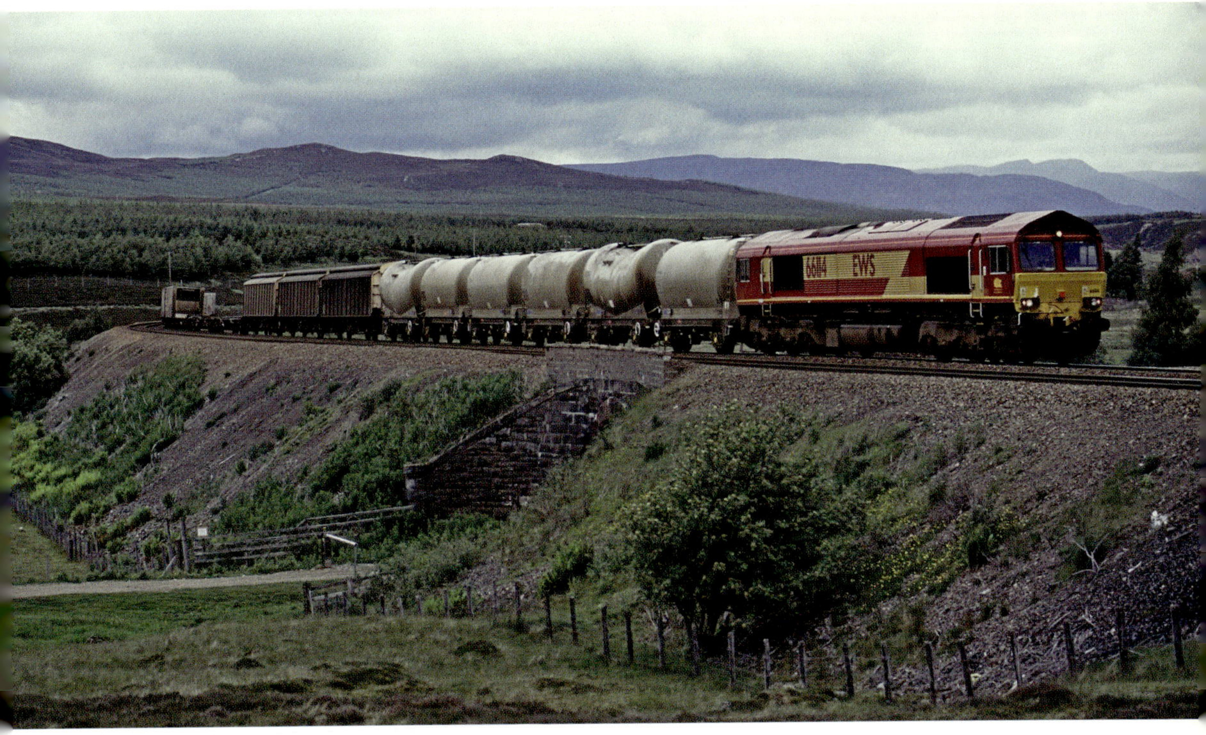

Class 66 No. 66114 leaves Dalwhinnie with a freight south in June 2000.

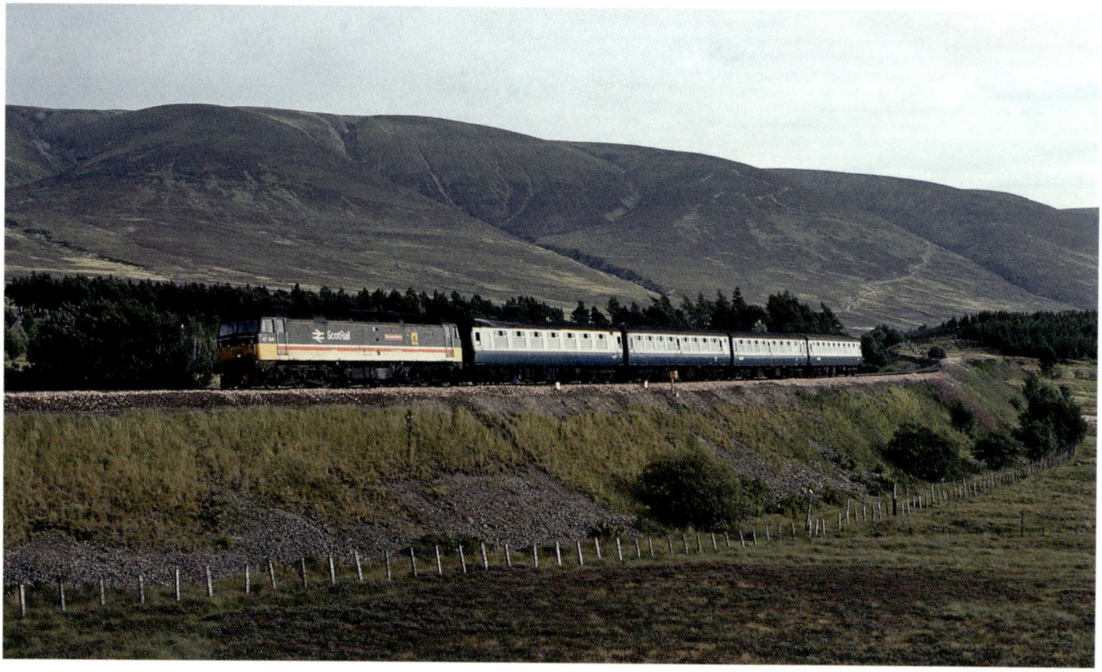

No. 47541 leans into the curve as it approaches Dalwhinnie with a train for Inverness on 1 September 1990.

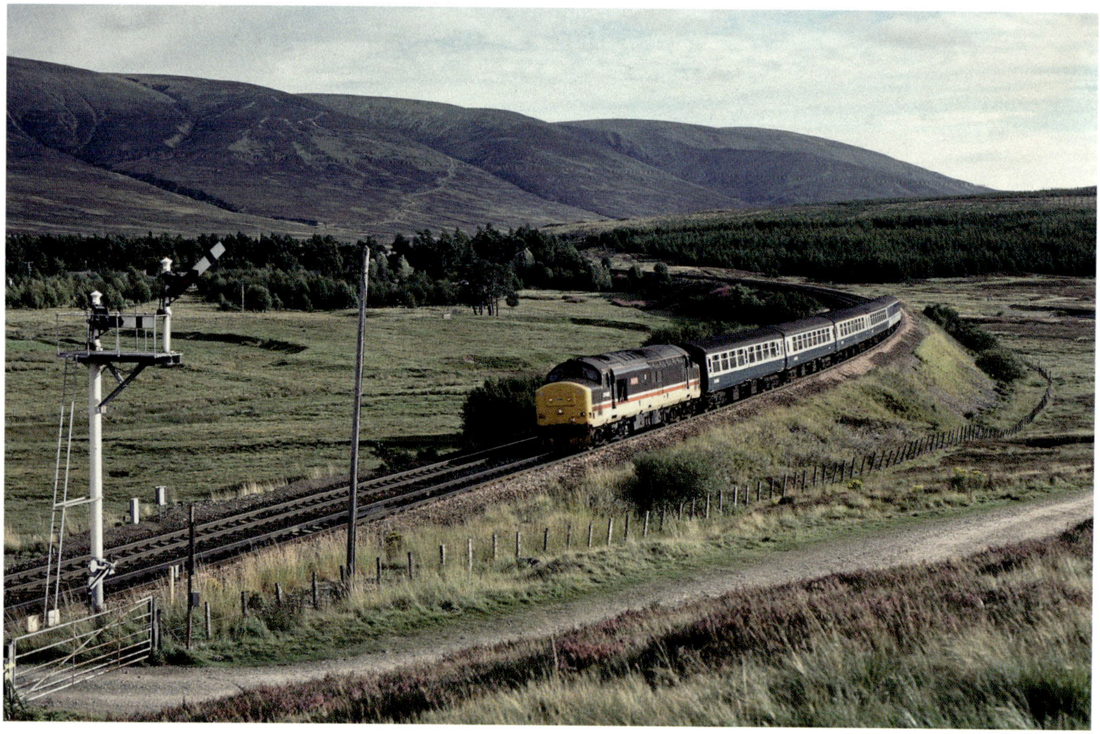

No. 37402 gets the road into Dalwhinnie with a Glasgow to Inverness service on 10 September 1990.

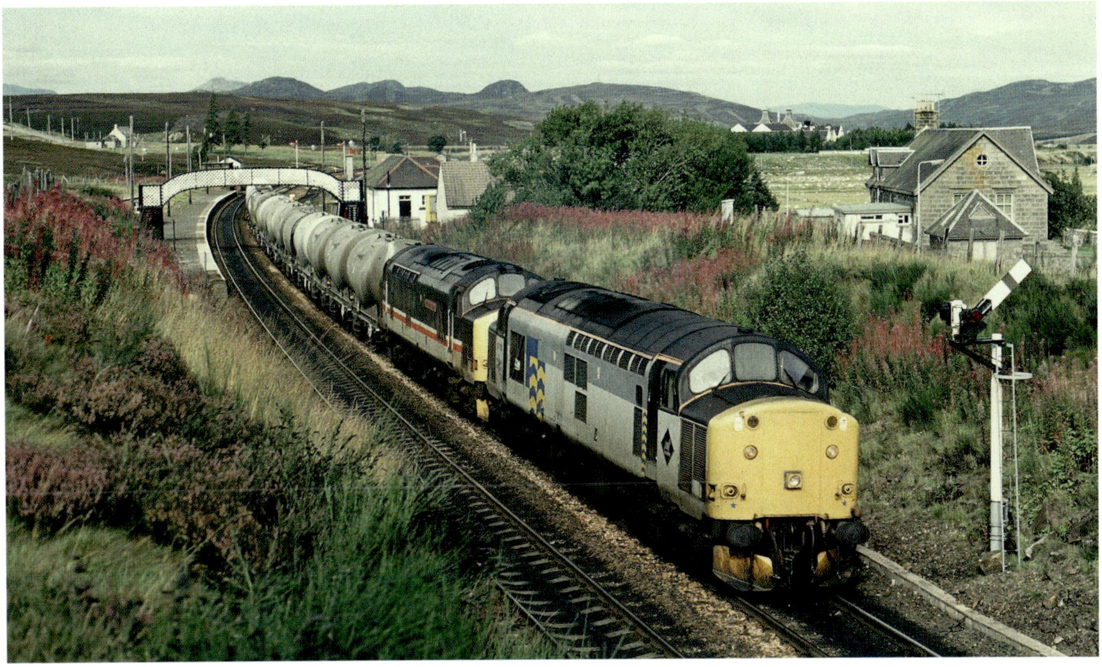

A pair of Class 37s, led by No. 37708, pass Dalwhinnie station with a freight south on 10 September 1990.

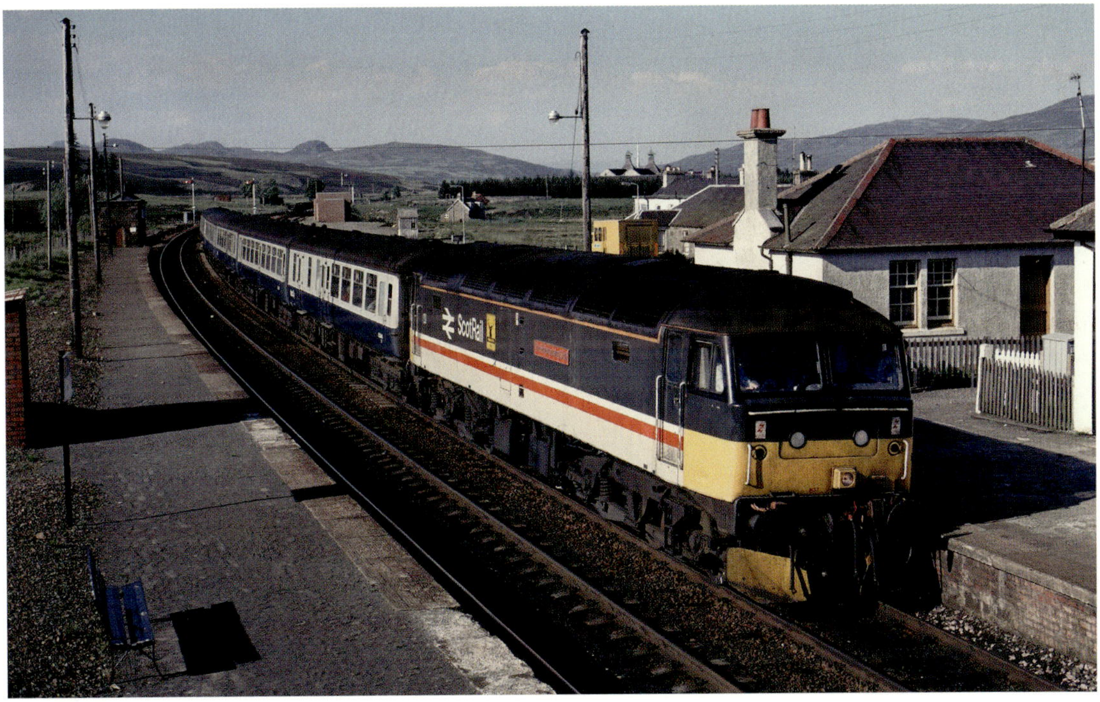

No. 47492 *The Enterprising Scot* pauses at Dalwhinnie station with a train to Glasgow on 18 June 1989.

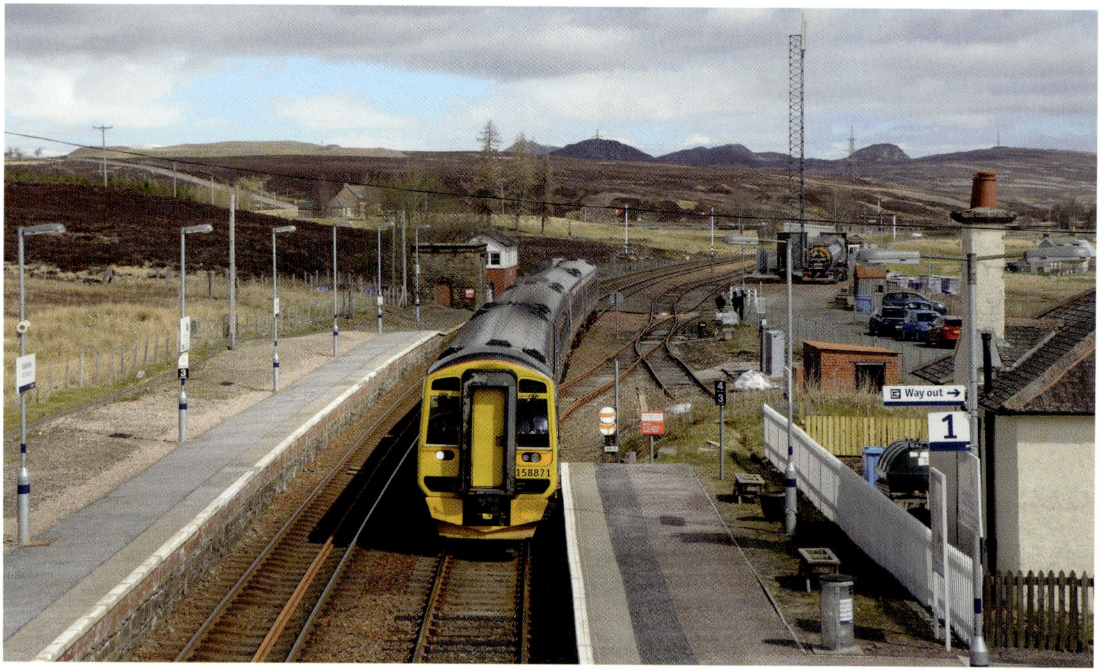

A 158 unit enters Dalwhinnie station with a service south on 30 April 2016. A water tanker waits by the sidings for a steam special.

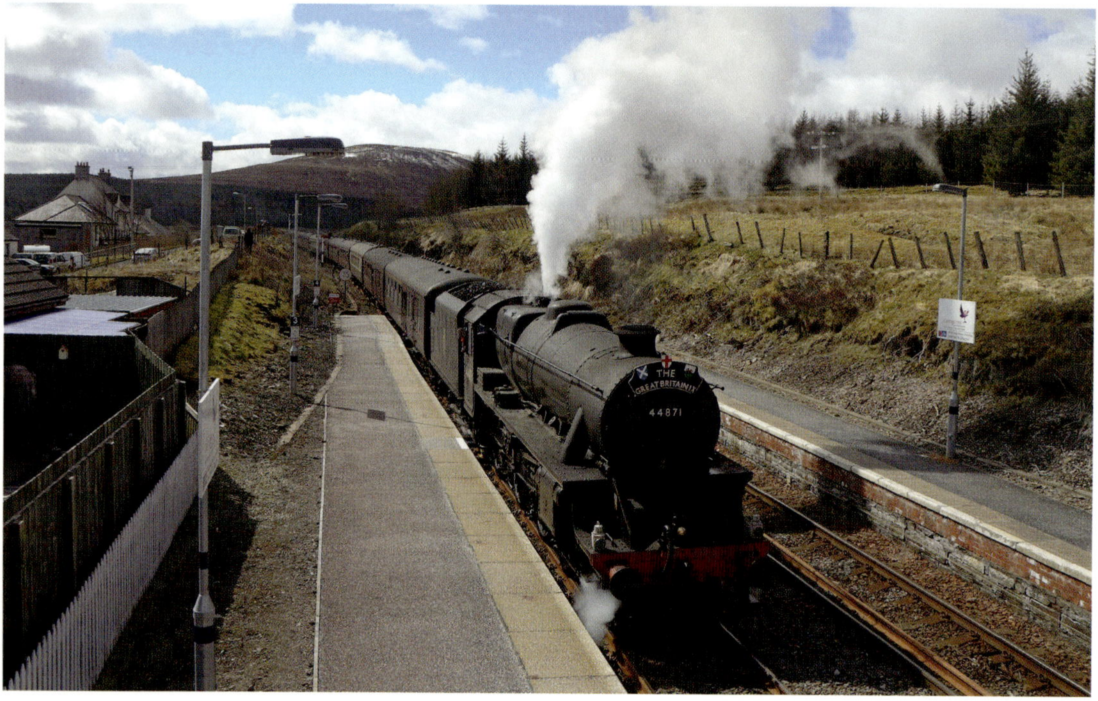

No. 44871 moves slowly through the station and will receive a water top up from the tanker shown in the previous picture.

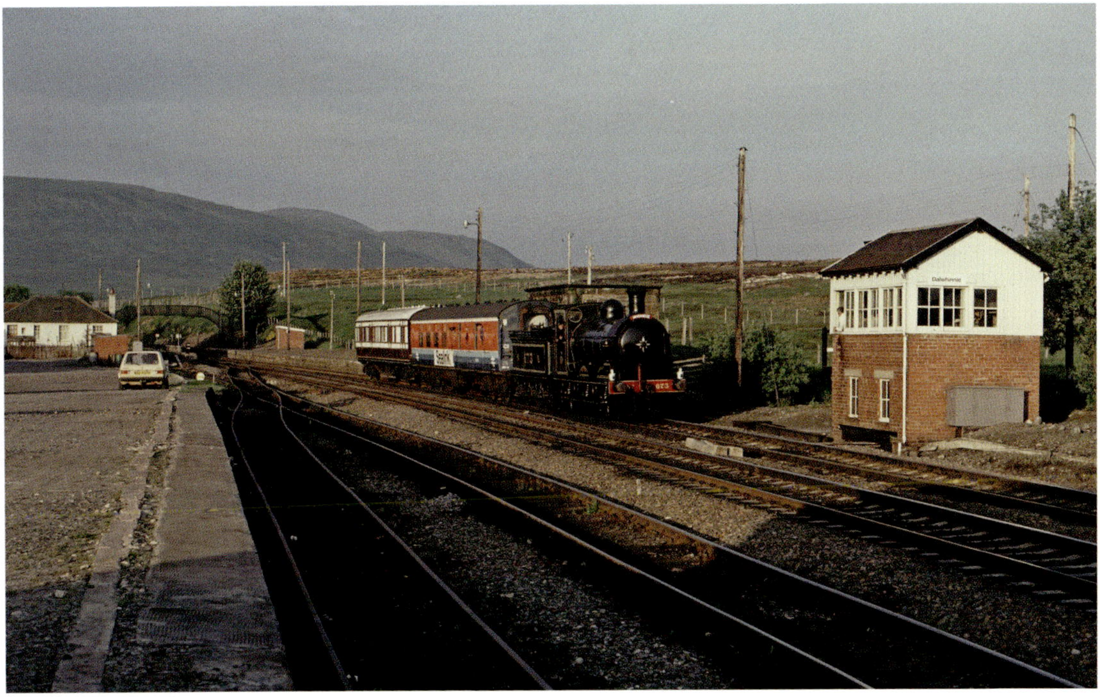

No. 673 *Maude* waits by the signal cabin on the way north on 27 June 1986.

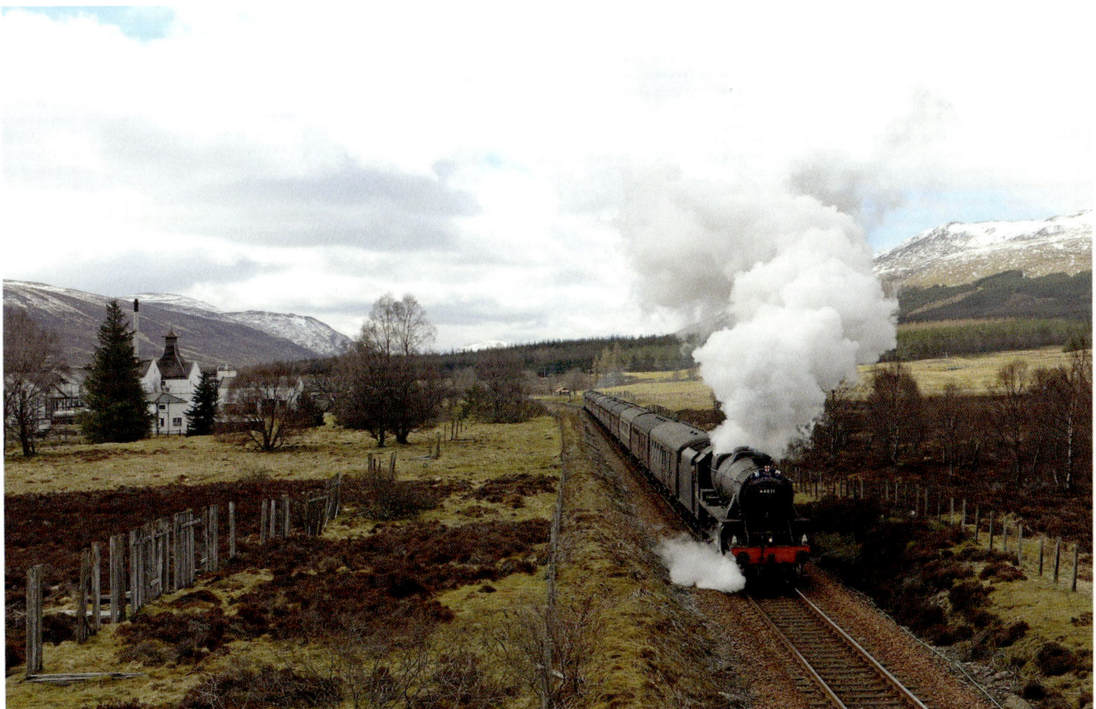

No. 44871 passes the distillery as it leaves Dalwhinnie with GB IX to Inverness on 30 April 2016.

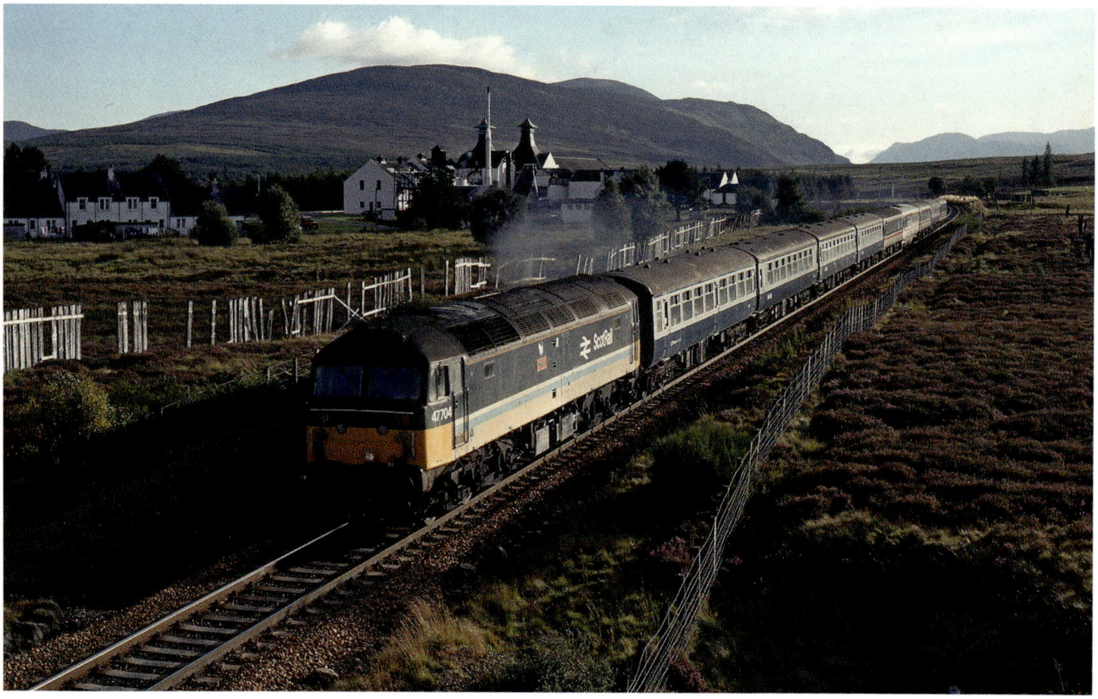

With the distillery in the background, No. 47704 heads north on 10 September 1990.

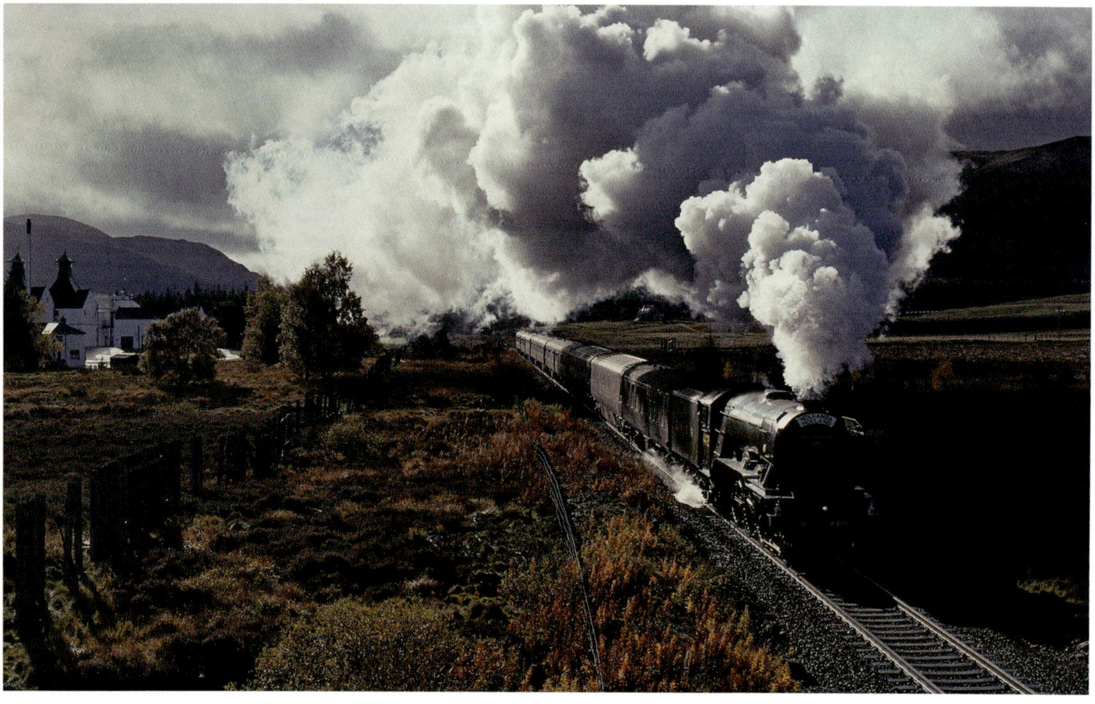

No. 4472 *Flying Scotsman* makes a spirited departure from Dalwhinnie with the private charter to Inverness on 19 October 2000.

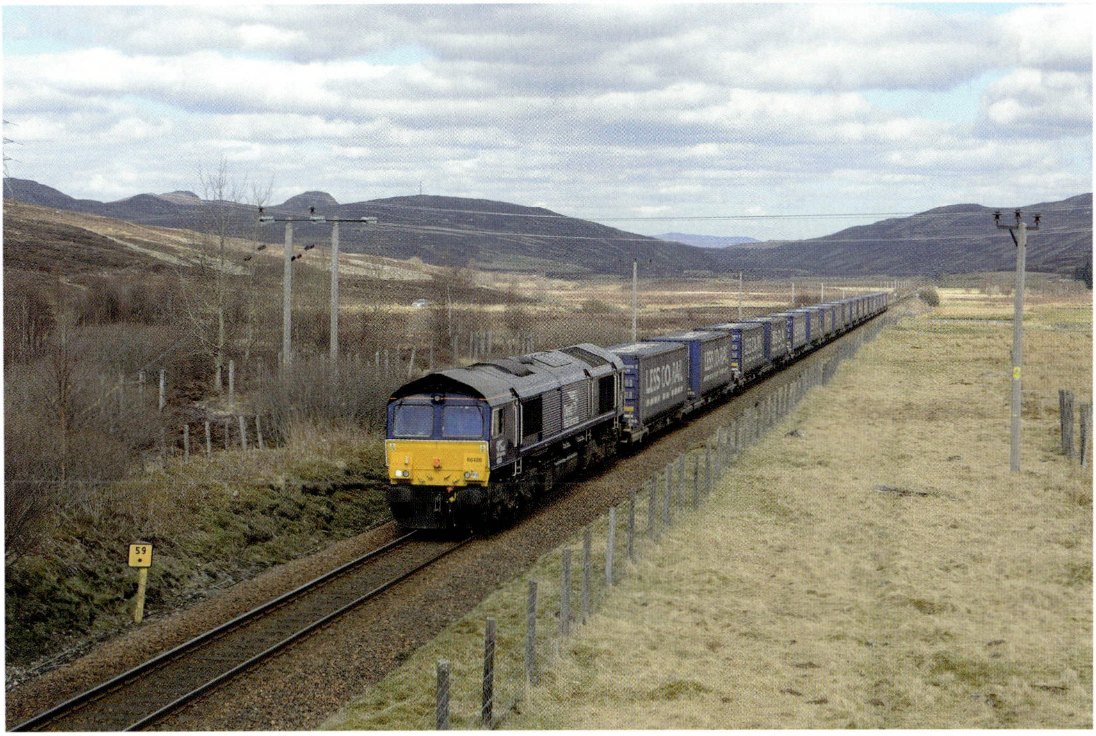

Class 66 No. 66426 approaches Dalwhinnie with the Inverness to Mossend Tesco service on 21 April 2018.

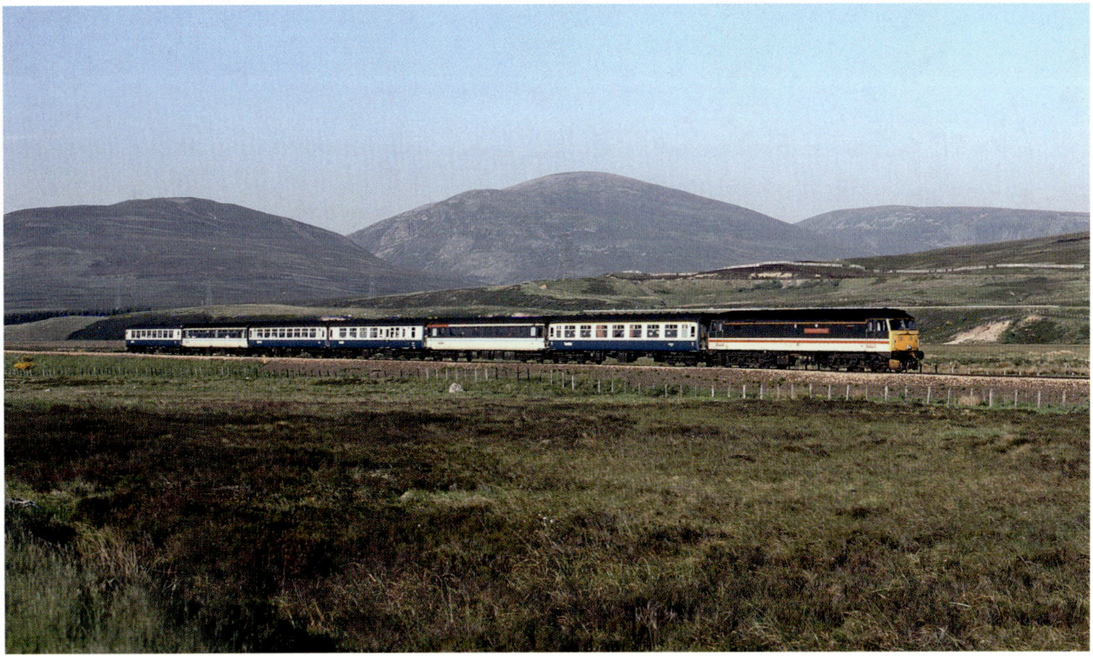

No. 47470 nears Dalwhinnie southbound on 5 September 1989.

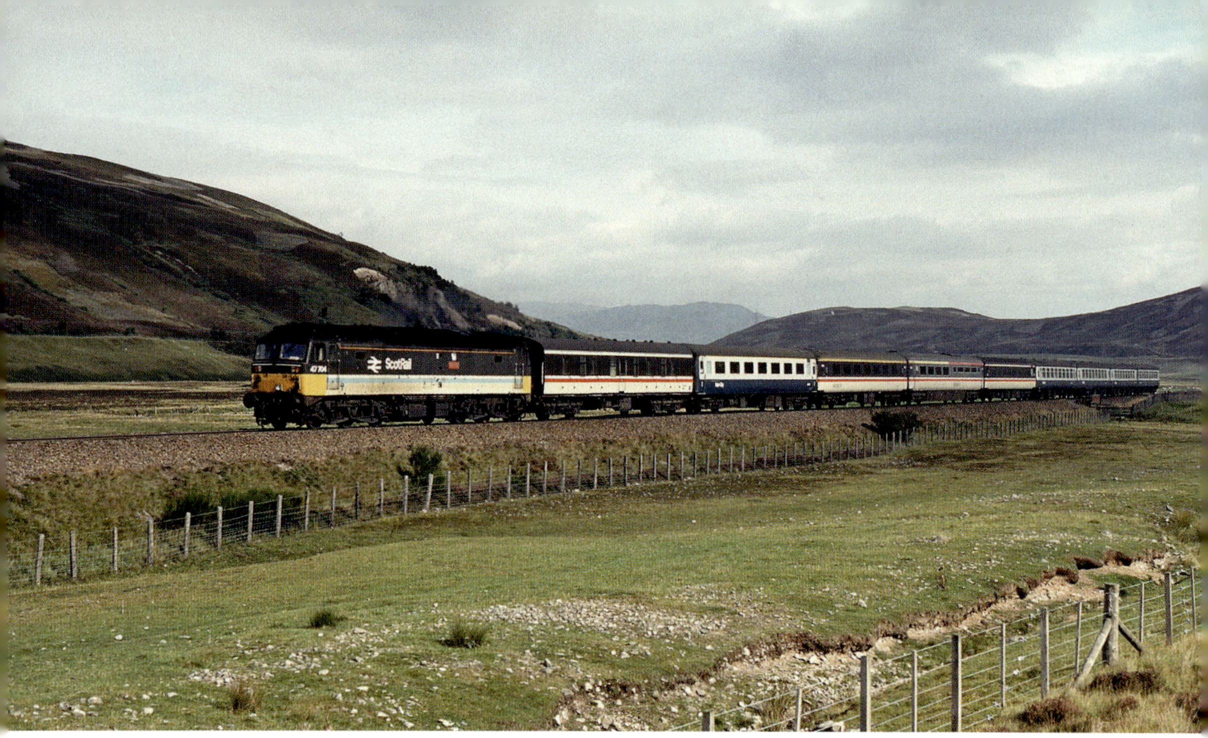

No. 47704 in Glentruim with an Inverness to Glasgow service on 11 September 1990. The mixed livery of the coaches is typical of that period.

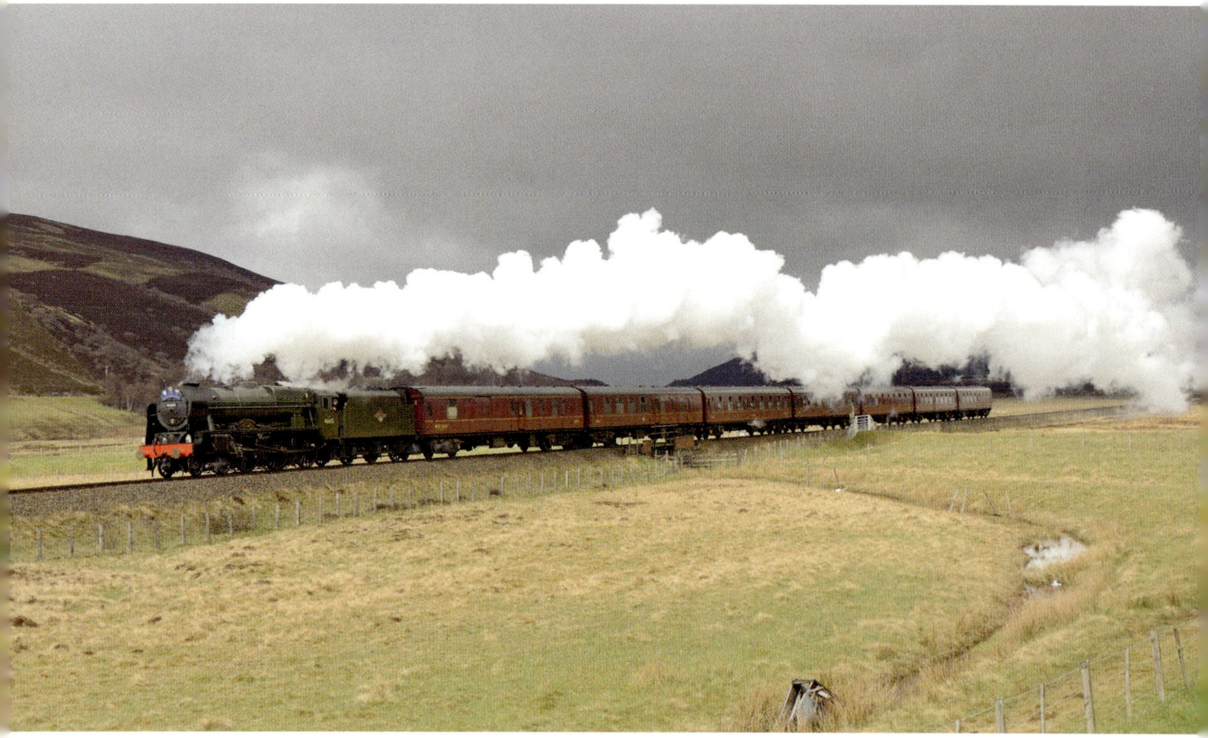

No. 46115 *Scots Guardsman* in Glentruim with the Inverness to Glasgow leg of GB V on 24 April 2012.

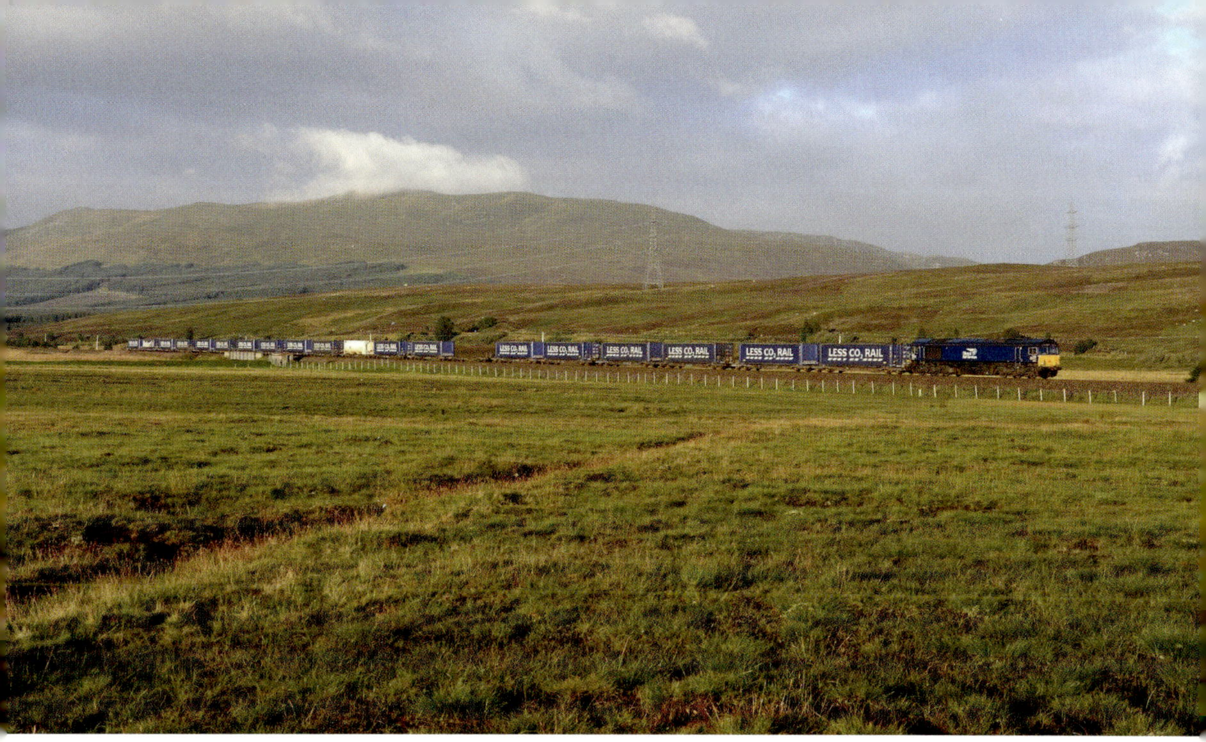

No. 66434 with the Mossend to Inverness Tesco working in Glentruim on 13 September 2019.

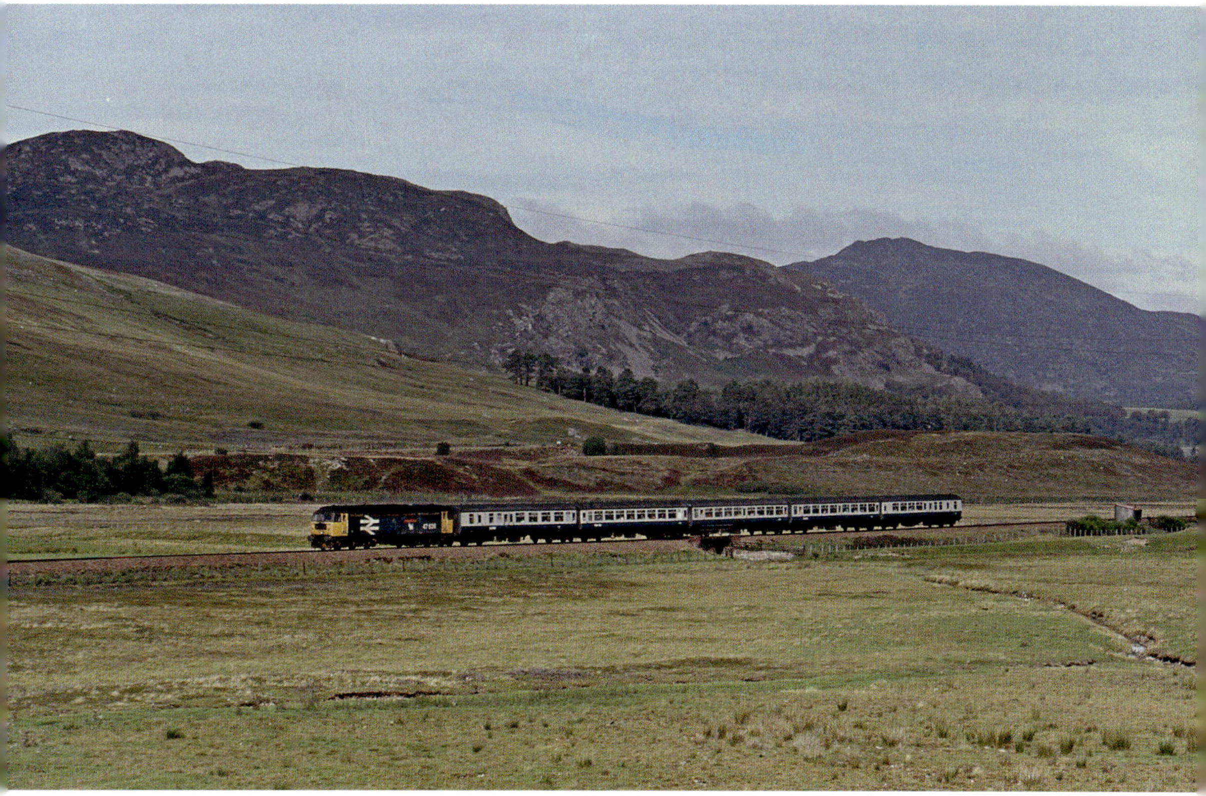

No. 47636 near Crubenmore with a train to Glasgow on 10 September 1990.

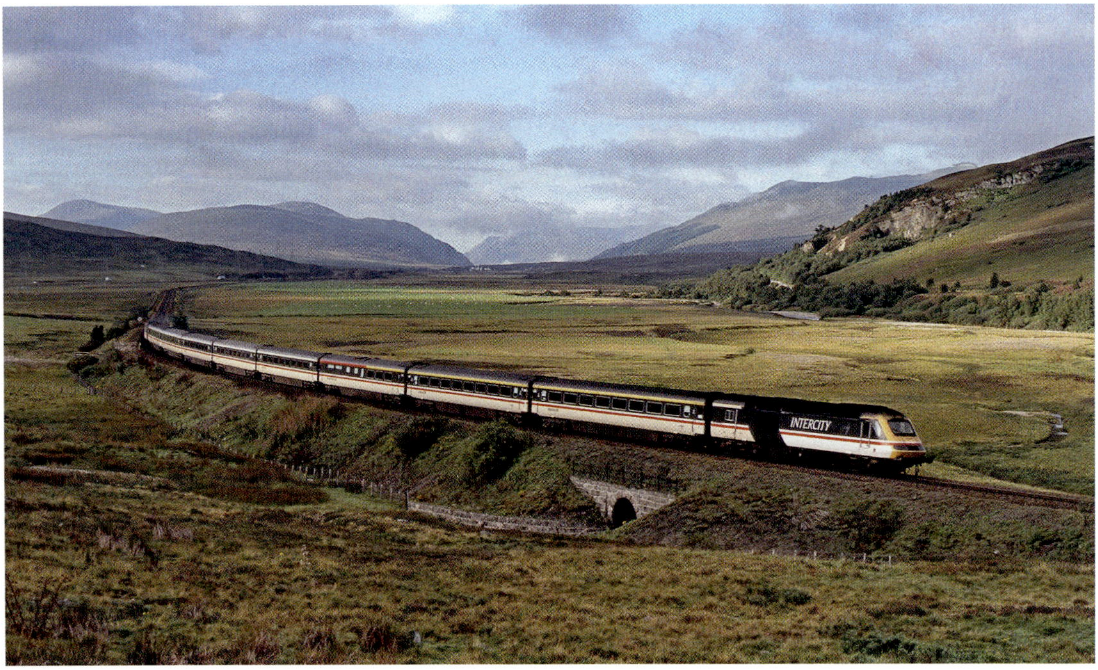

The Inverness to Kings Cross HST heads away from the camera at Crubenmore on 11 September 1990.

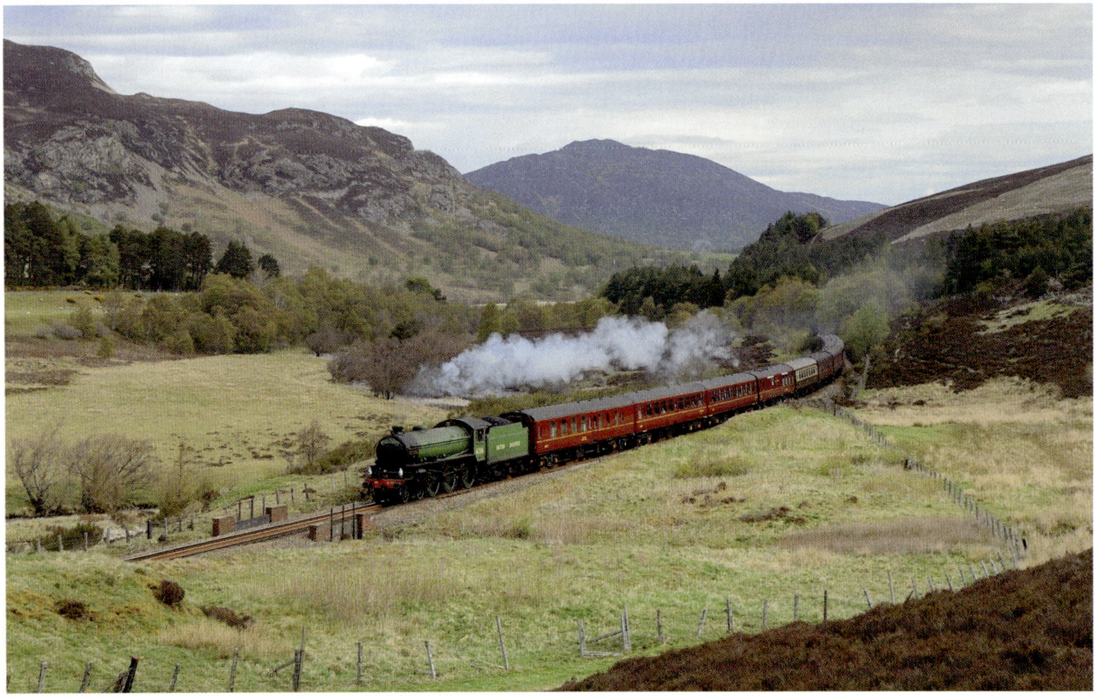

B1 No. 61306 *Mayflower* at Crubenmore with the Inverness to Fort William via Glasgow leg of the Steam Dreams tour on 13 May 2019.

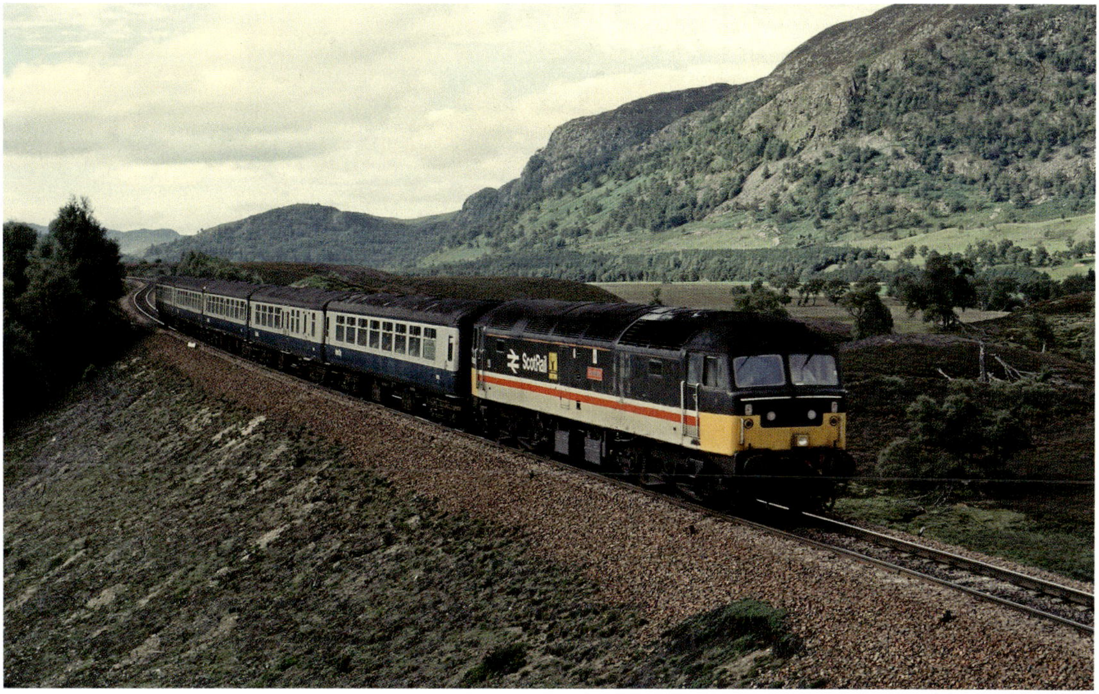

No. 47462 with a northbound working at Ralia on 10 September 1990.

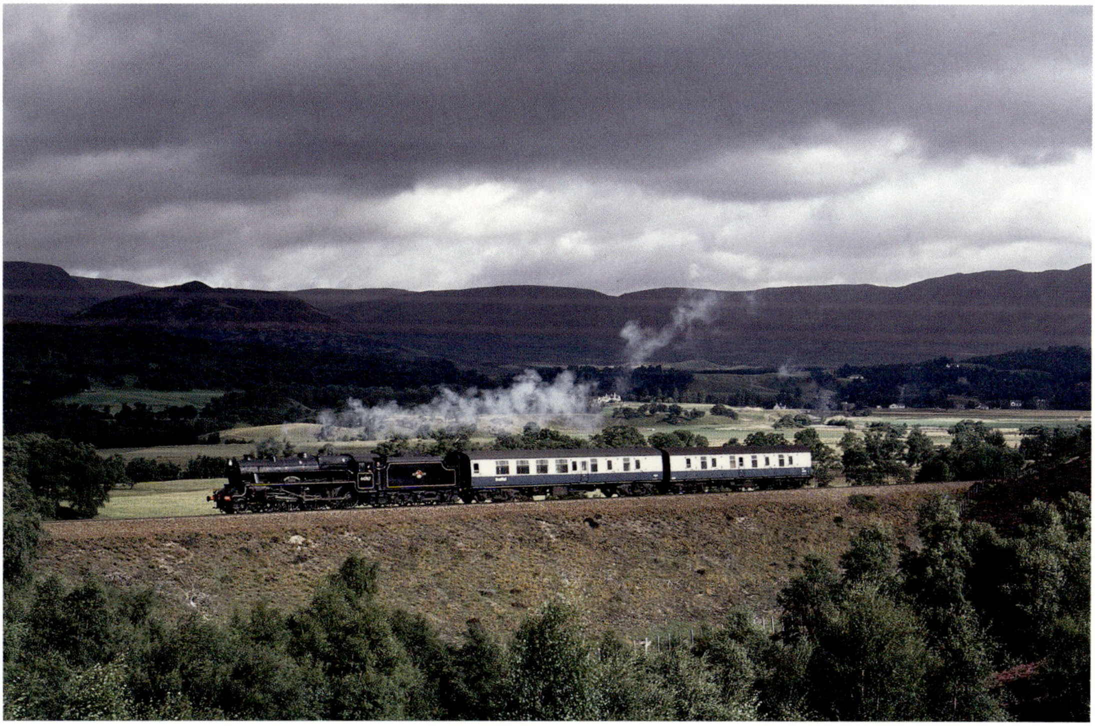

Class 5 No. 44767 passes Ralia heading south with two coaches on 1 September 1986.

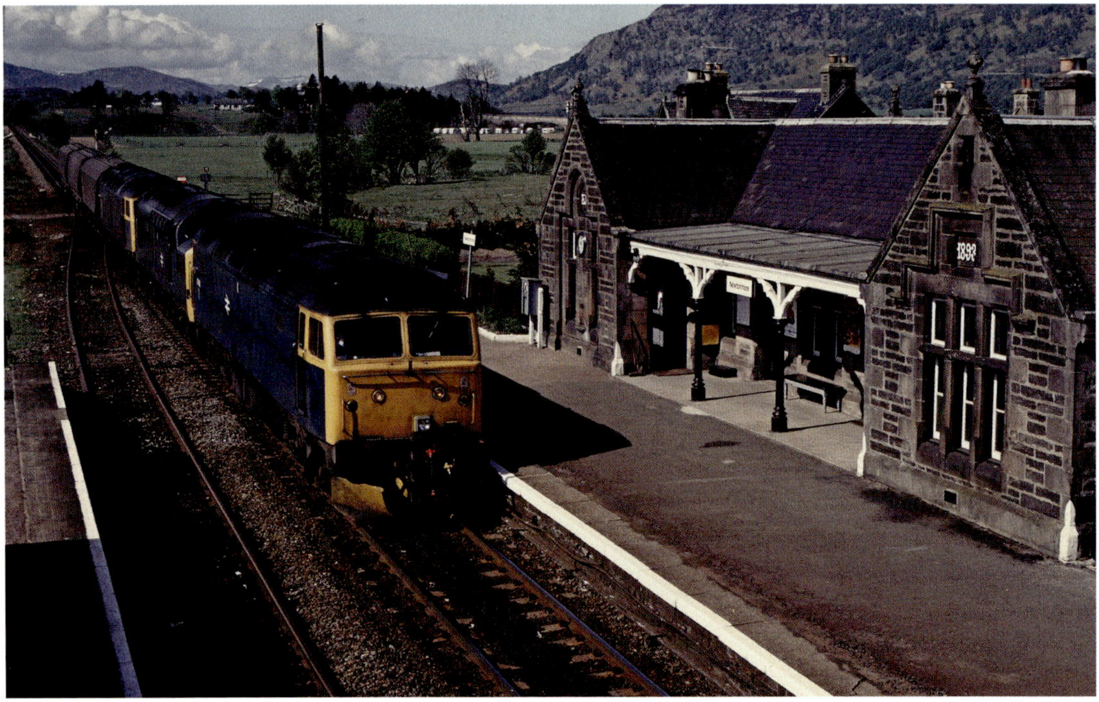

Two Class 47s and a Class 37 provide superpower for a short freight to Inverness on 29 May 1984.

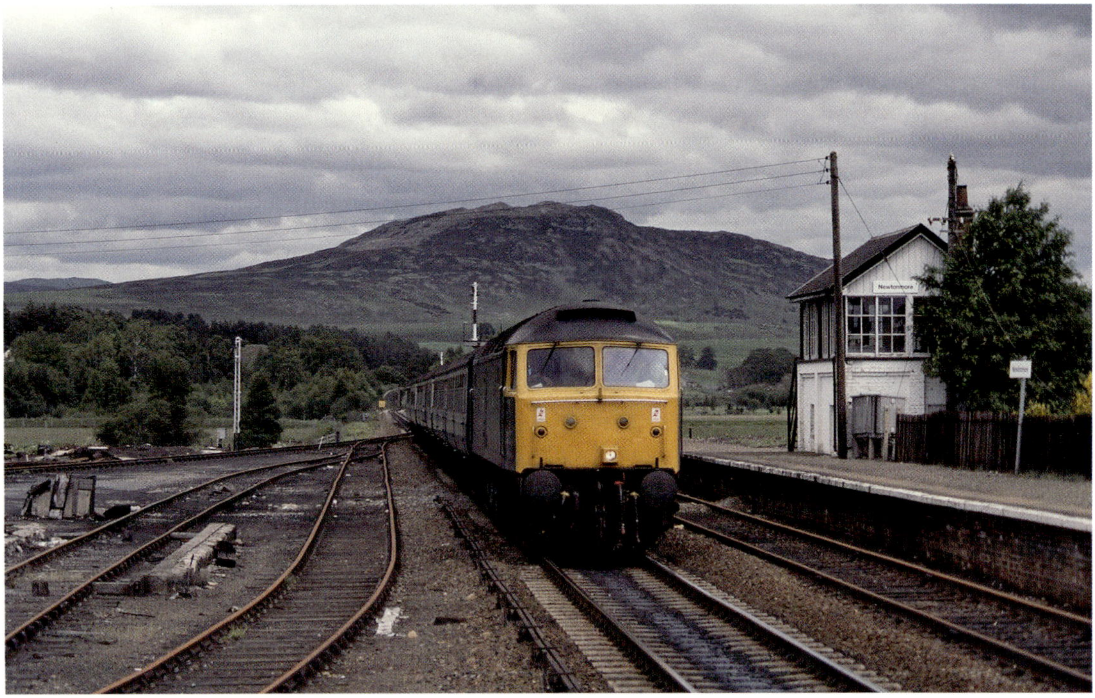

On 29 June 1985 a Class 47 with a train to Glasgow passes the closed signal cabin at Newtonmore after the passing loop there had been taken out of use.

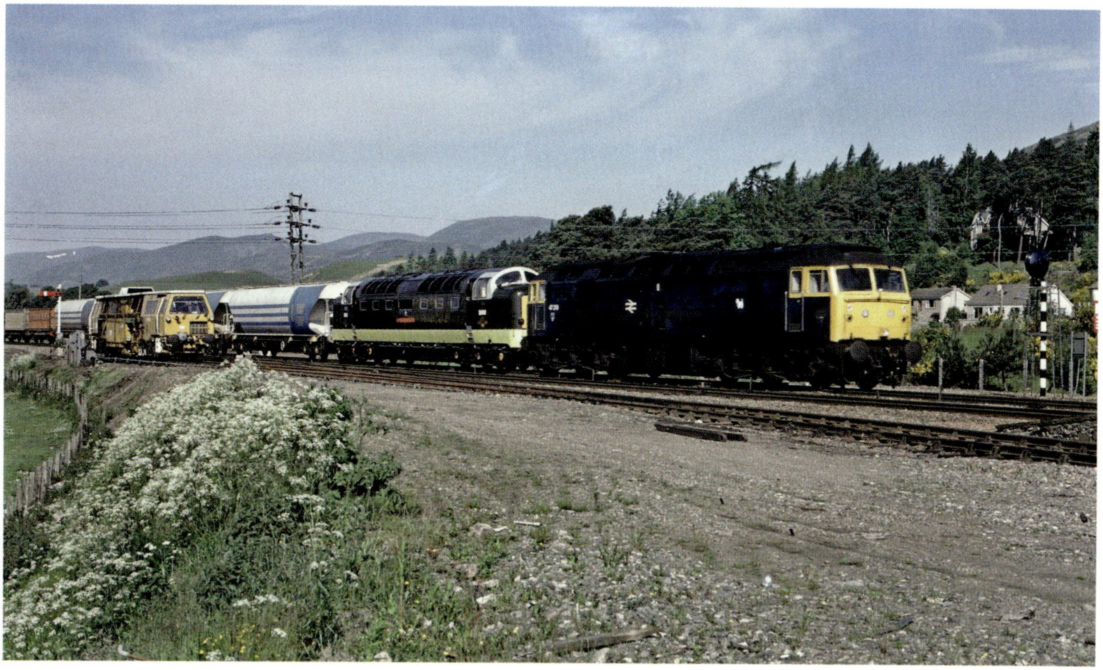

No. 47210 approaches Kingussie with a freight for Inverness on 27 June 1986. The train included a Deltic locomotive being towed to the Inverness Railfair.

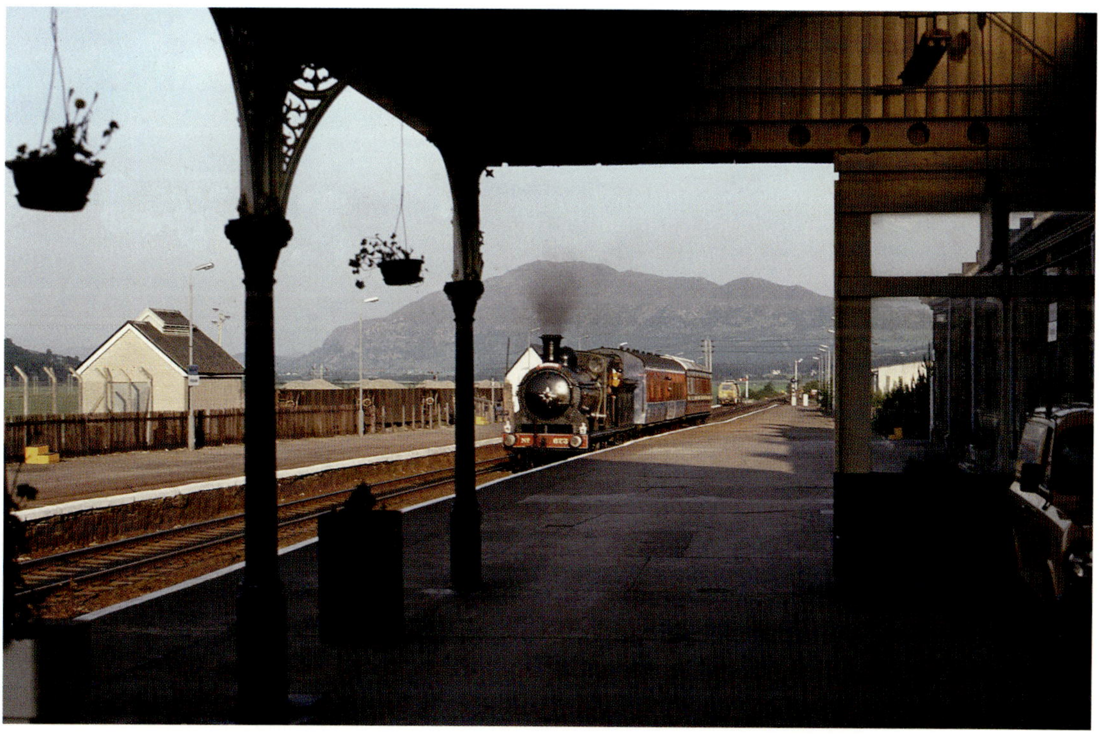

No. 673 *Maude* drifts into Kingussie station on the way north on 27 June 1986.

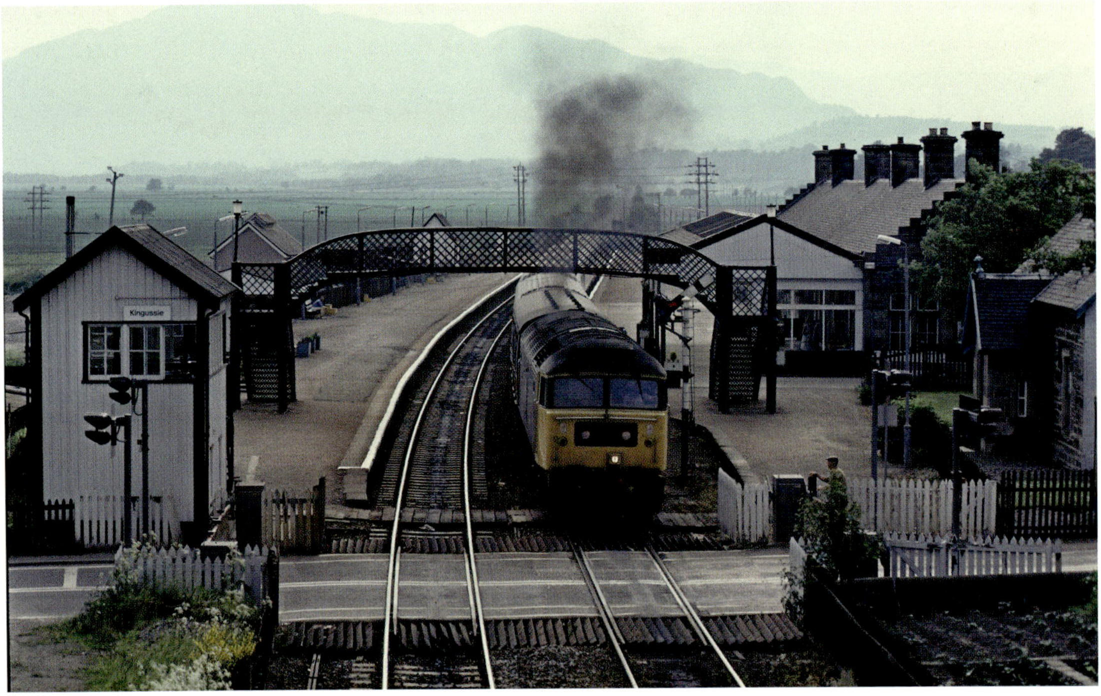

No. 47604 powers away from Kingussie station on 26 June 1986.

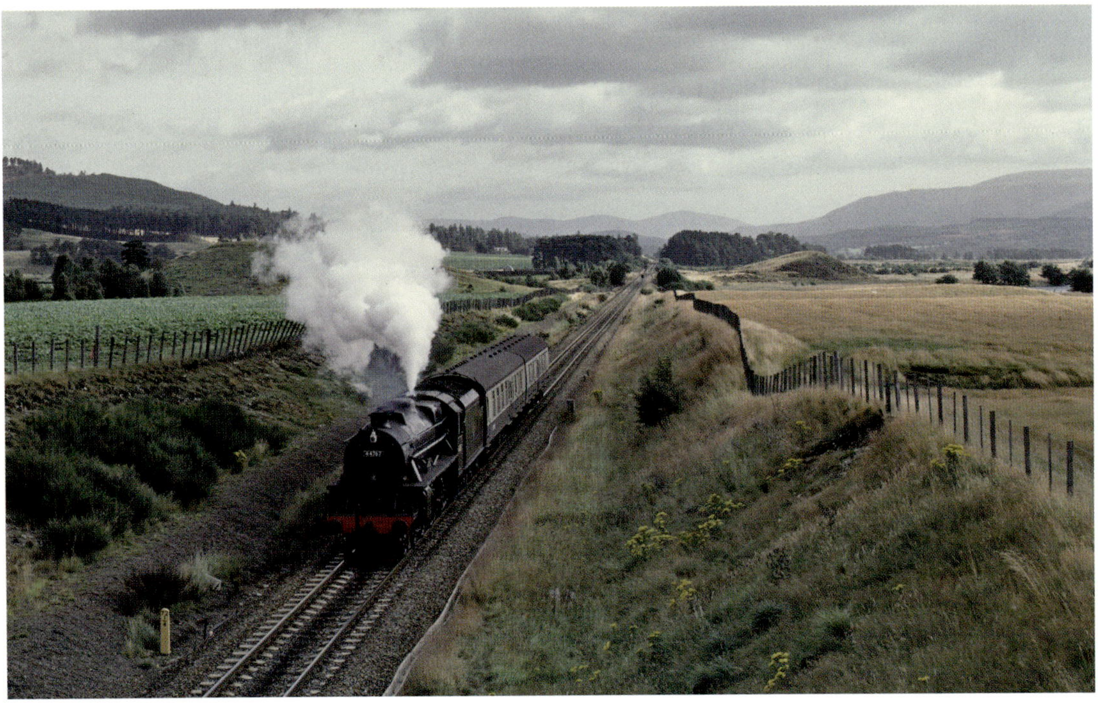

No. 44767 nears Kingussie on 1 September 1986, returning south after working a special on the Far North line to Helmsdale the previous day.

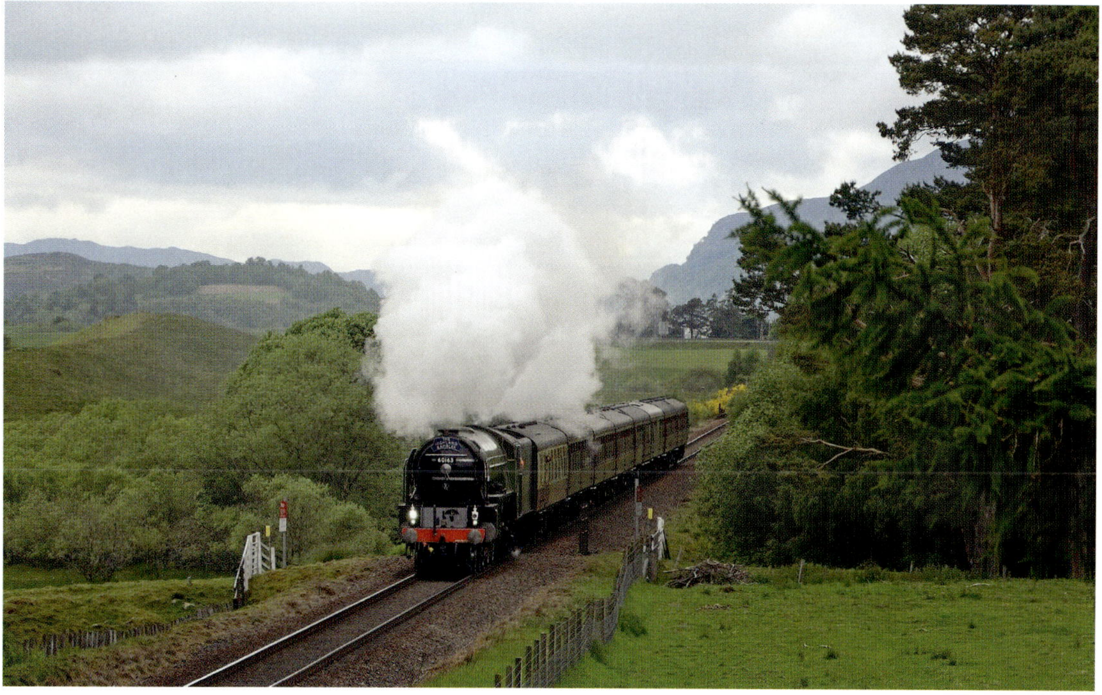

No. 60163 *Tornado* at Lynchat with the ScotRail sponsored trip to Inverness on 20 June 2015.

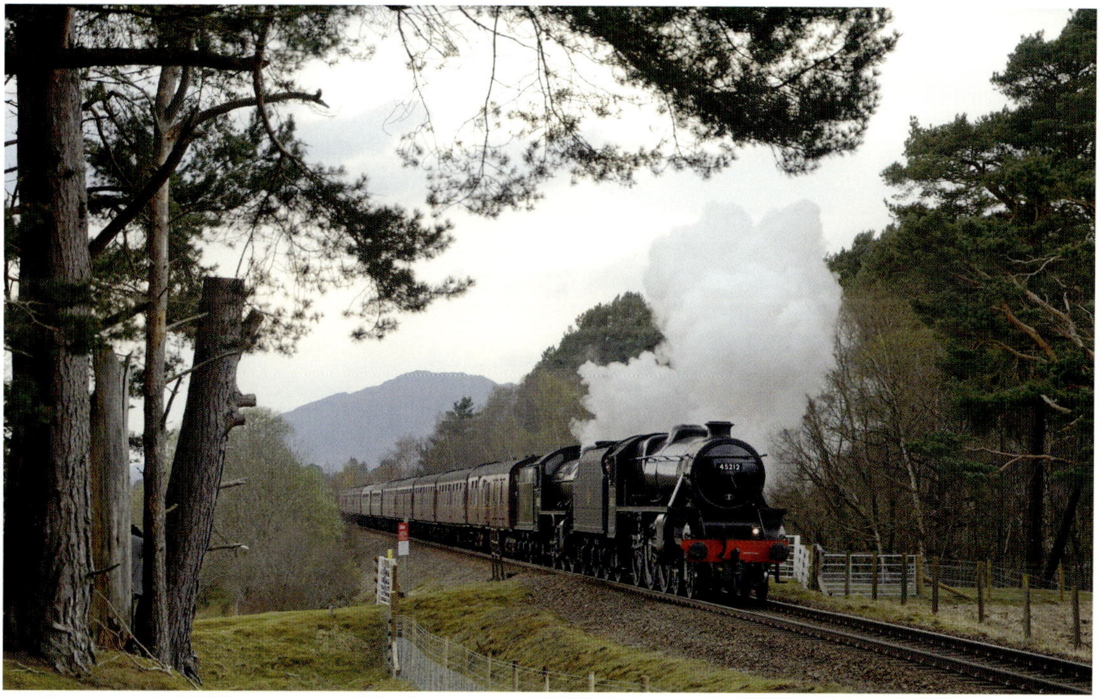

Nos 45212 and 62005 pass the farm crossing at Lynchat while working the GB X leg to Inverness on 30 April 2017.

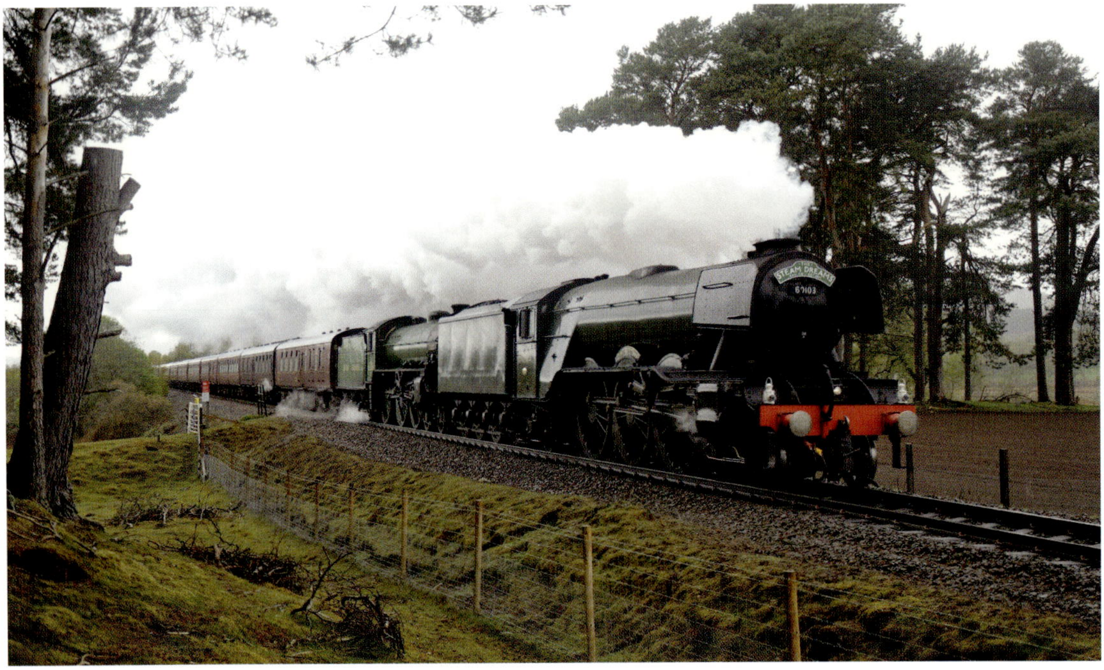

Nos 60103 *Flying Scotsman* and 61306 *Mayflower* pass Lynchat with the Steam Dreams tour on 10 May 2019. The A3 is running in BR livery.

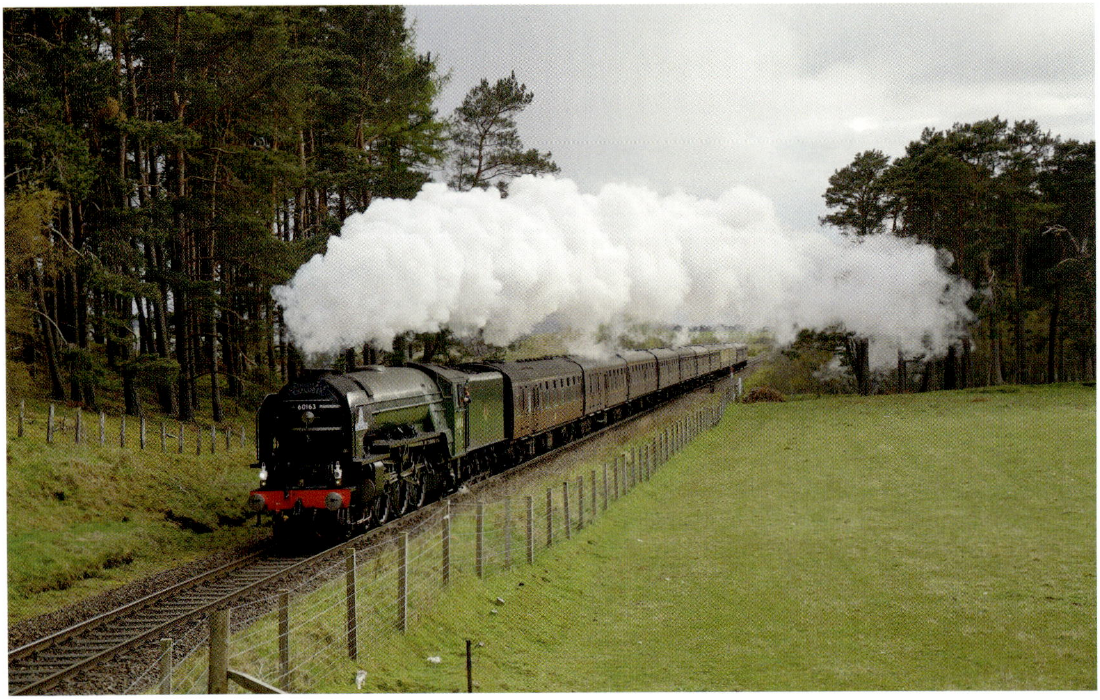

Seen from the other side of the line, No. 60163 *Tornado* hauls the Cathedrals Explorer to Inverness on 19 May 2012.

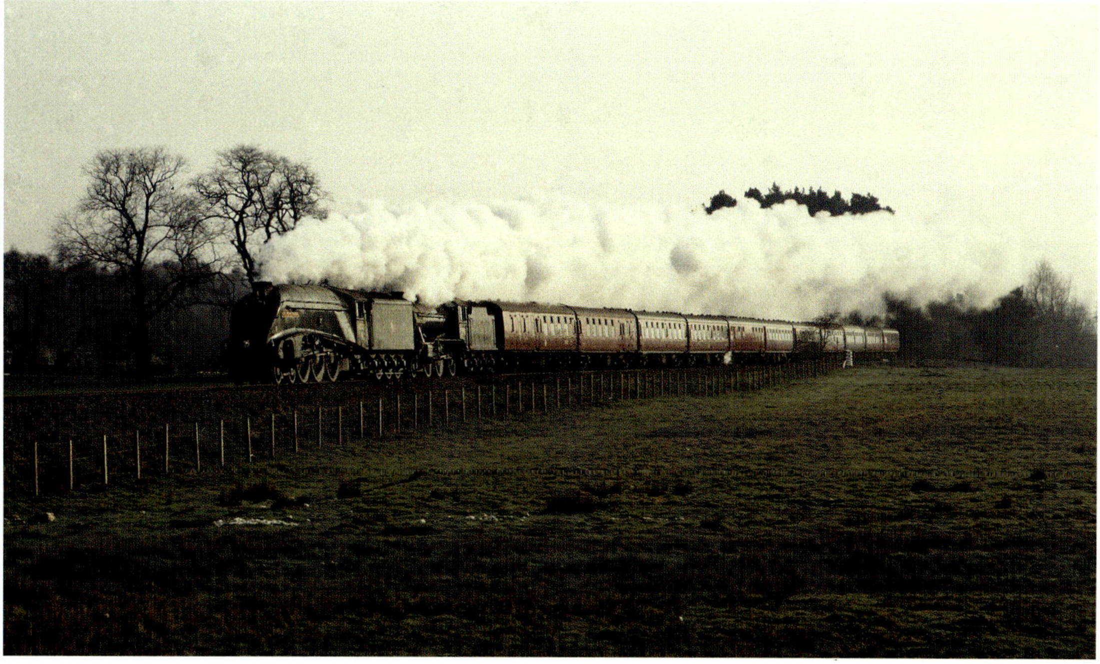

Nos 60009 and 61994, both owned by John Cameron, approach Lynchat on the way south on 14 April 2007 with the Railway Touring Company's first Great Britain tour.

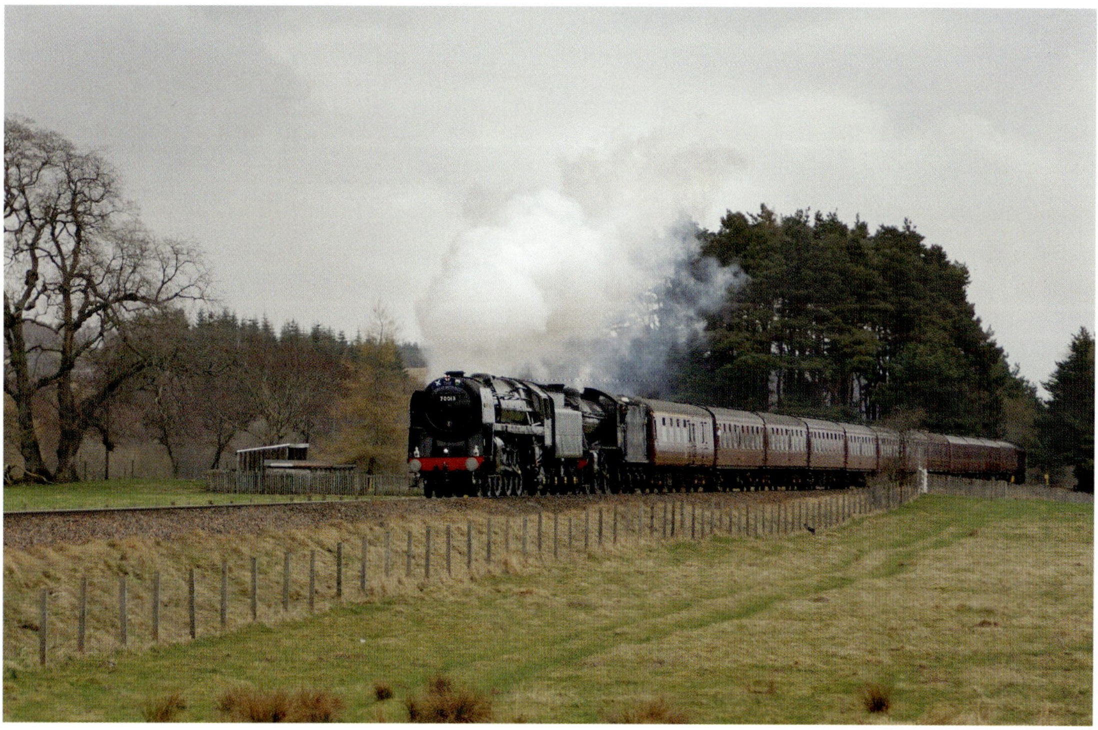

A different pairing, this time Nos 70013 and 61994, near Lynchat on 13 April 2010.

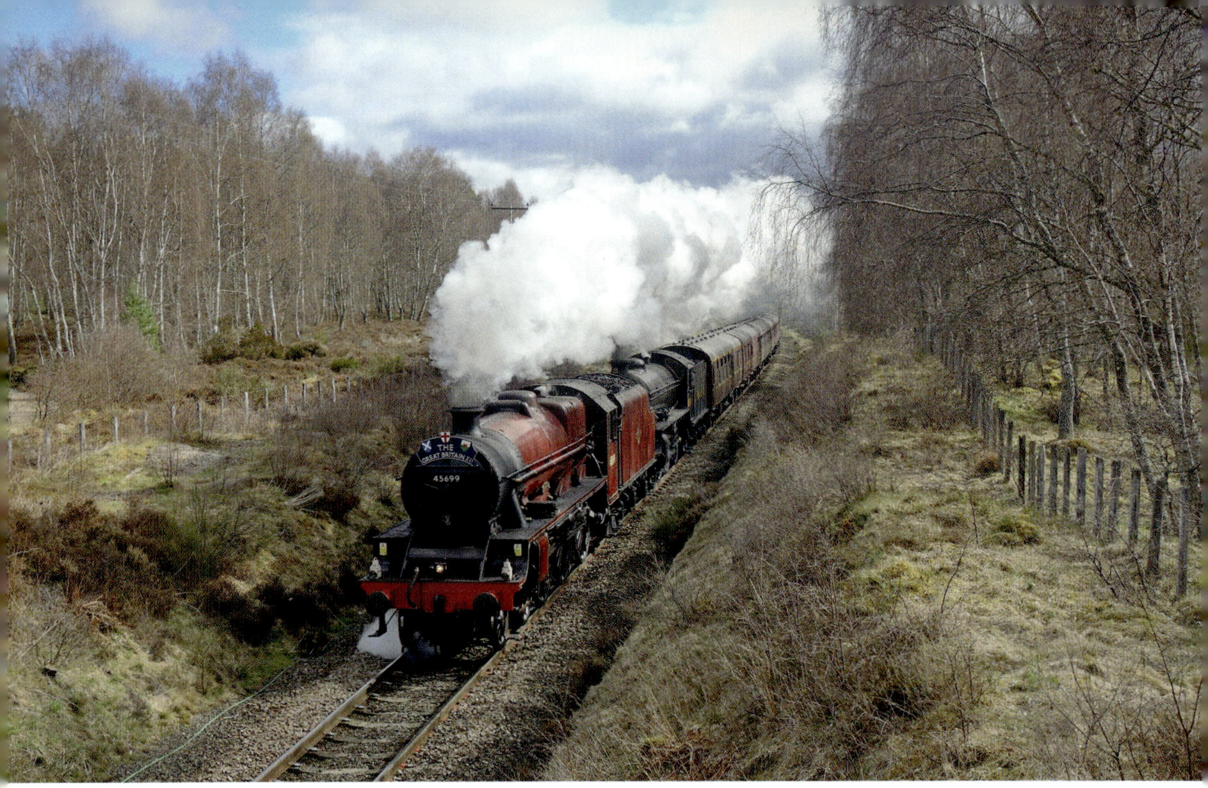

Nos 45699 and 1264 pass through the birch woods near Kincraig as they return south with GB XI on 23 April 2018.

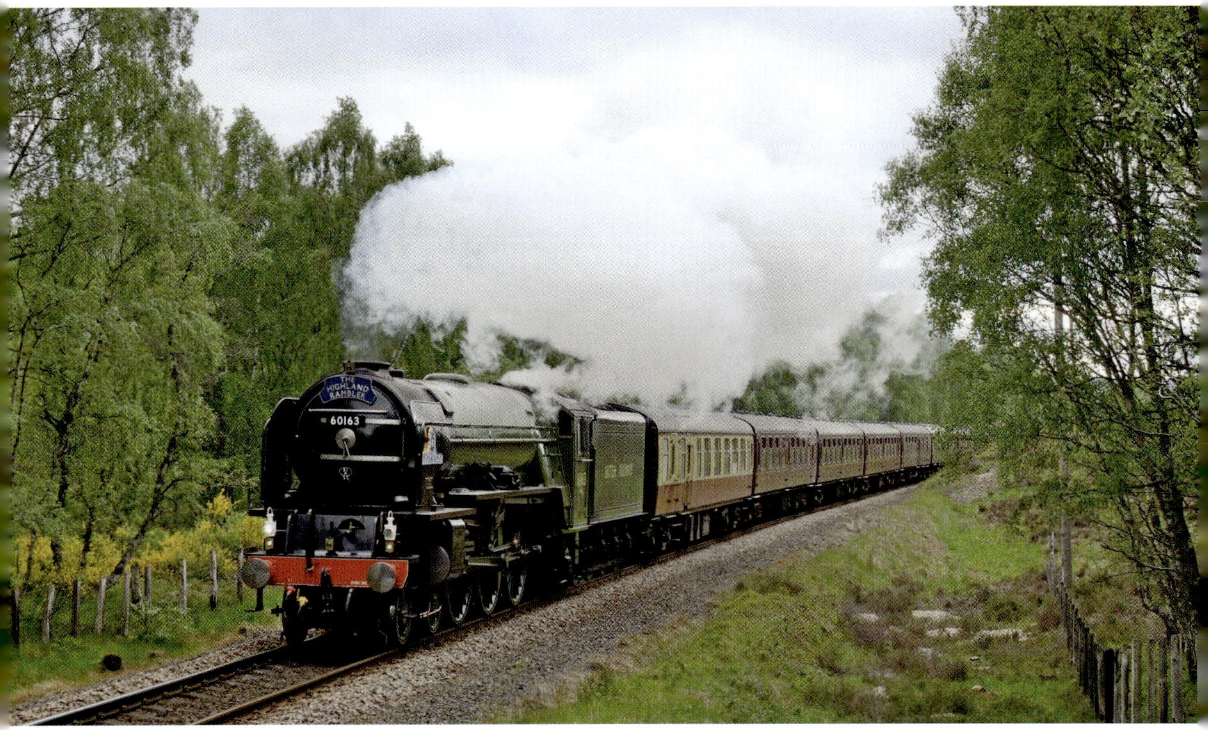

No. 60163 *Tornado* at Speybank with the northbound Highland Rambler on 20 June 2015.

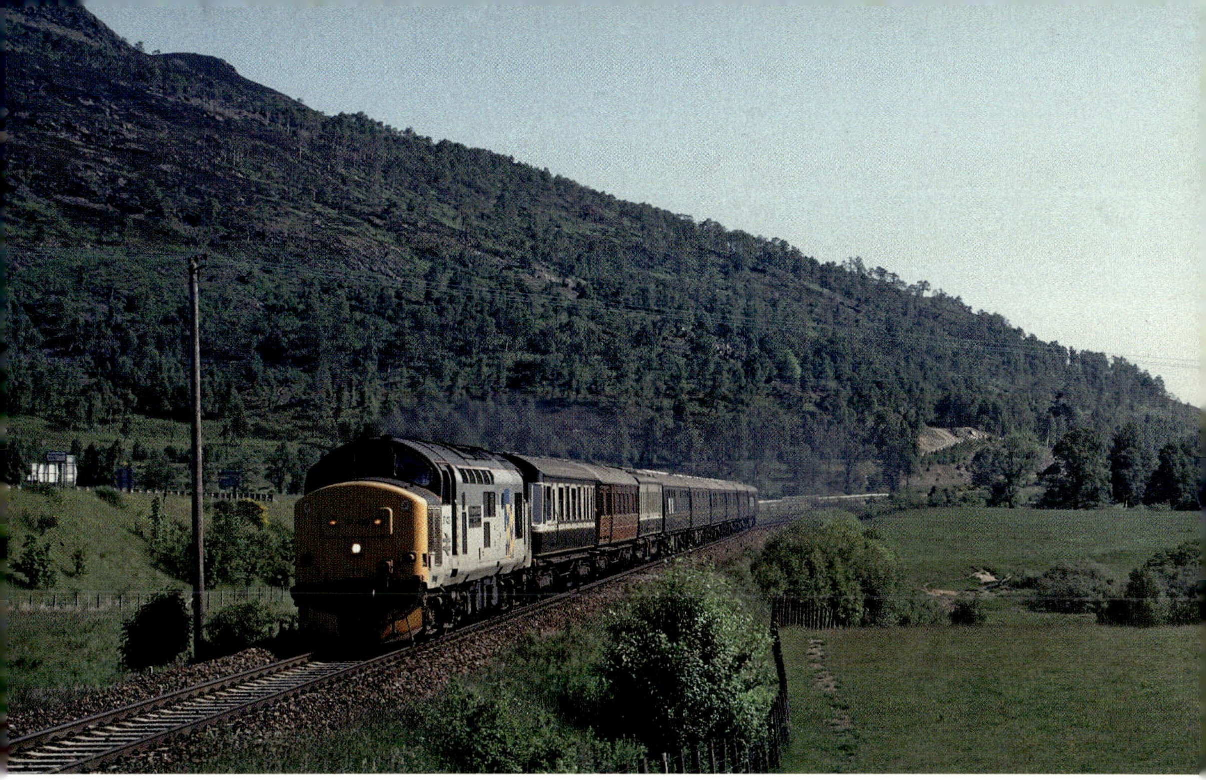

No. 37423 heads south at Lynwilg with the Royal Scotsman on 18 June 1989. The train had been stabled overnight on the Strathspey Railway.

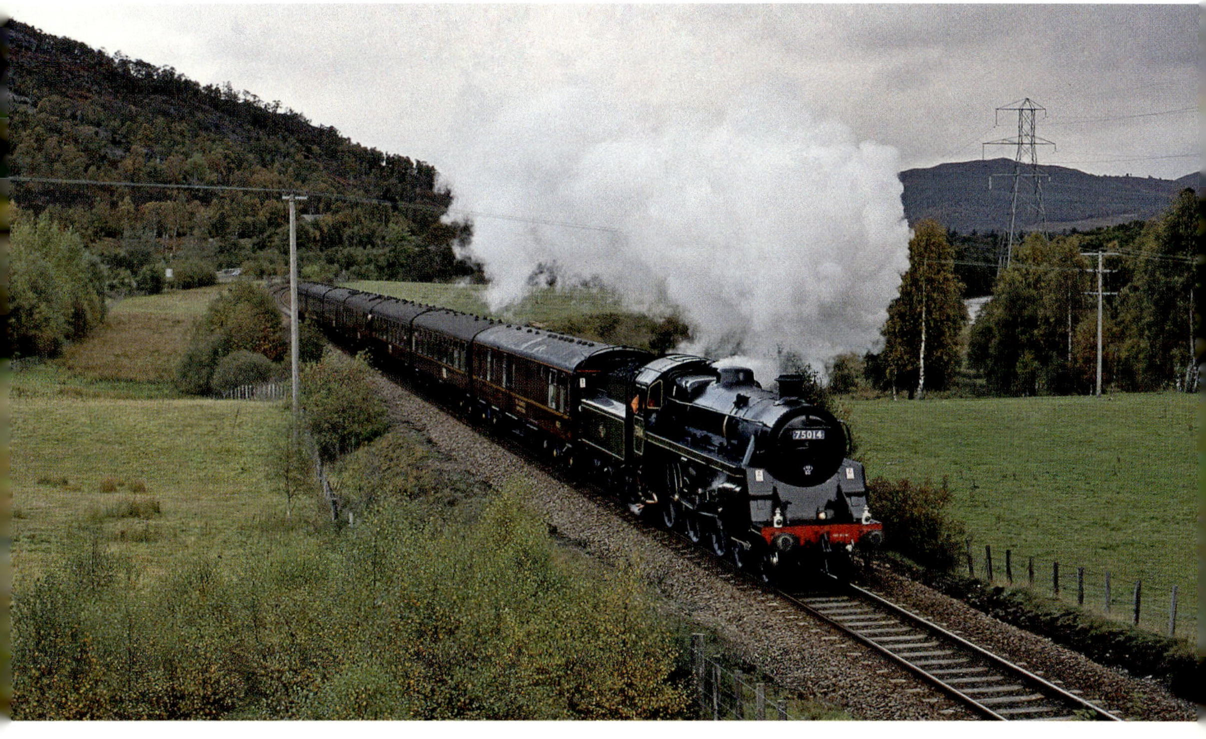

No. 75014 works south at Lynwilg, near Aviemore, on 12 October 1997.

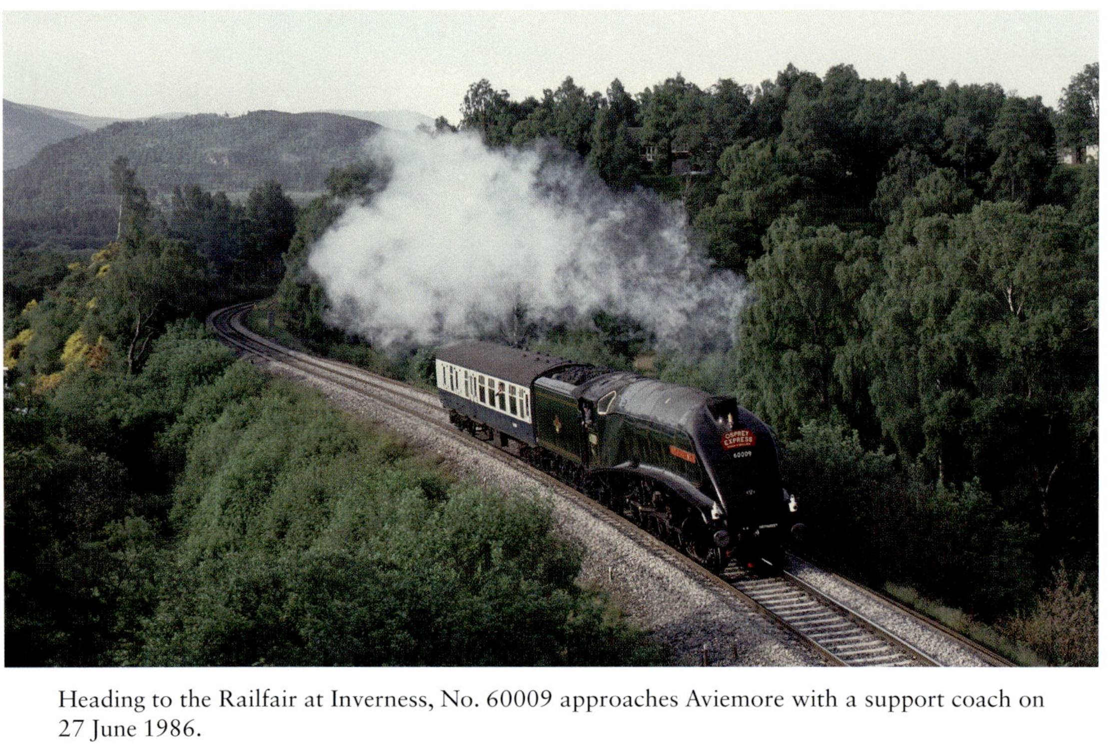

Heading to the Railfair at Inverness, No. 60009 approaches Aviemore with a support coach on 27 June 1986.

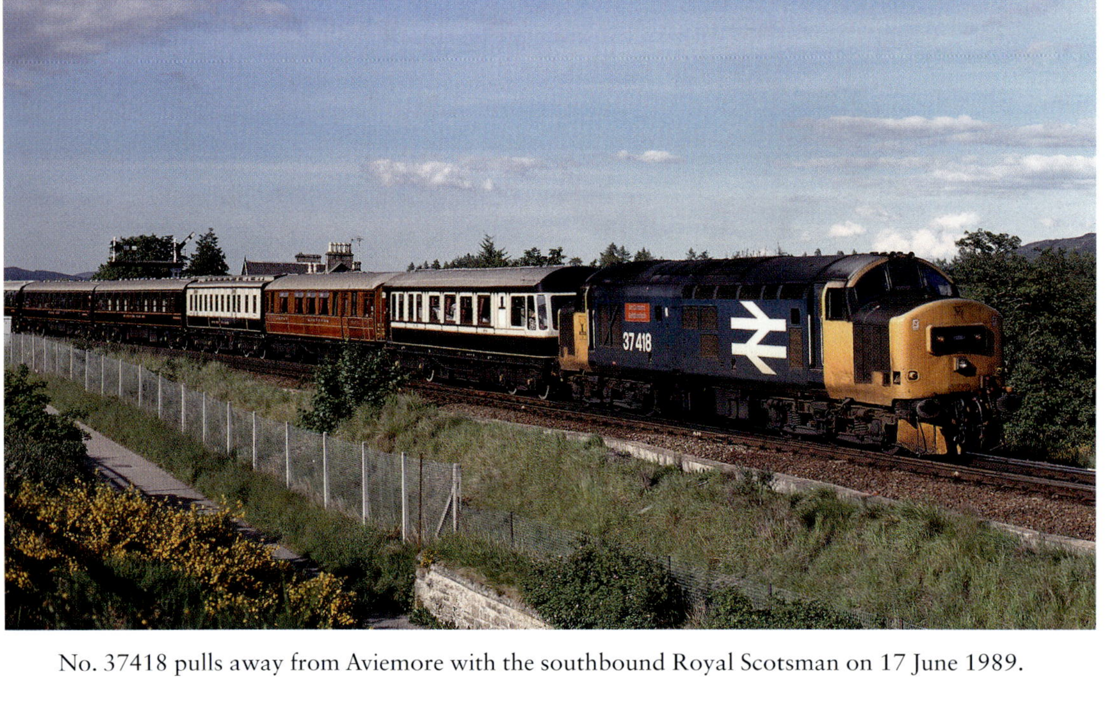

No. 37418 pulls away from Aviemore with the southbound Royal Scotsman on 17 June 1989.

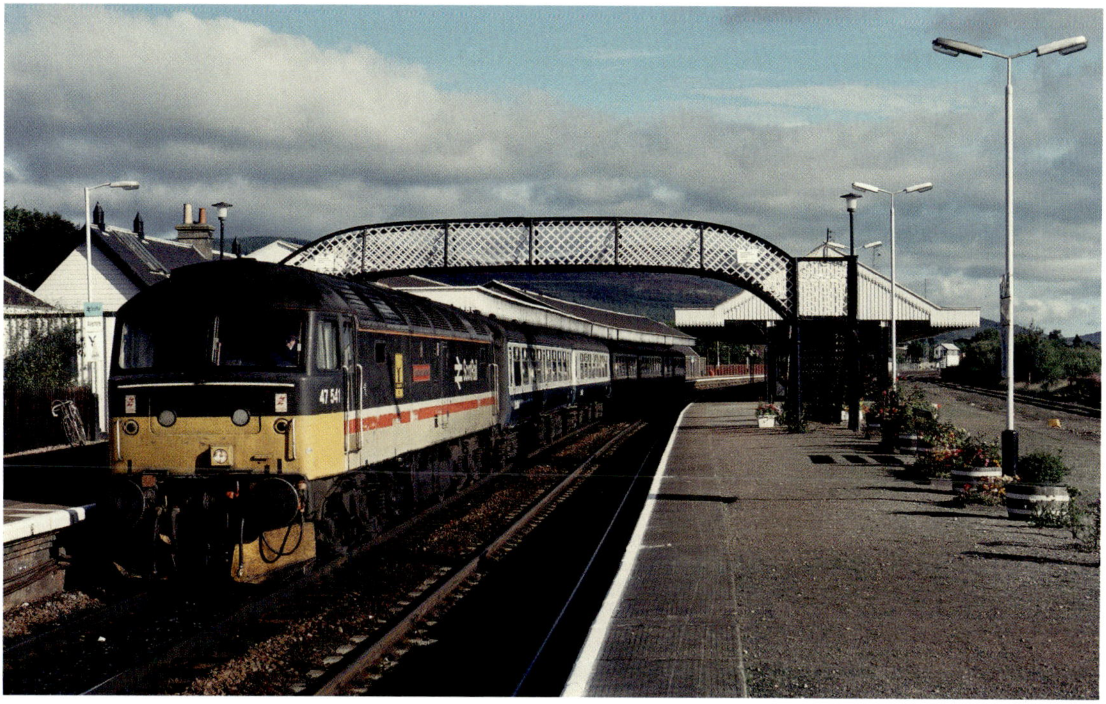

No. 47451 pauses at Aviemore with a Glasgow train on 10 September 1990. The Strathspey Railway now uses the platform face on the right of shot.

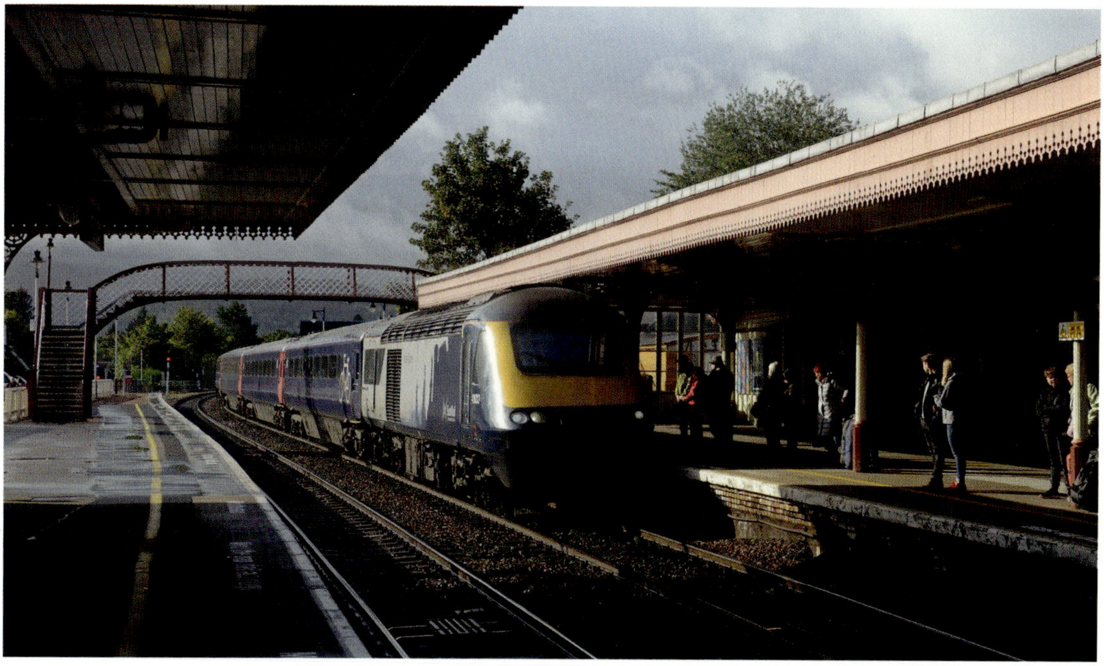

Power car No. 43033 leads a ScotRail InterCity HST set into Aviemore on the way to Inverness on 11 September 2019.

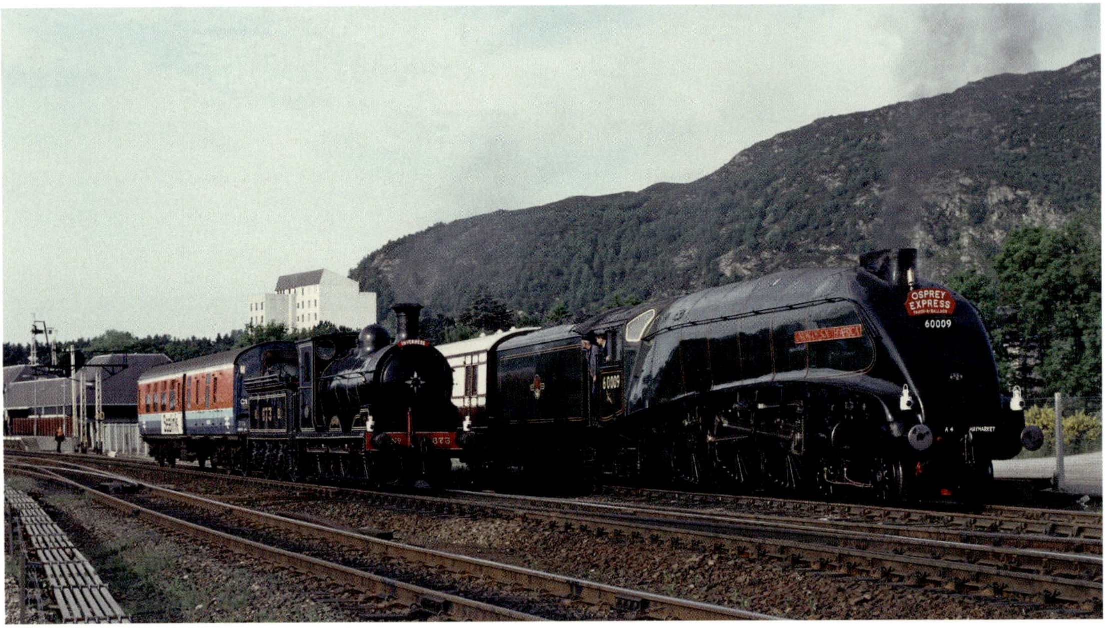

Nos 673 *Maude* and 60009 *Union of South Africa* pose at Aviemore on 27 June 1986.

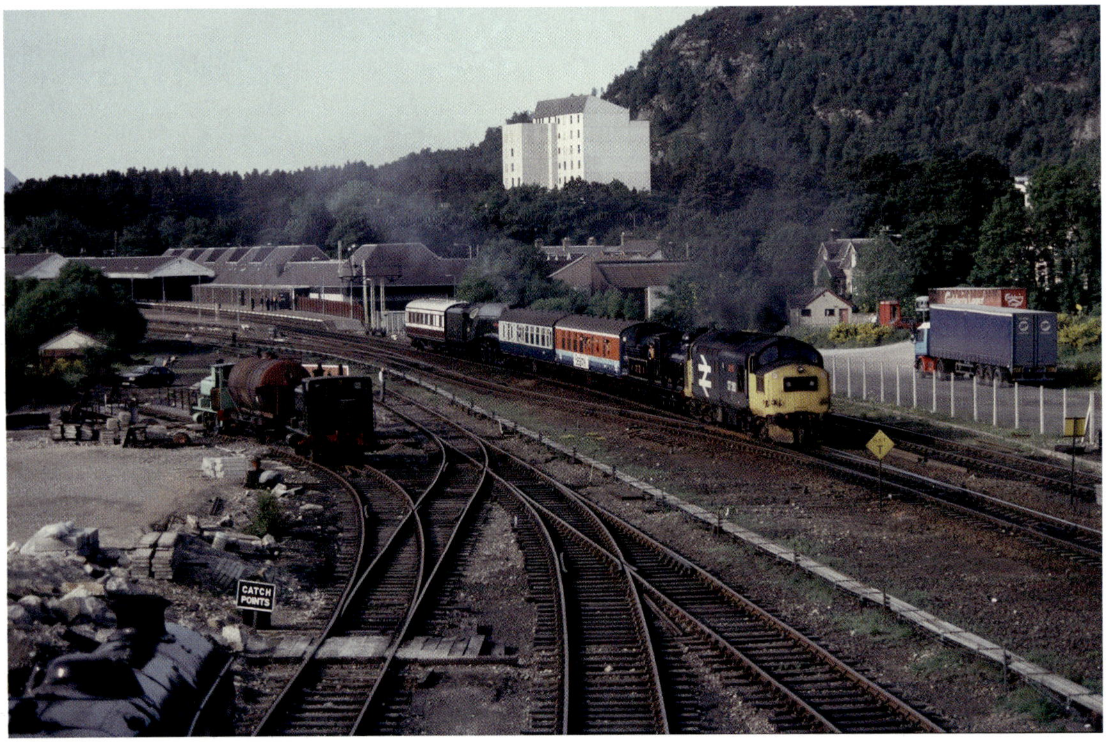

Unassisted steam beyond Aviemore was not allowed at the time so Class 37 No. 37262 heads a convoy of Nos 60009, 673 and their coaches on 27 June 1986. The lines to the left are used by the Strathspey Railway.

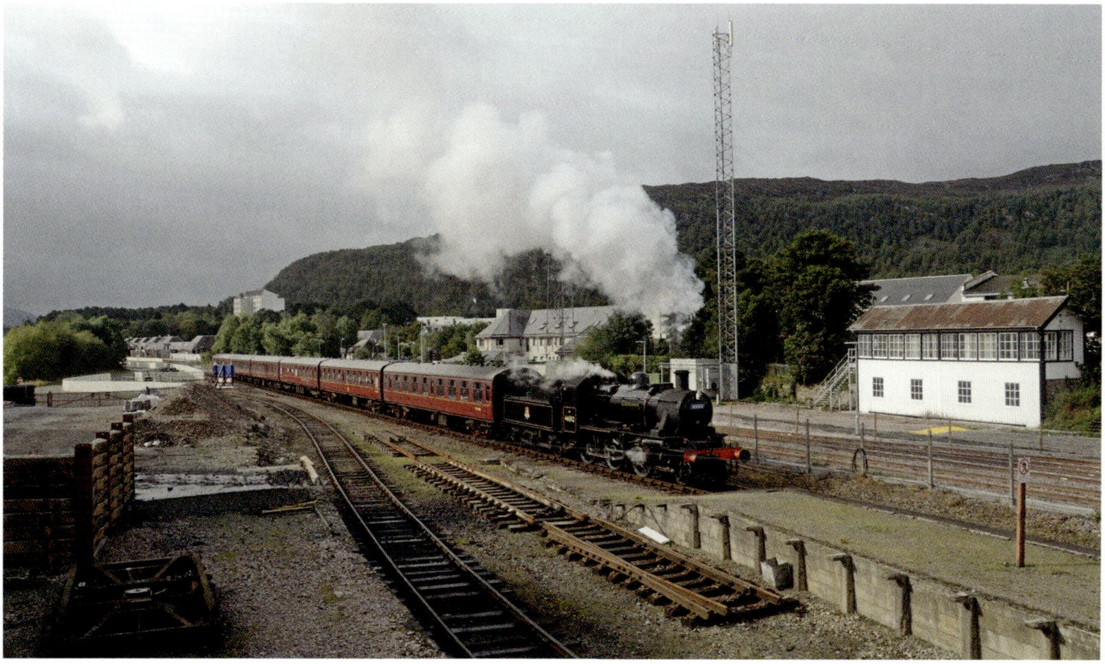

Ivatt Class 2 No. 46512 leaves Aviemore on the Strathspey line on 11 September 2019. The large signal cabin is now disused after the area was re-signalled.

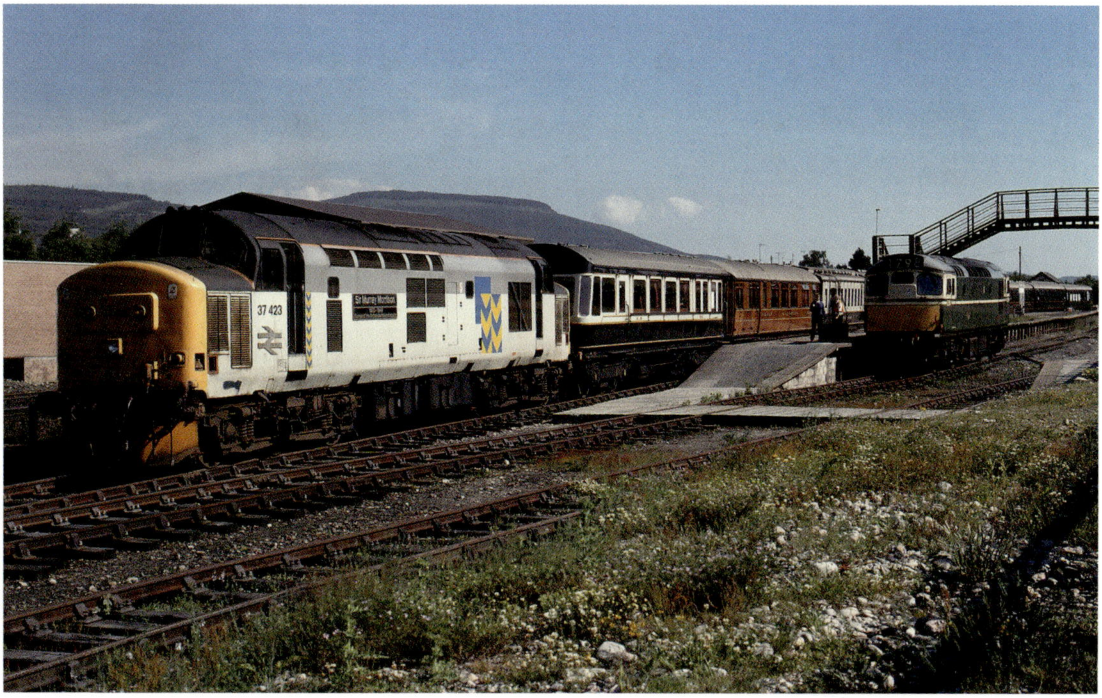

A locomotive change at Aviemore Speyside on 18 June 1989. Class 26 D5394 brought the Royal Scotsman train from Boat of Garten and No. 37423 will take it on south on the mainline.

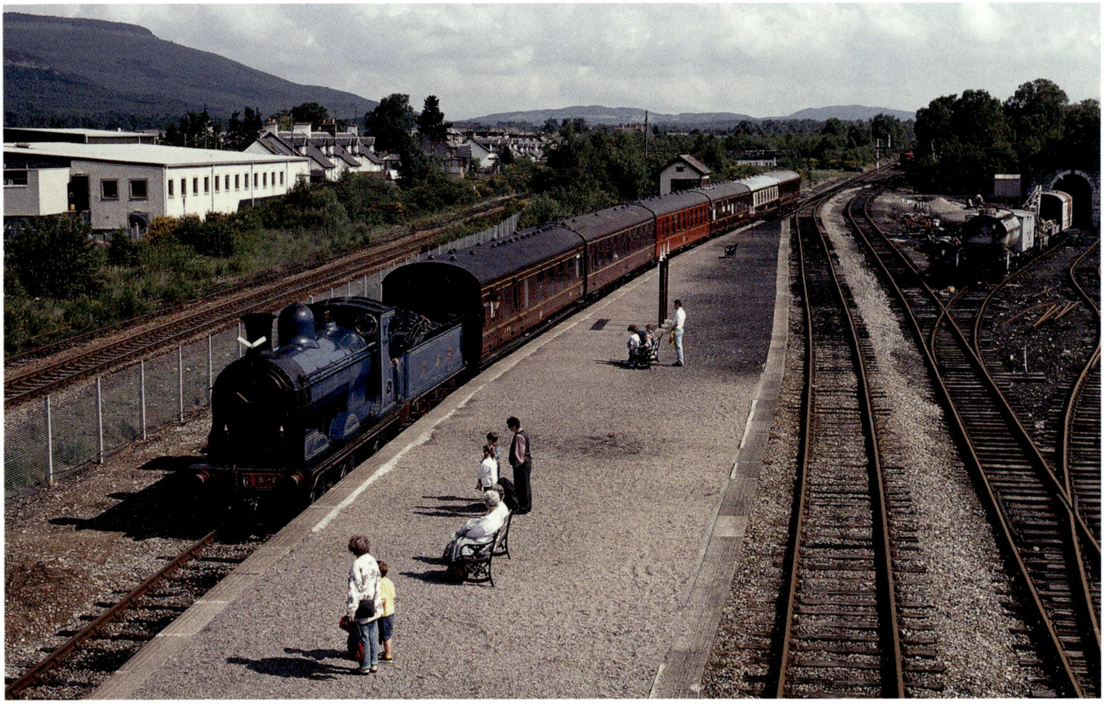

Before the Stathspey were allowed to run into the main Aviemore station they operated from a newly built one – Aviemore Speyside. Ex-Caledonian Railway Class 812 No. 828 arrives on 6 July 1994.

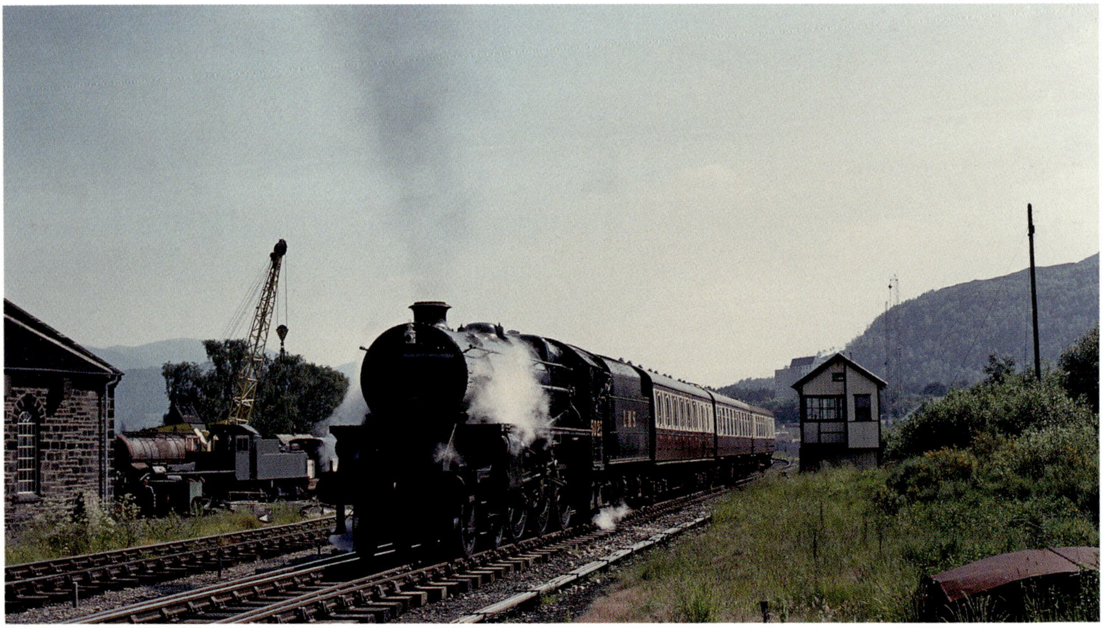

Class 5 5025 leaves Aviemore Speyside on 18 June 1989, heading to Boat of Garten. The signal cabin was recovered from Garve on the Kyle line.

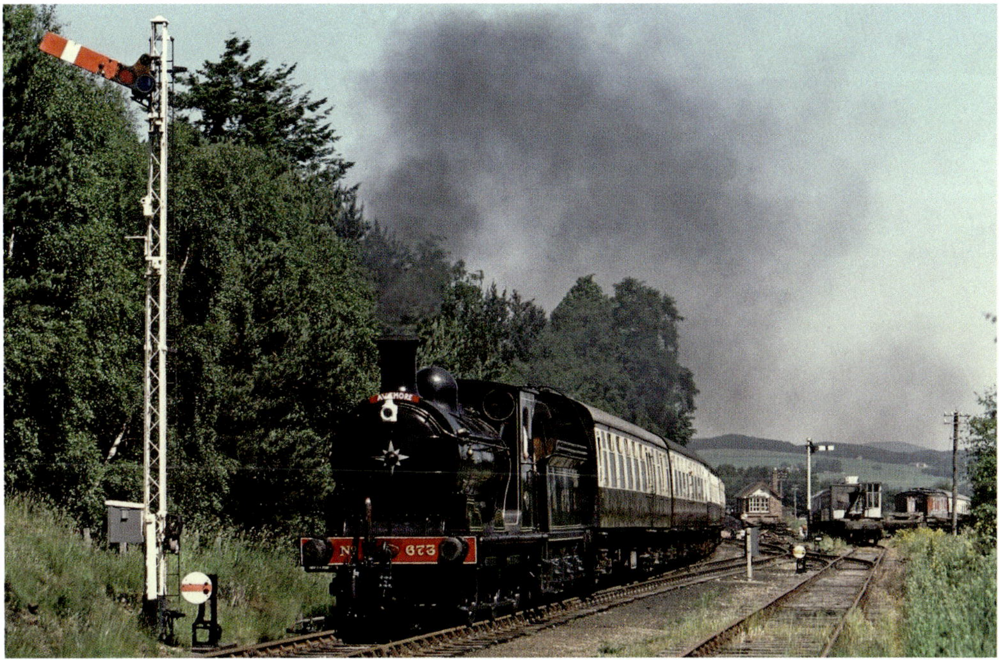

No. 673 *Maude* visited the Stathspey in 1986 and is seen heading south from Boat of Garten on 29 June.

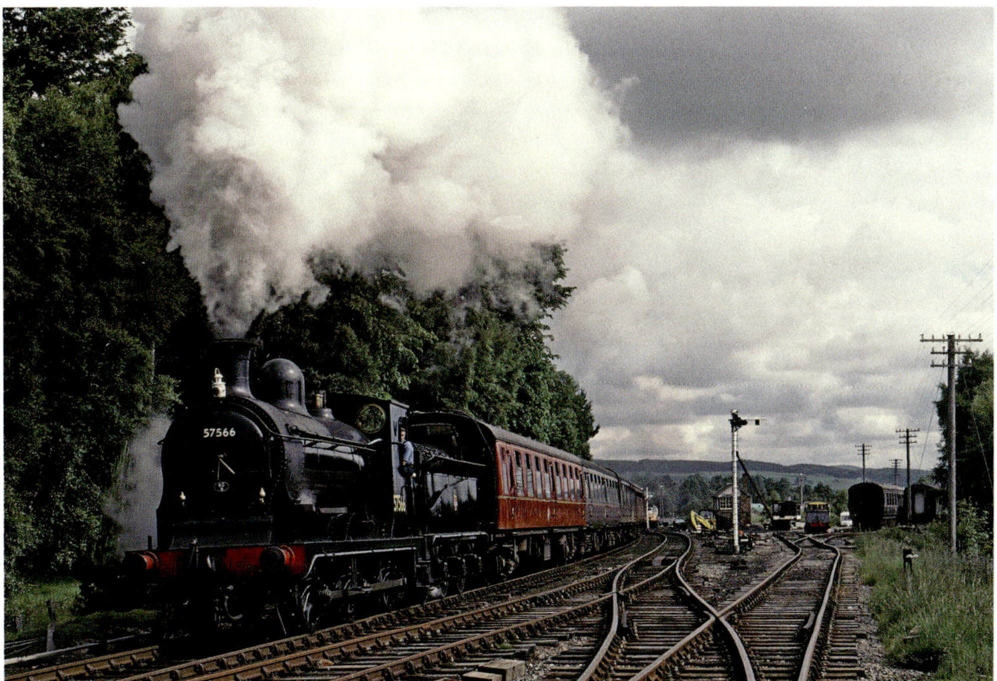

The preserved Caledonian Class 812 engine has also run in BR livery as No. 57566. It's seen here in this guise heading south on 27 June 2000.

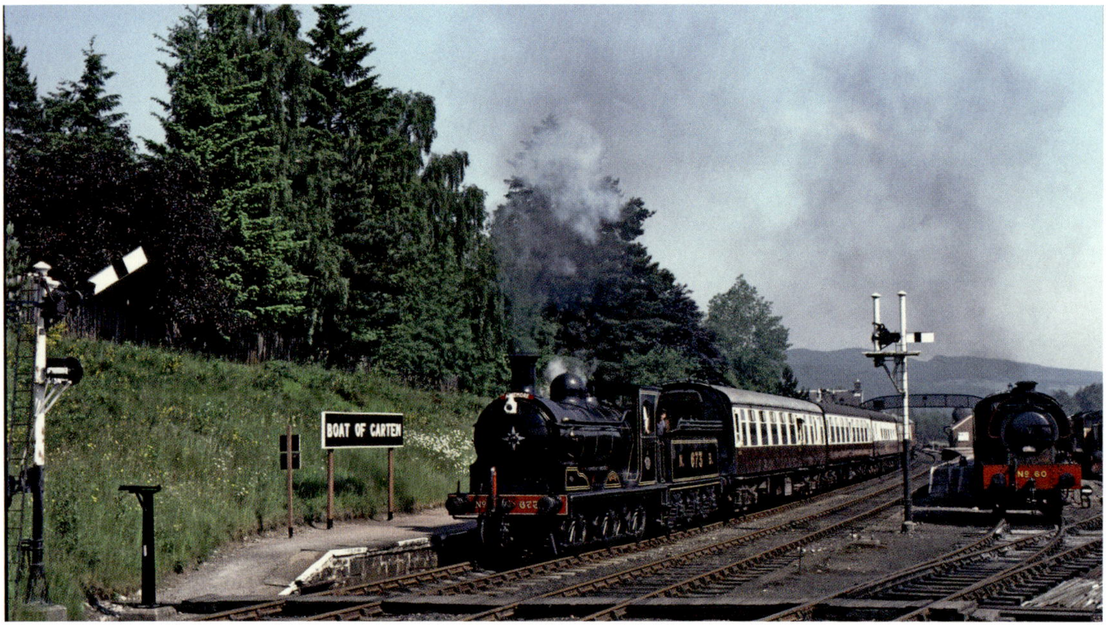

No. 673 *Maude* pulls out of Boat of Garten on 29 June 1986. Austerity class No. 60 is on the right.

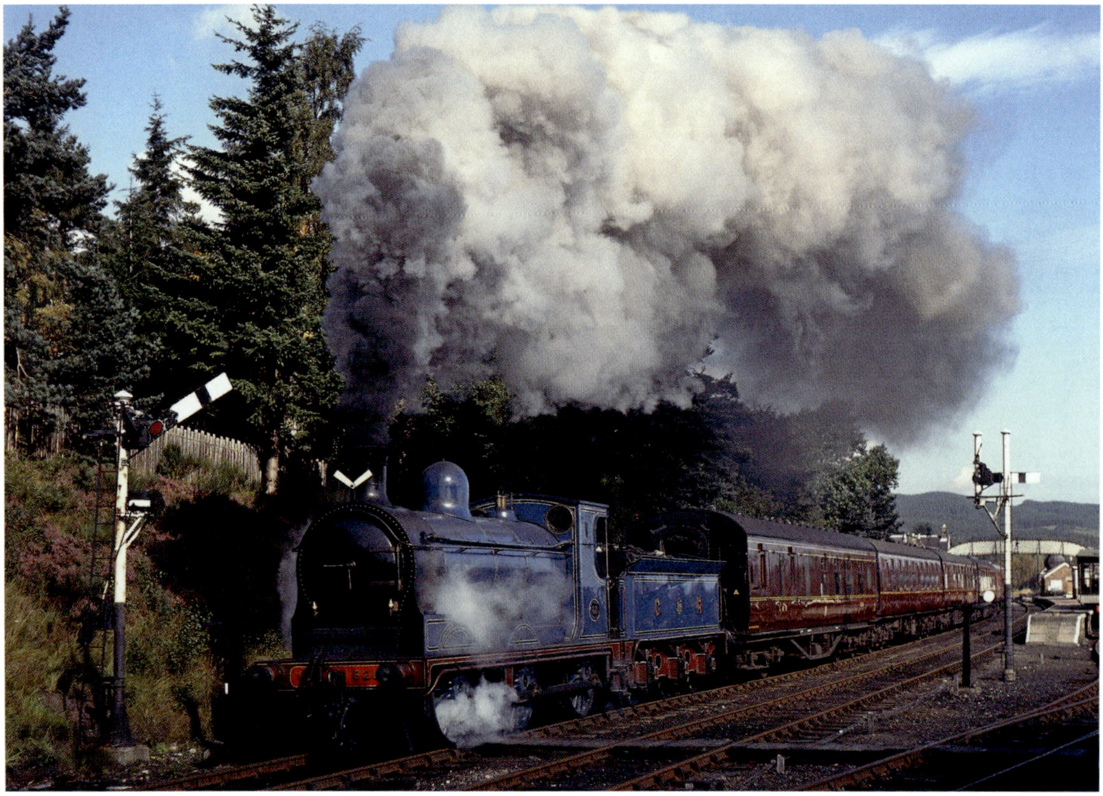

No. 828 leaves Boat of Garten on 17 September 1993.

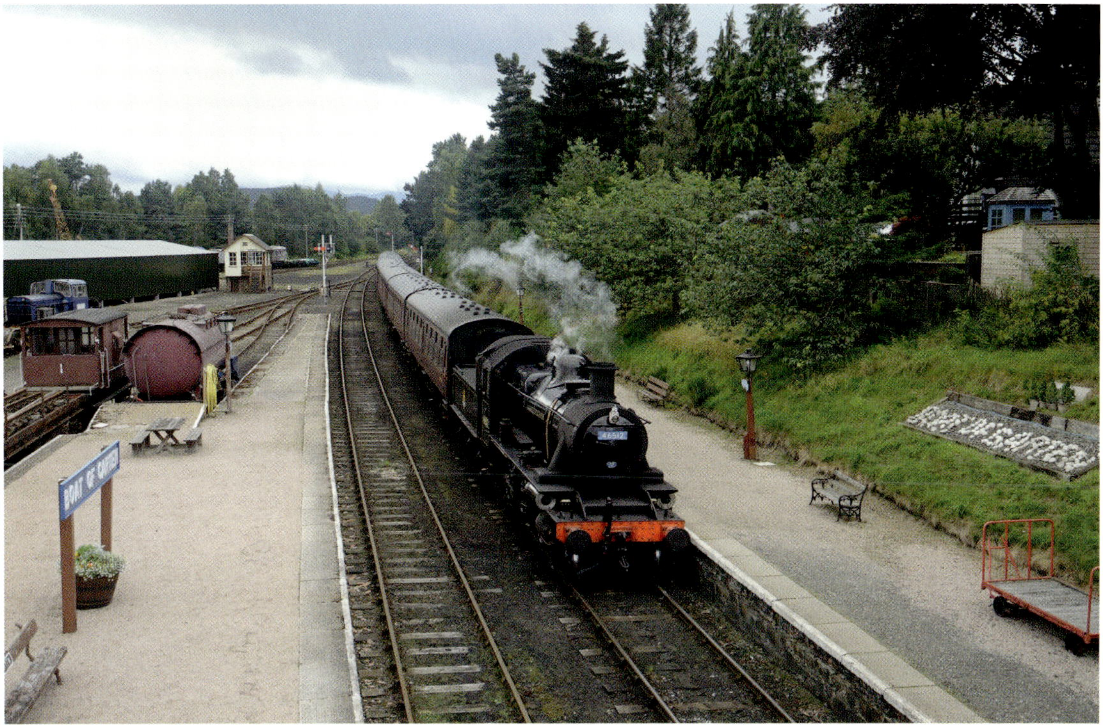

No. 46512 enters Boat of Garten with a train to Broomhill on 12 September 2019.

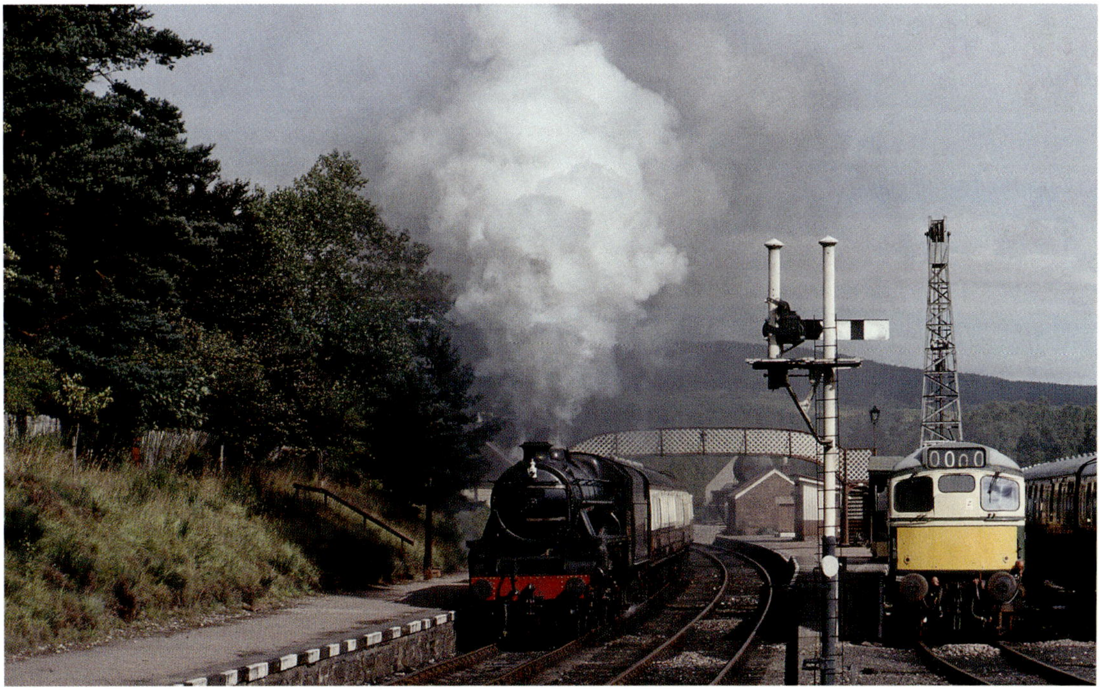

Class 5 No. 5025 makes an impressive departure south from Boat of Garten on 10 September 1990.

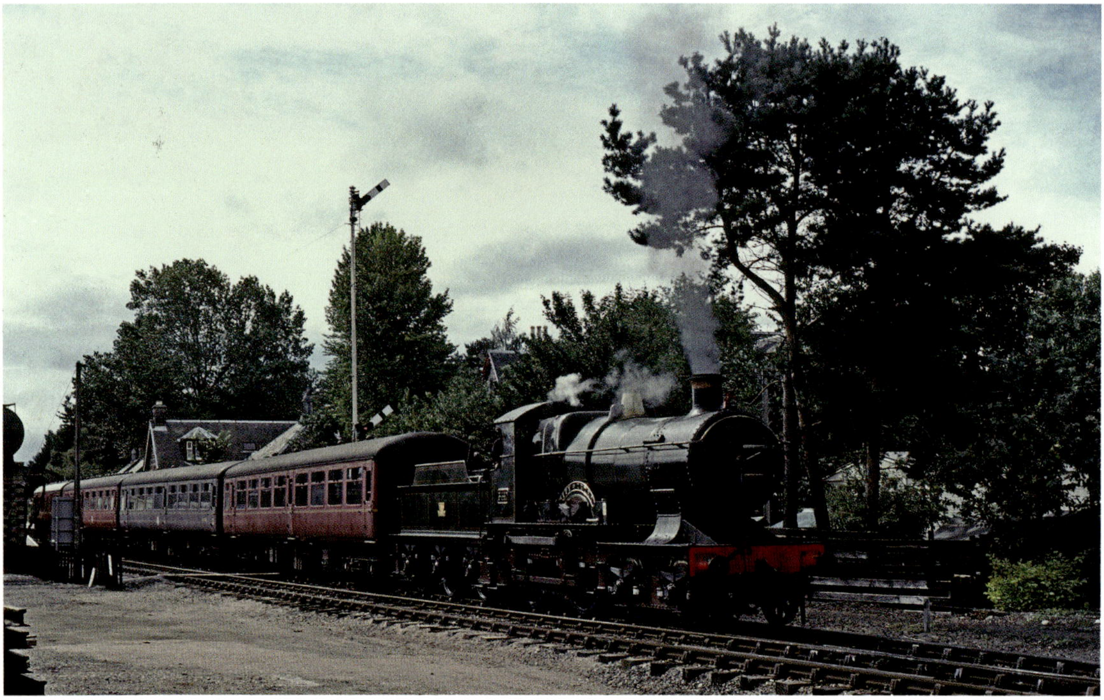

Great Western 4-4-0 No. 3440 *City of Truro* was a long way from home when it visited the Strathspey in 2006. It is heading to Broomhill on 2 September.

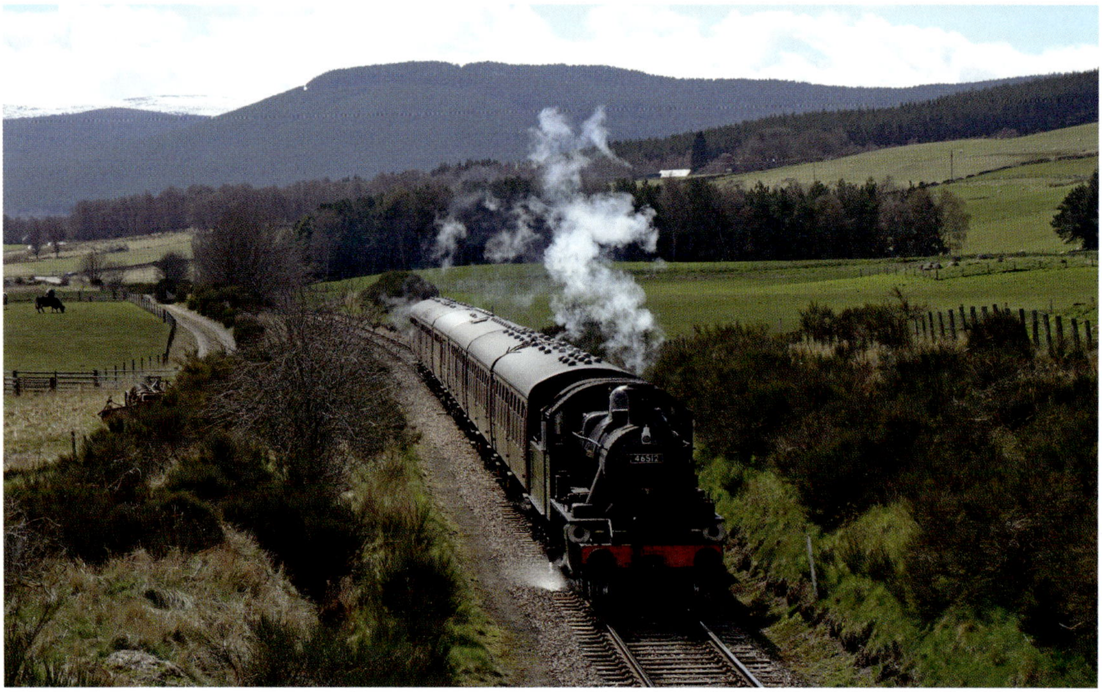

No. 46512 works north to Broomhill at Tullochgorum on 30 April 2016.

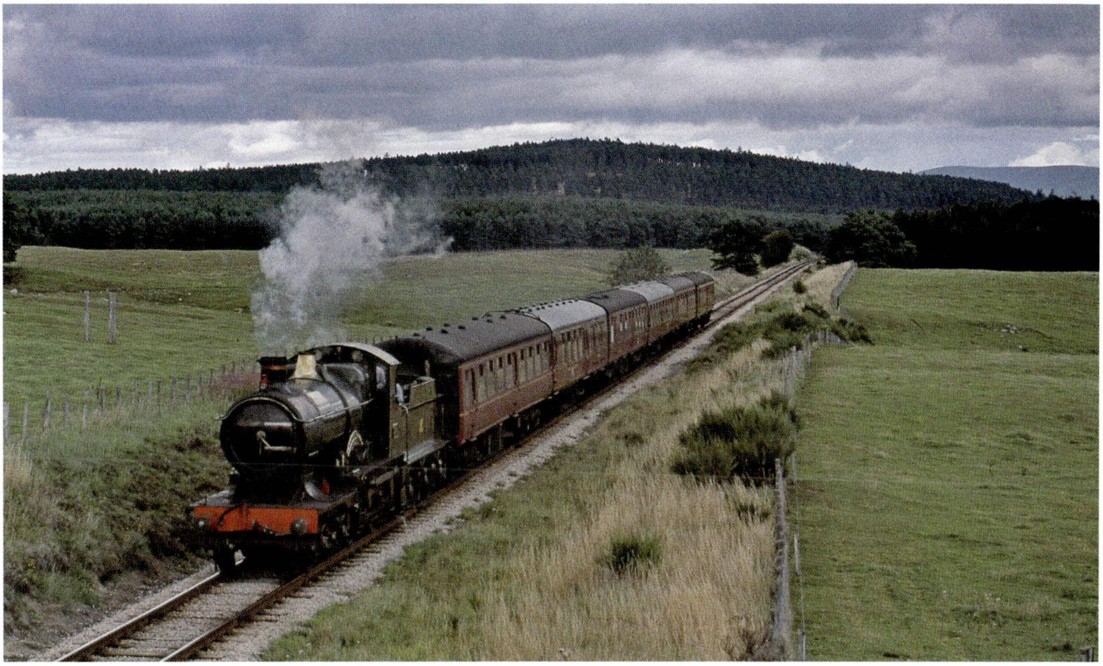

No. 3440 *City of Truro* at Tullochgorum with a working to Aviemore on 3 September 2006. The engine had been turned on the Aviemore turntable.

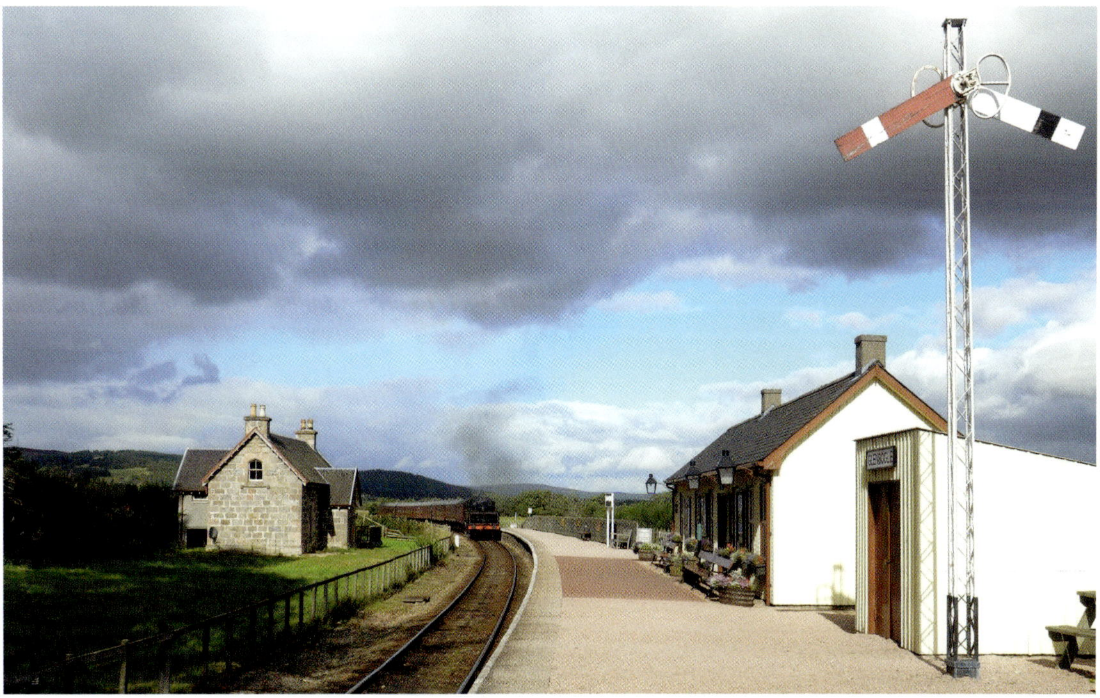

A run-round loop north of Broomhill is the current limit of the Strathspey operations pending the extension to Grantown. Ivatt No. 46512 works back into the station on 12 September 2019.

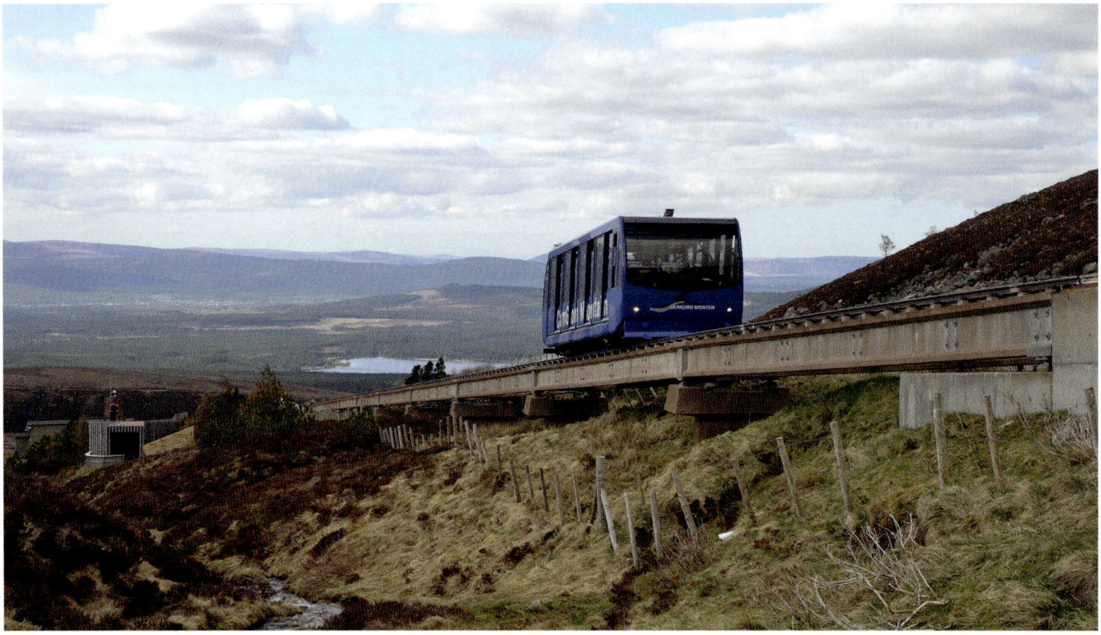

A much more recent addition to railways in the Central Highlands is the Cairngorm Mountain Railway, a 2-km funicular line that opened on Cairngorm Mountain in 2001. A vehicle ascends on 2 May 2014.

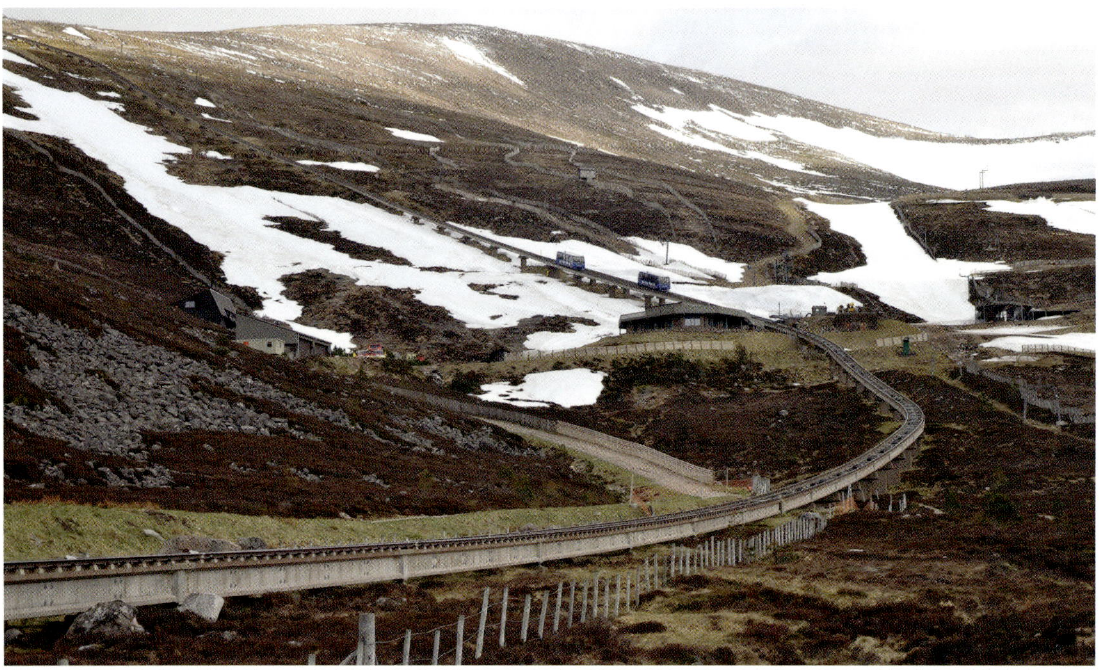

Vehicles pass on the loop near the summit of the Cairngorm Mountain Railway on 2 May 2014. Structural faults were discovered on the line in 2018 and at the time of writing it has been closed pending a decision on its future.

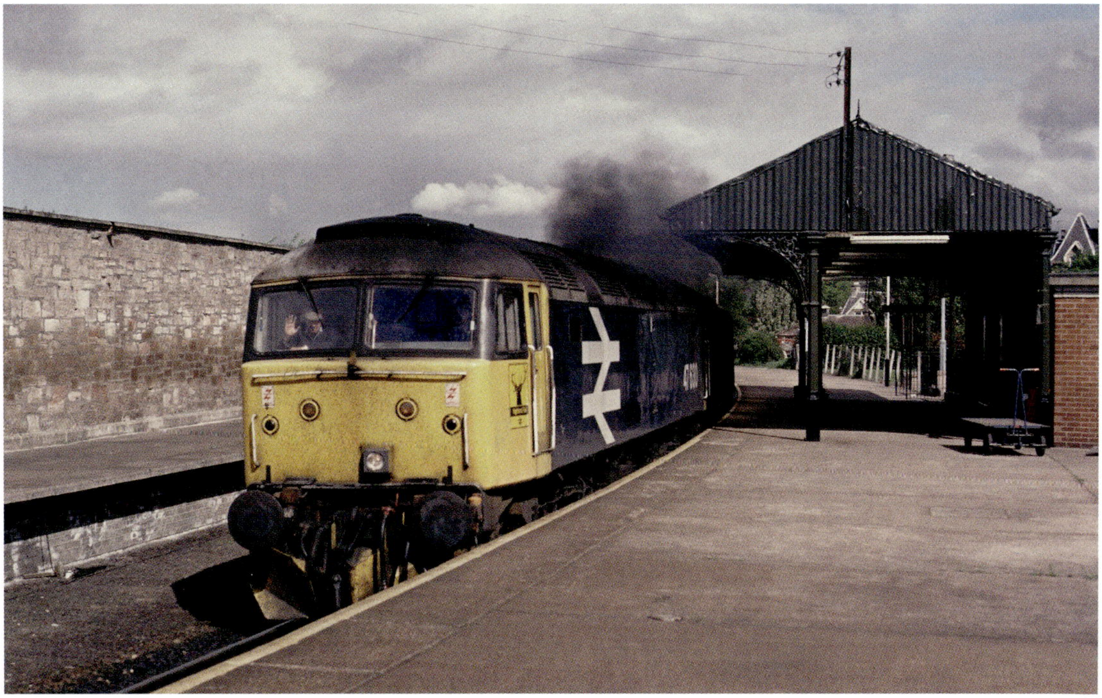

The line north from Grantown has been closed for some time, so we join the original route at Forres as No. 47630 works from Aberdeen to Inverness on 17 May 1988.

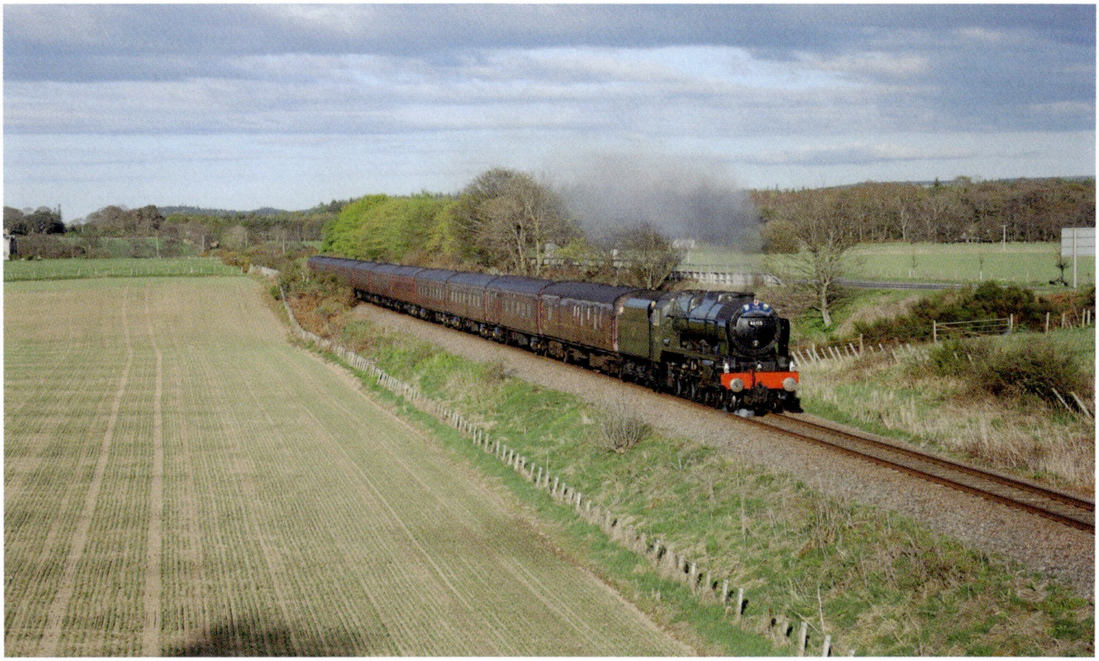

No. 46115 *Scots Guardsman* passes Brodie with the GB IV leg from Edinburgh to Inverness via Aberdeen on 17 April 2011.

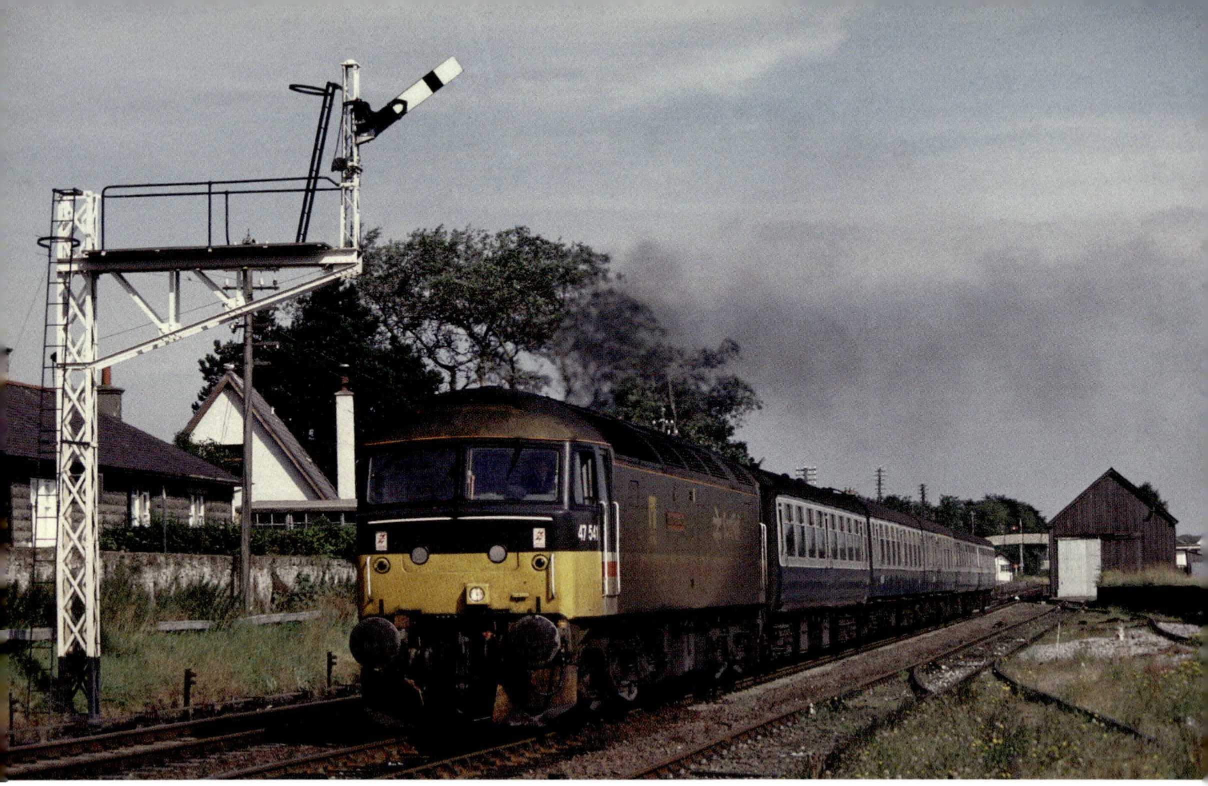

No. 47541 leaves Nairn with an Aberdeen to Inverness service on 31 August 1987.

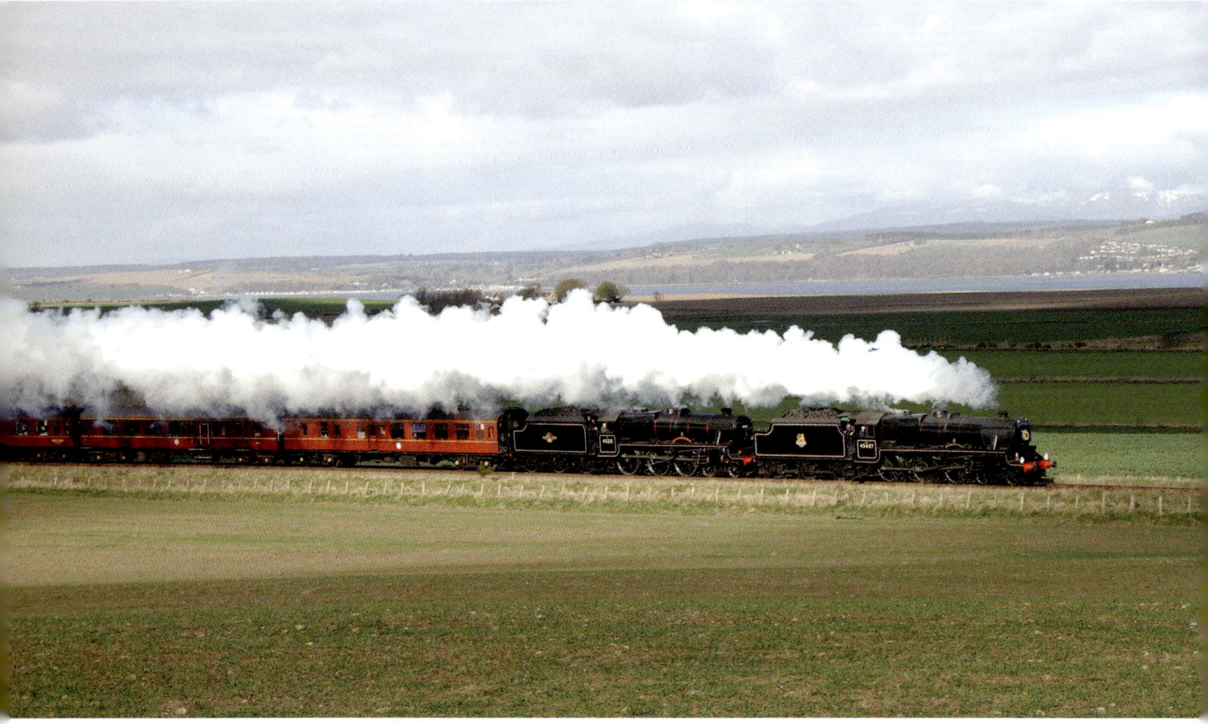

With the Moray Firth in the background, Class 5s Nos 45407 and 45231 take the GB II tour from Inverness to Aberdeen past Gollanfield on 12 April 2009.

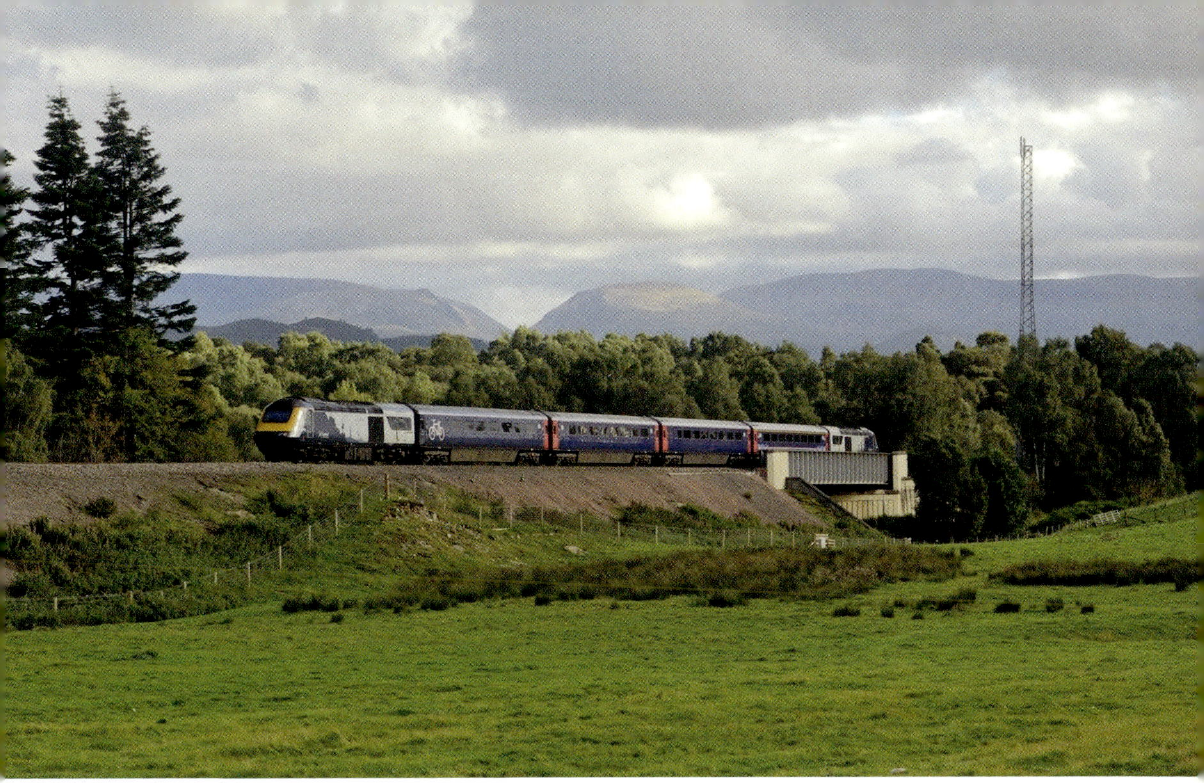

On the direct route from Aviemore, a northbound ScotRail HST crosses the rebuilt bridge over the A95 road on 12 September 2019.

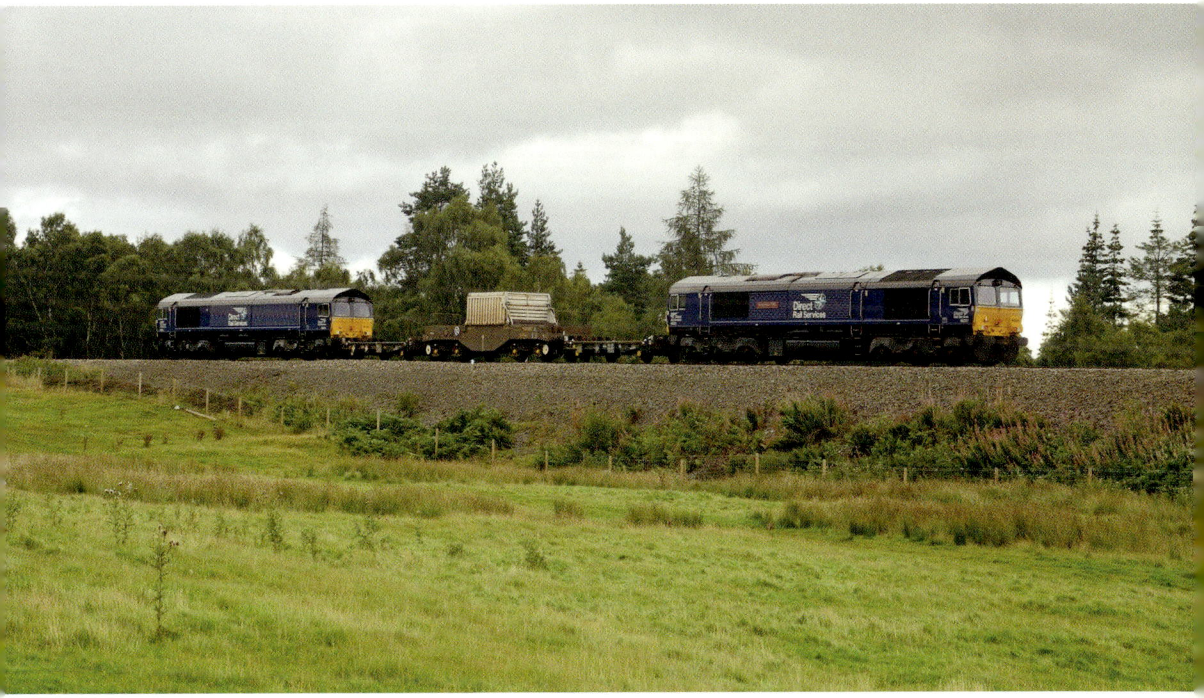

DRS Class 66s Nos 66304 and 66301 head north from Aviemore with a nuclear flask to Georgemas Junction, the railhead for the Dounreay site.

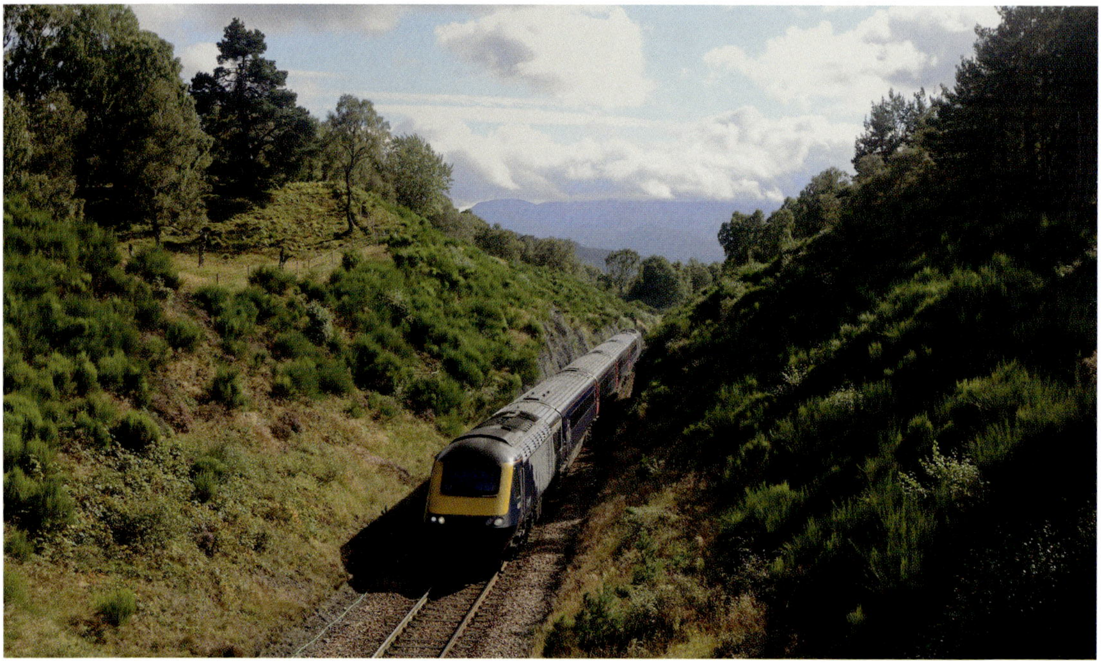

Seen from the overbridge at Kinveachy, a ScotRail HST set led by power car No. 43033 heads north on 12 September 2019.

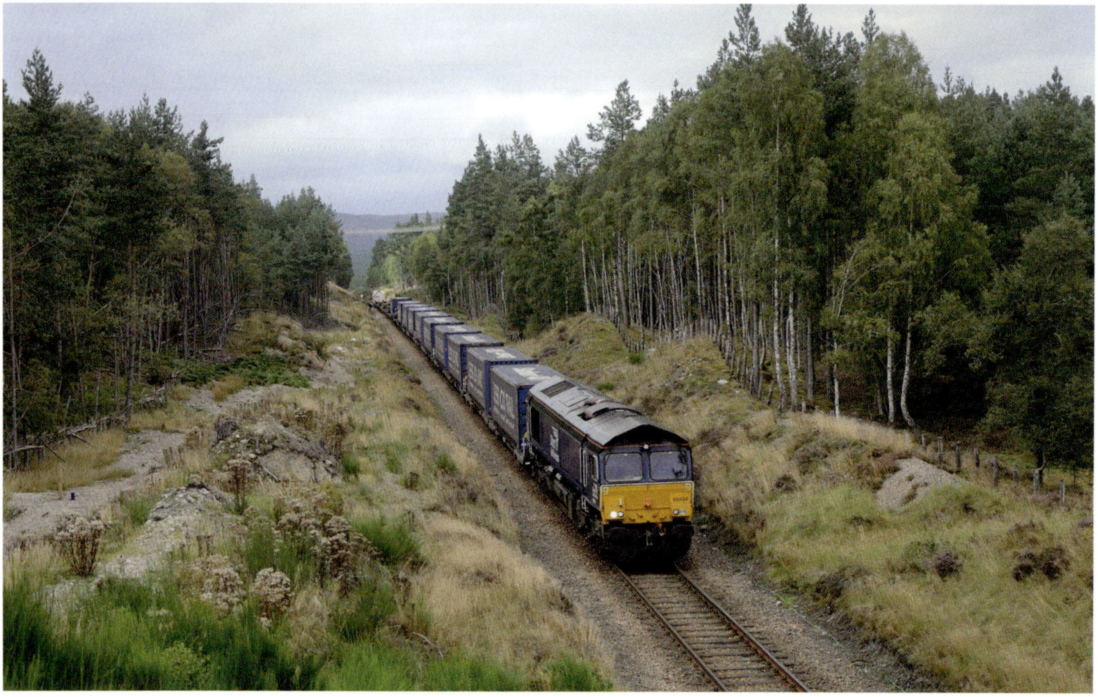

Looking north from the same bridge, No. 66434 works the Inverness to Mossend Tesco freight on 11 September 2019.

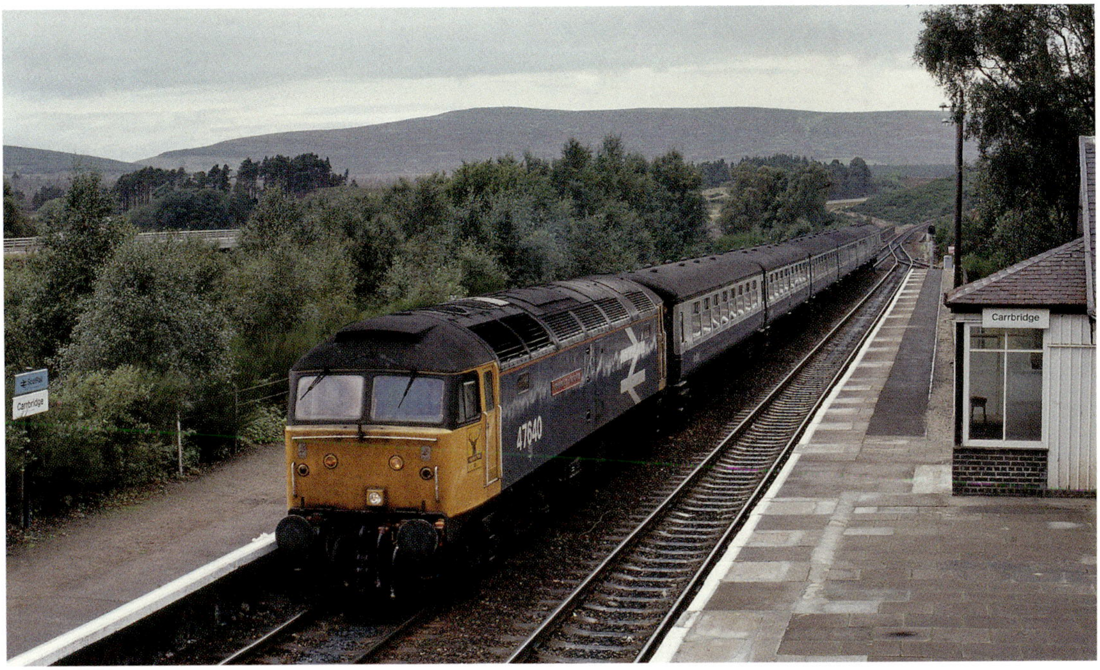

No. 47640 *University of Strathclyde* pulls into Carrbridge station with a service to Glasgow on 7 September 1989.

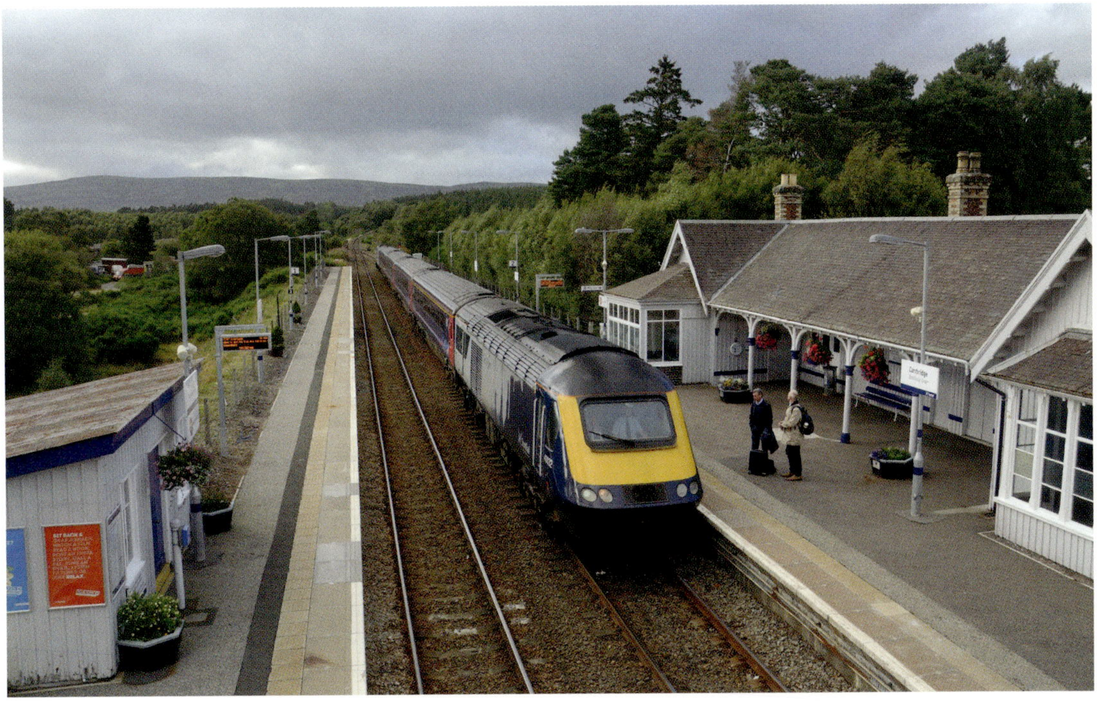

By 2019 Carrbridge station has been fitted with lighting and information boards as a ScotRail HST heads south on 11 September.

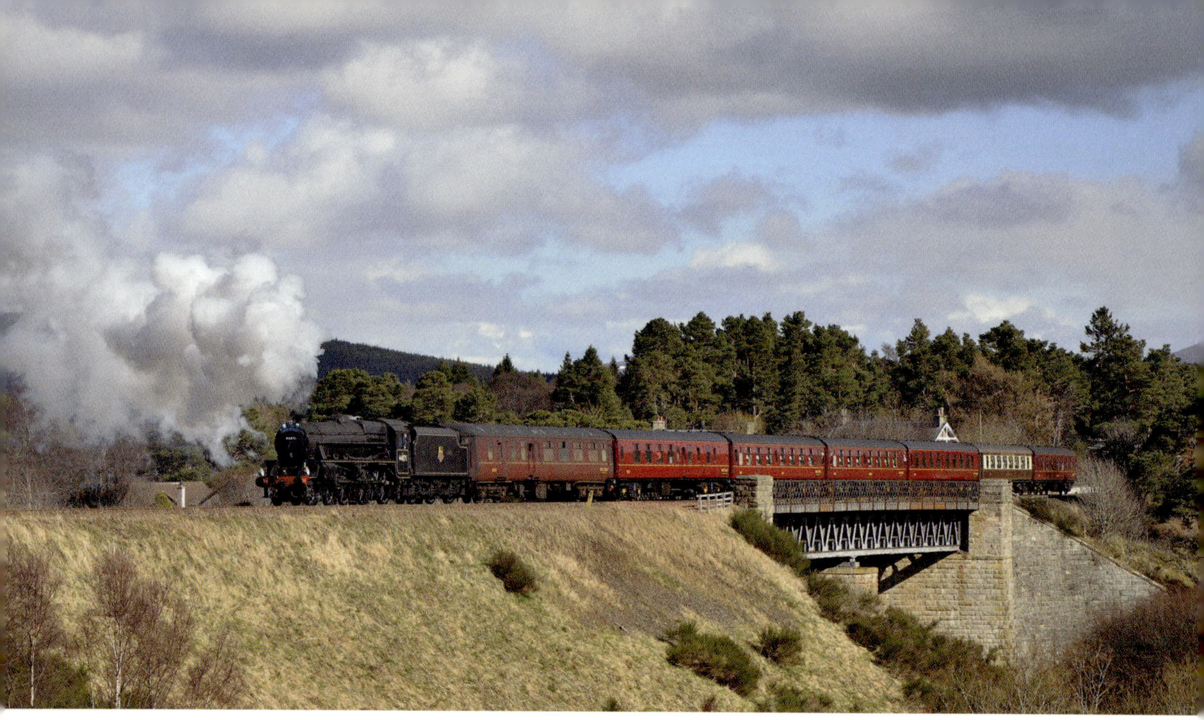

Class 5 44871 crosses the Dulnain Viaduct with GB VI to Inverness on 25 April 2013.

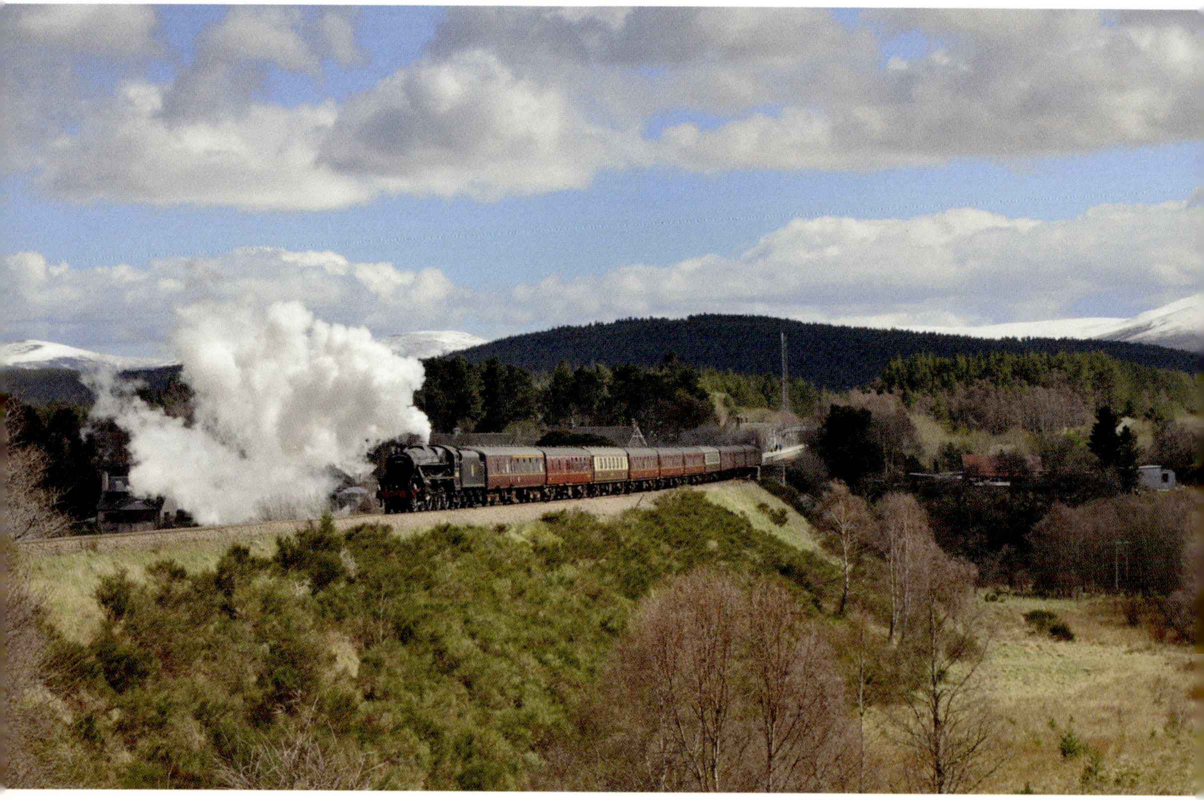

The same engine was working GB IX on 30 April 2016 and is seen on the embankment north of Carrbridge.

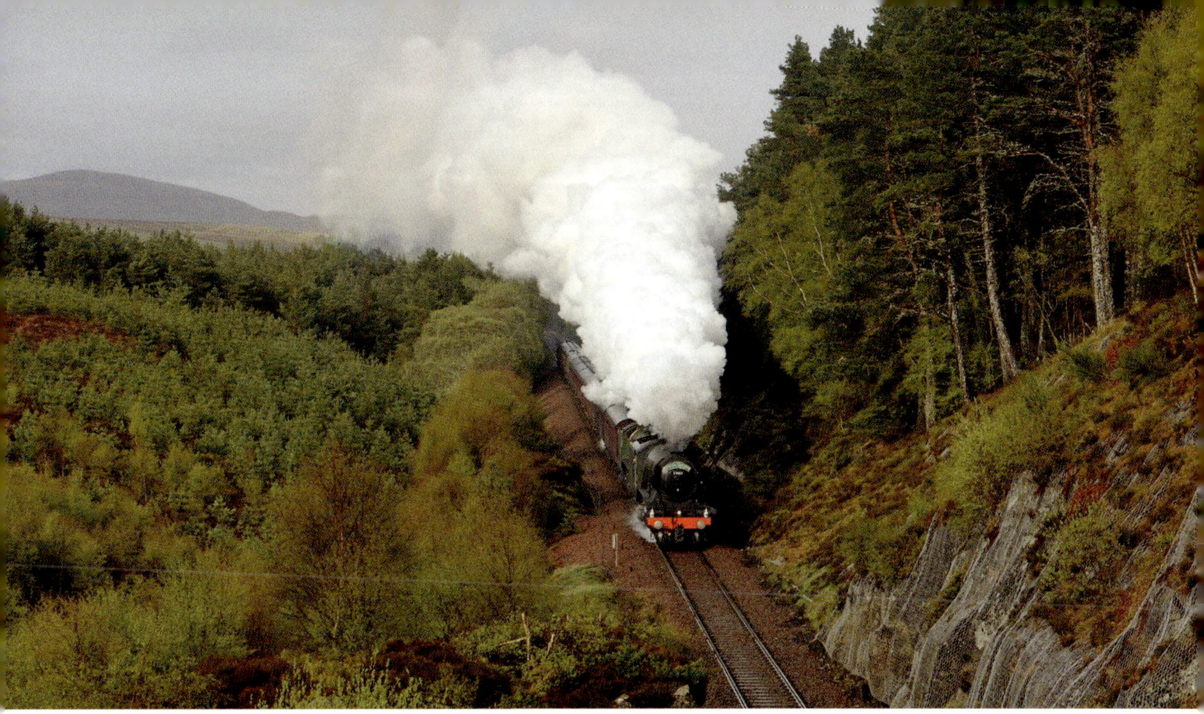

Nos 60103 *Flying Scotsman* and 61306 *Mayflower* near the old railway cottages at Slochd on the way north on 10 May 2019.

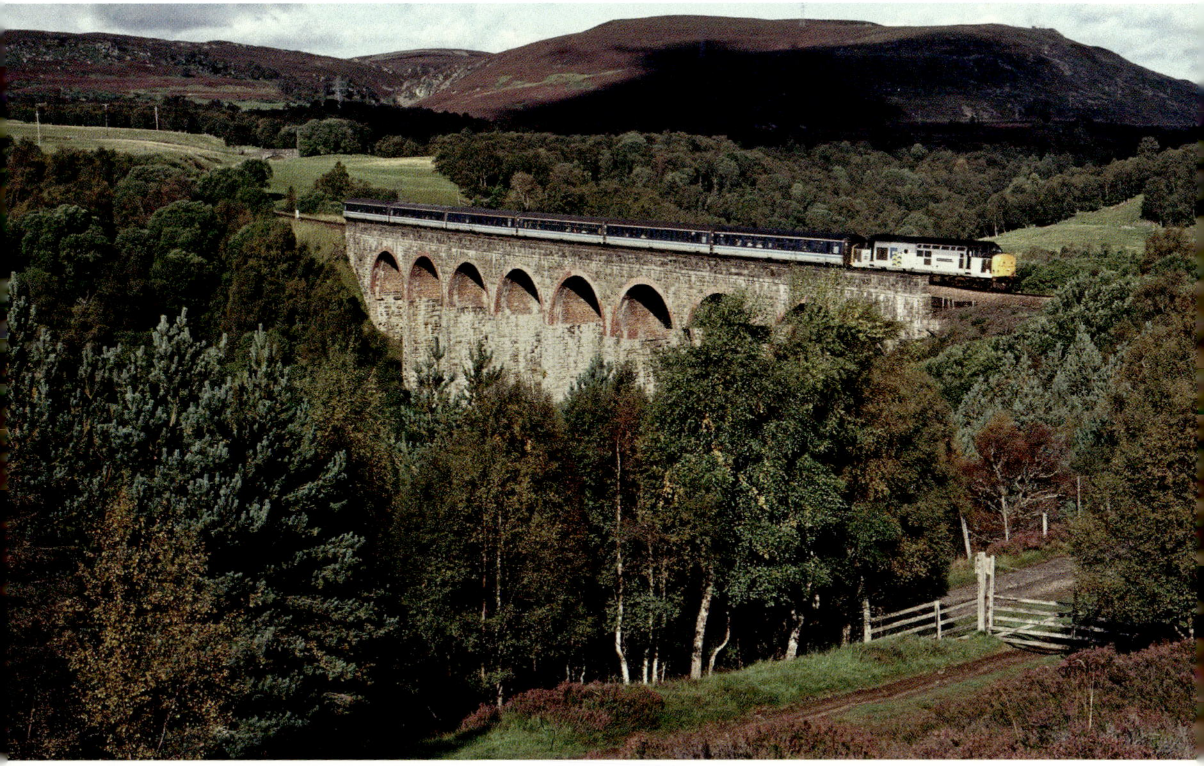

There is a fine show of heather as No. 37428 *David Lloyd George* heads south over Slochd viaduct on 17 September 1993.

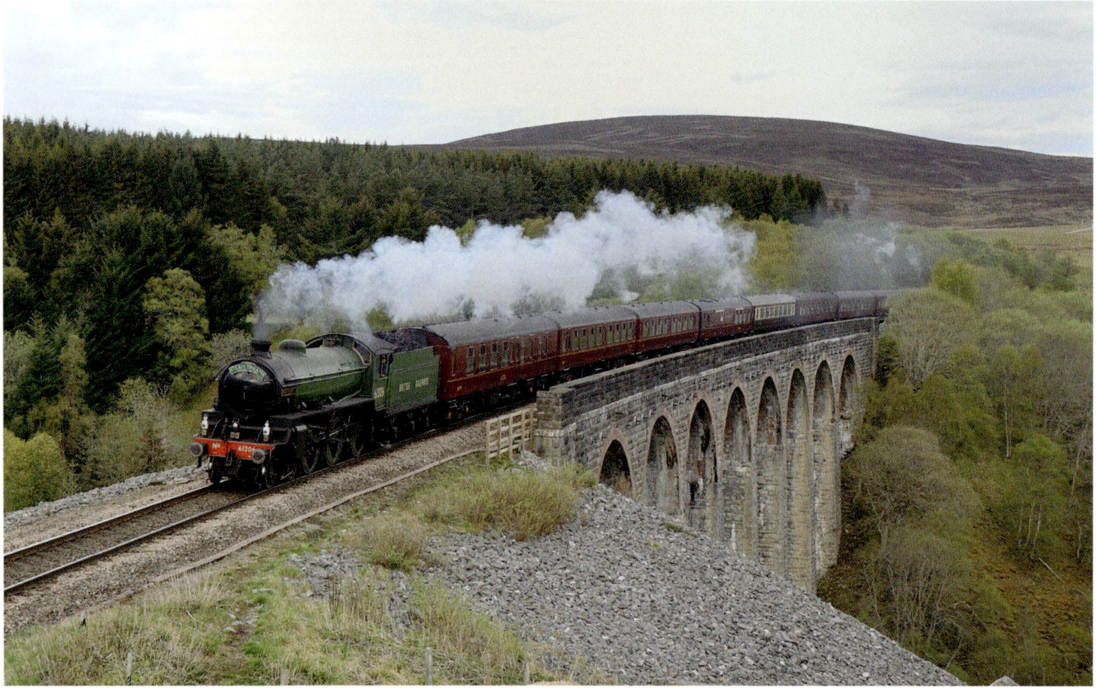

B1 No. 61306 crosses Slochd viaduct on the way south on 13 May 2019.

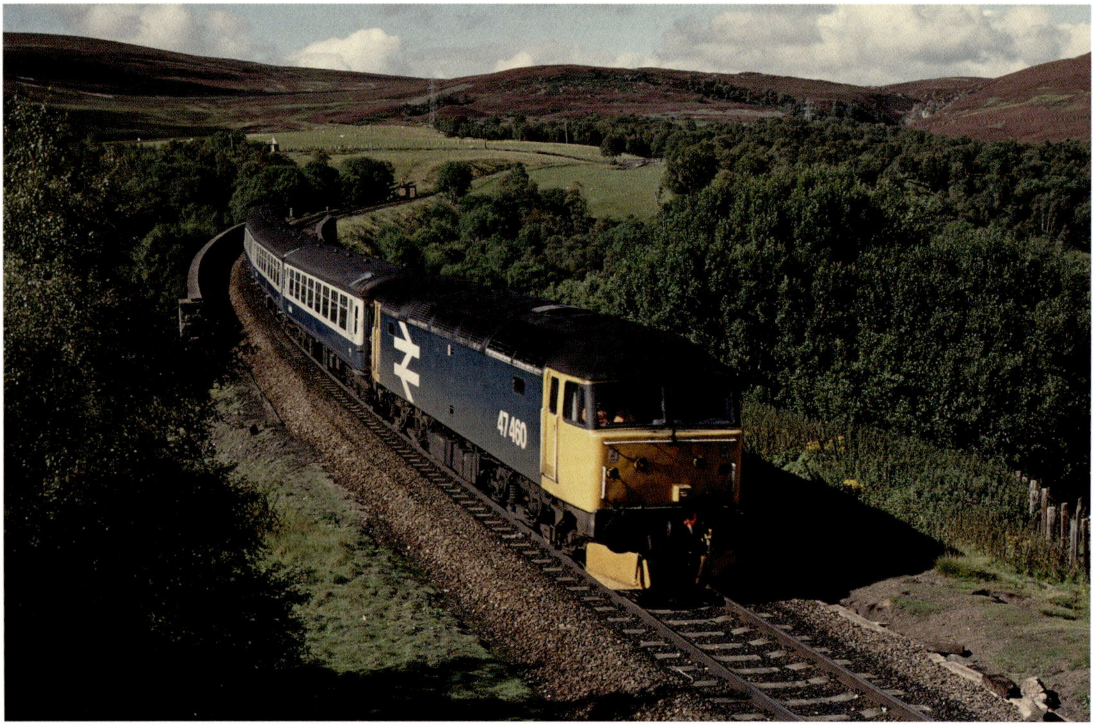

No. 47460 leaves Slochd viaduct with a service to Glasgow on 8 September 1989.

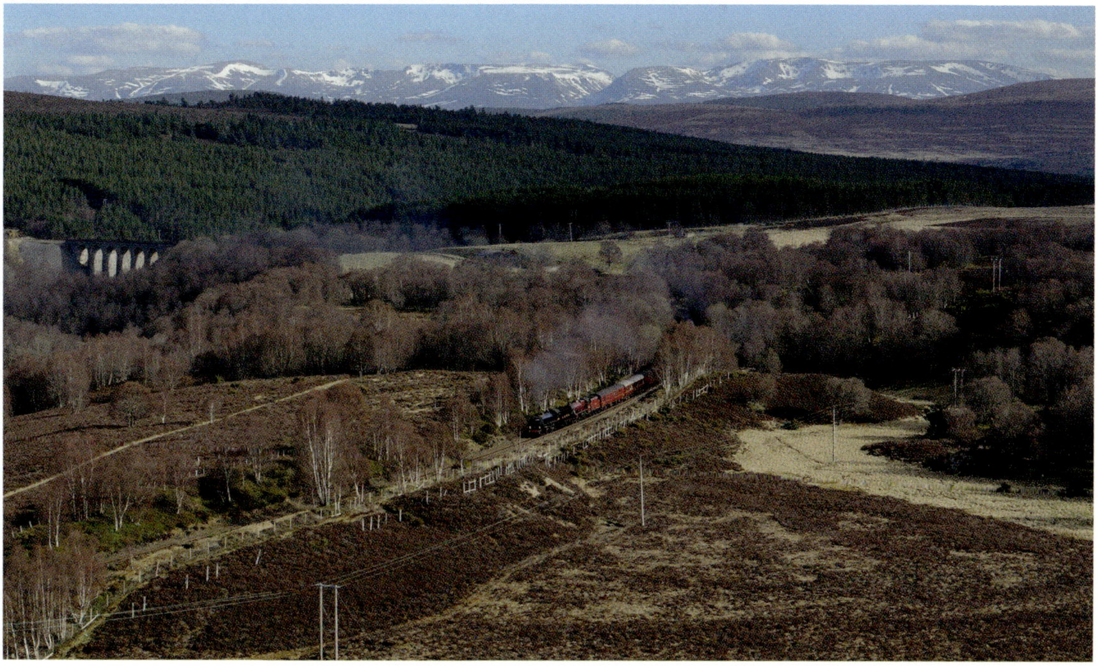

With the Cairngorms as backdrop, B1 No. 1264 and Jubilee No. 45699 *Galatea* climb to Slochd Summit with GB XI to Inverness on 21 April 2018.

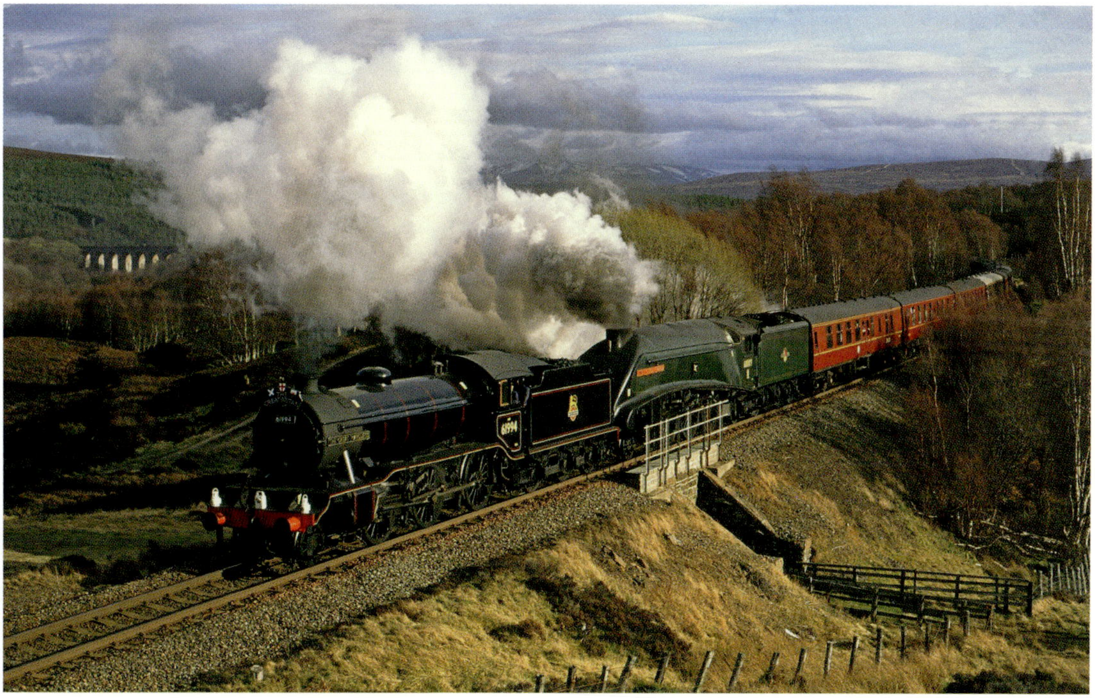

K1 No. 61994 and A4 No. 60009 work hard on the climb to Slochd with the Great Britain tour on 10 April 2007. The viaduct can be seen to the left.

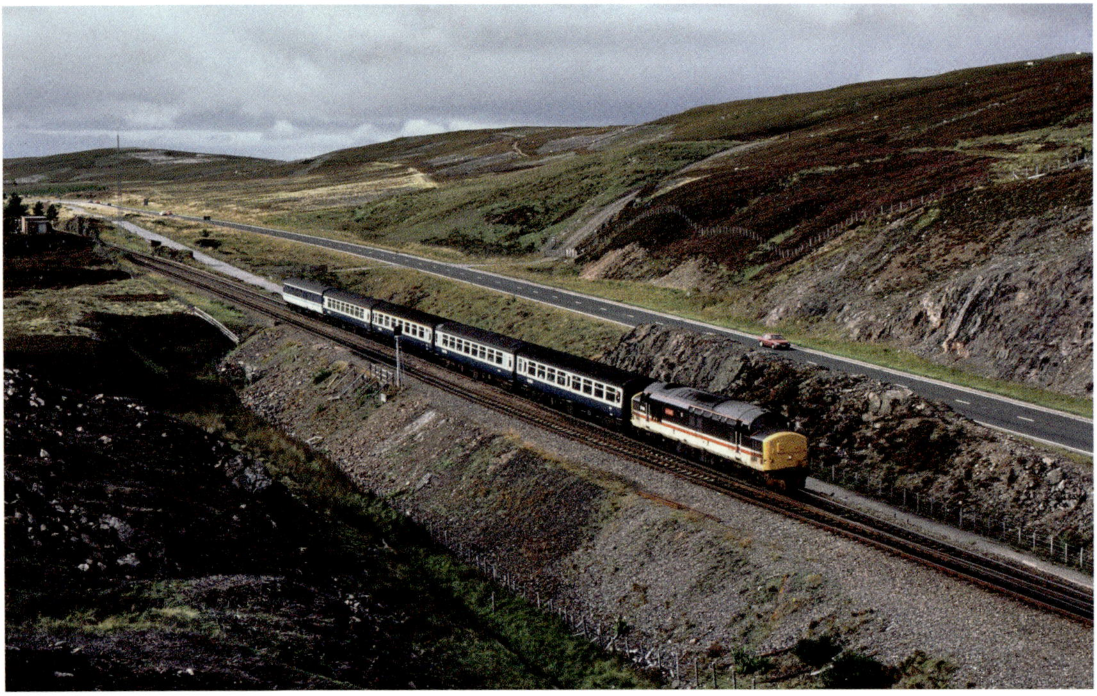

Class 37 No. 37424 passes Slochd Summit on the way south on 9 September 1990.

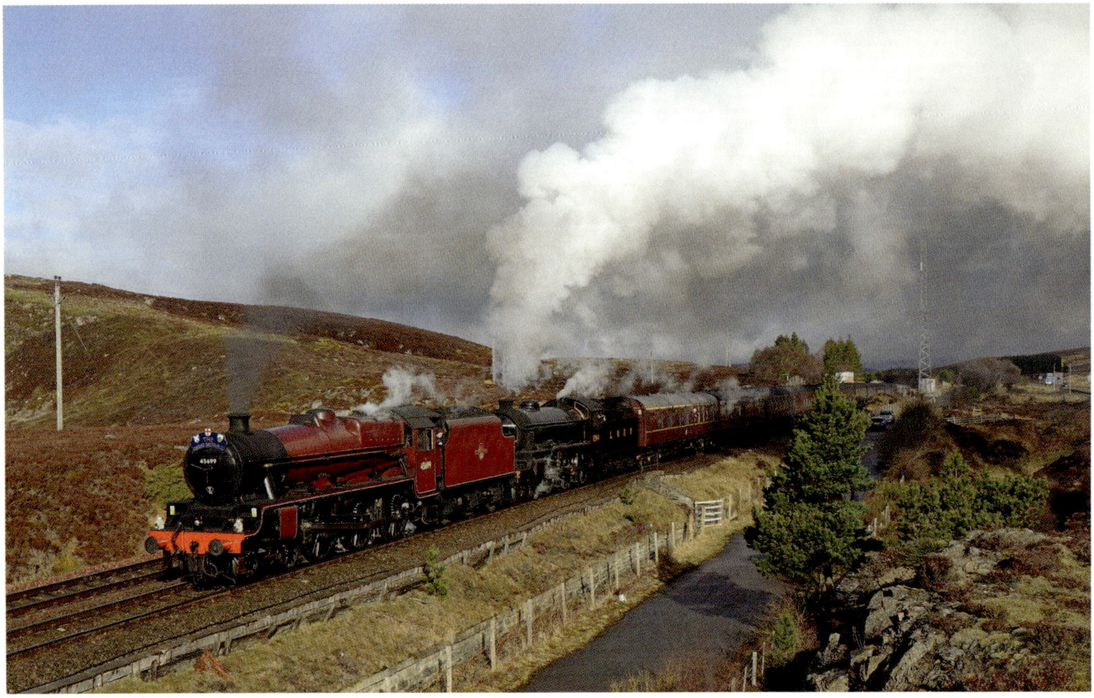

Nos 45699 and 1264 pause in the loop at Slochd Summit with GB XI from Inverness on 23 April 2018.

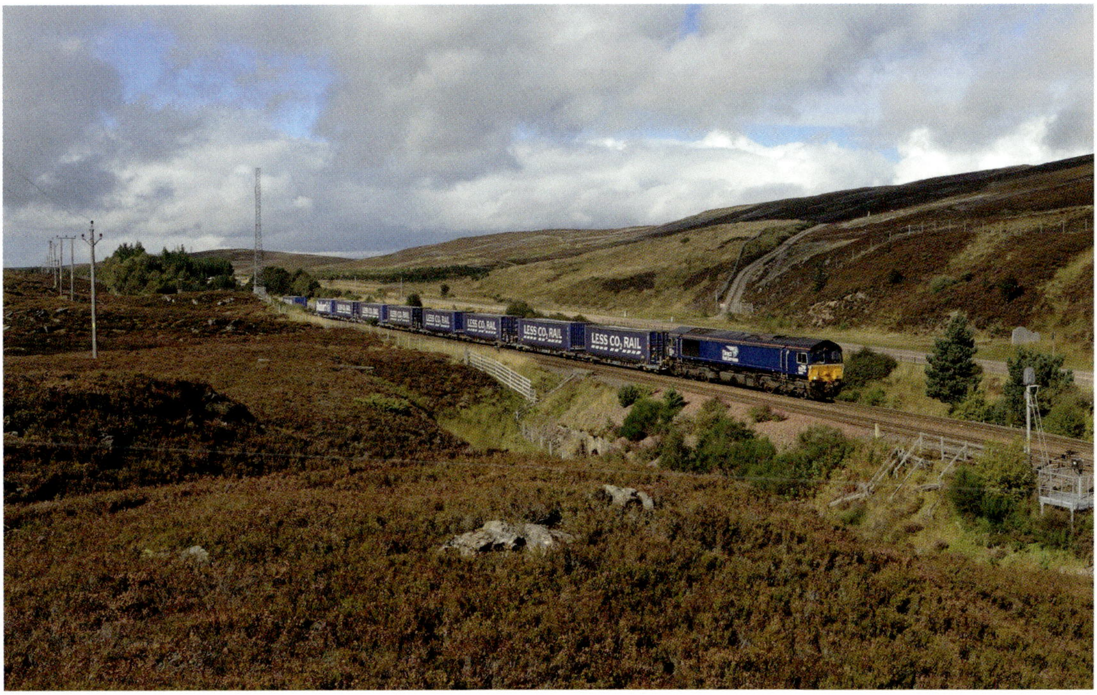

No. 66434 passes the summit with the Inverness to Mossend freight on 12 September 2019.

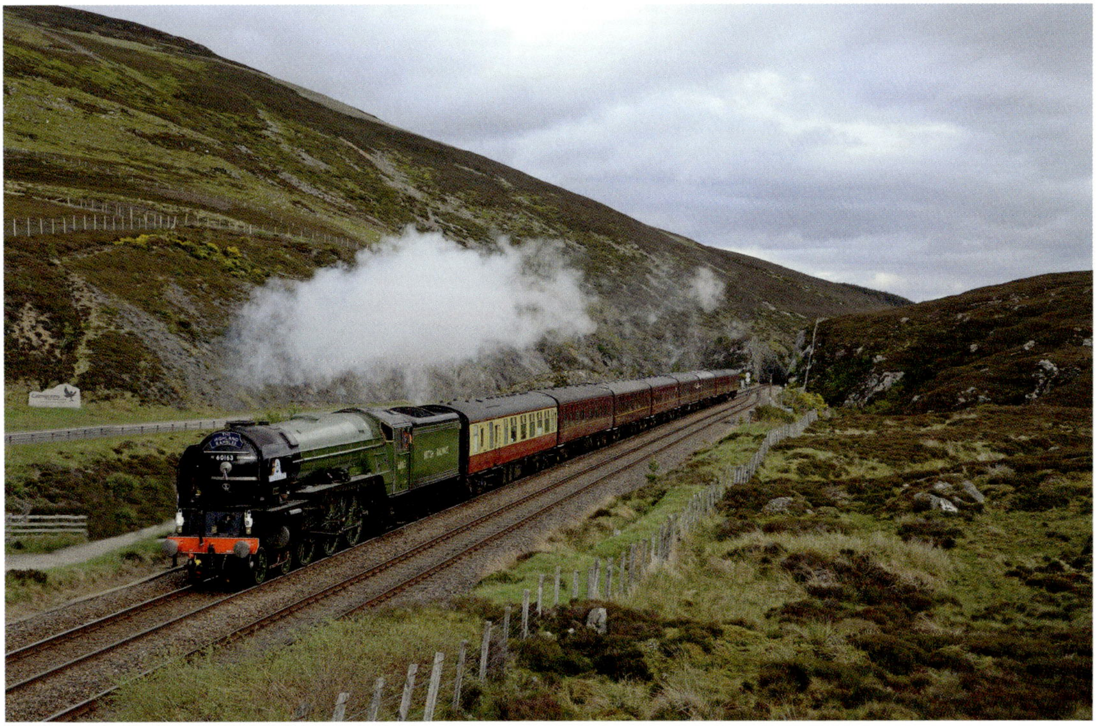

No. 60163 *Tornado* at Slochd Summit with the tour to Inverness on 20 June 2015.

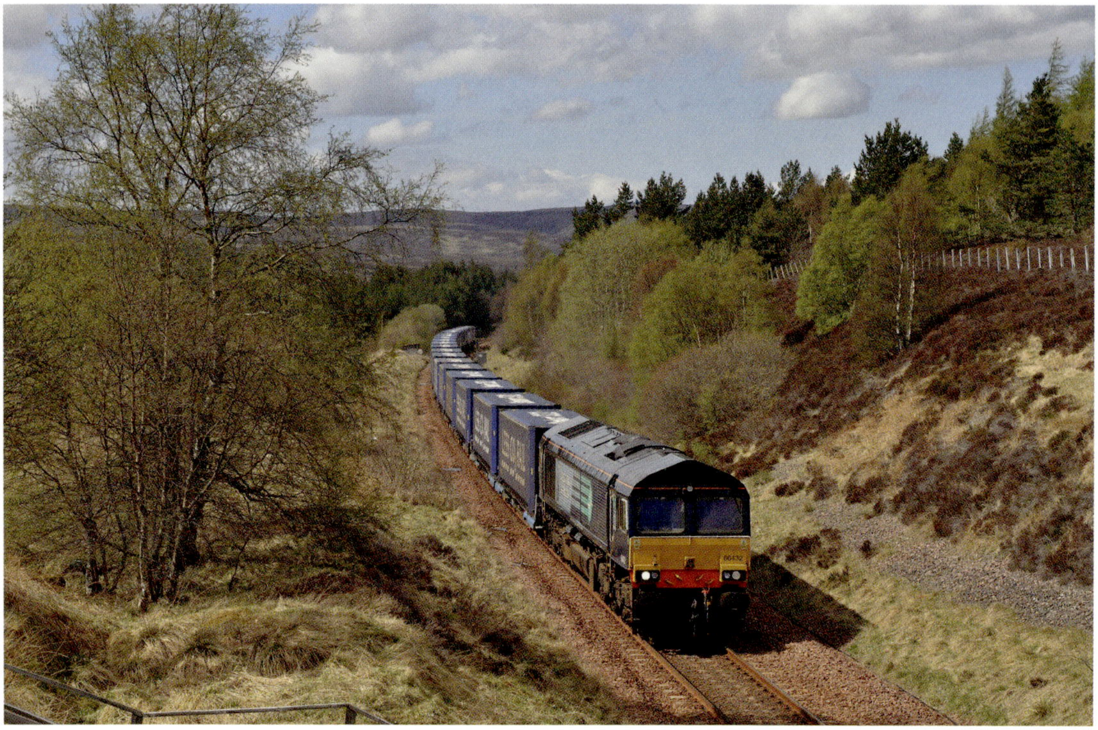

No. 66432 nears the summit with a southbound freight on 2 May 2014.

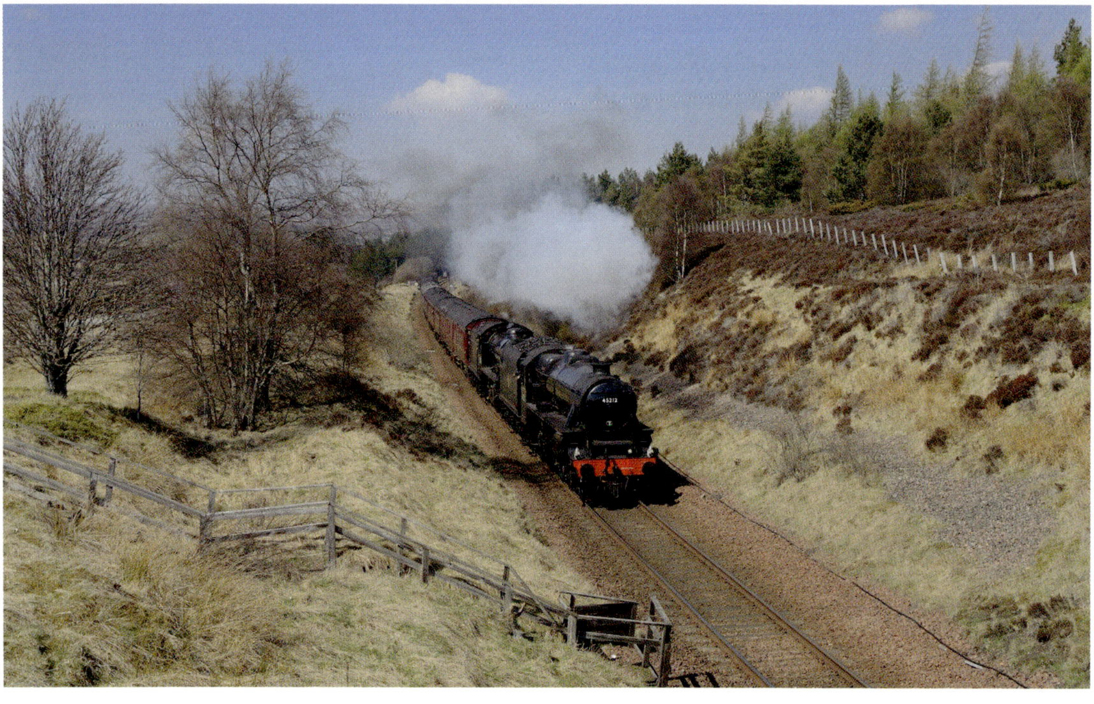

Nos 45212 and 62005 on the southbound climb with GB X on 2 May 2017.

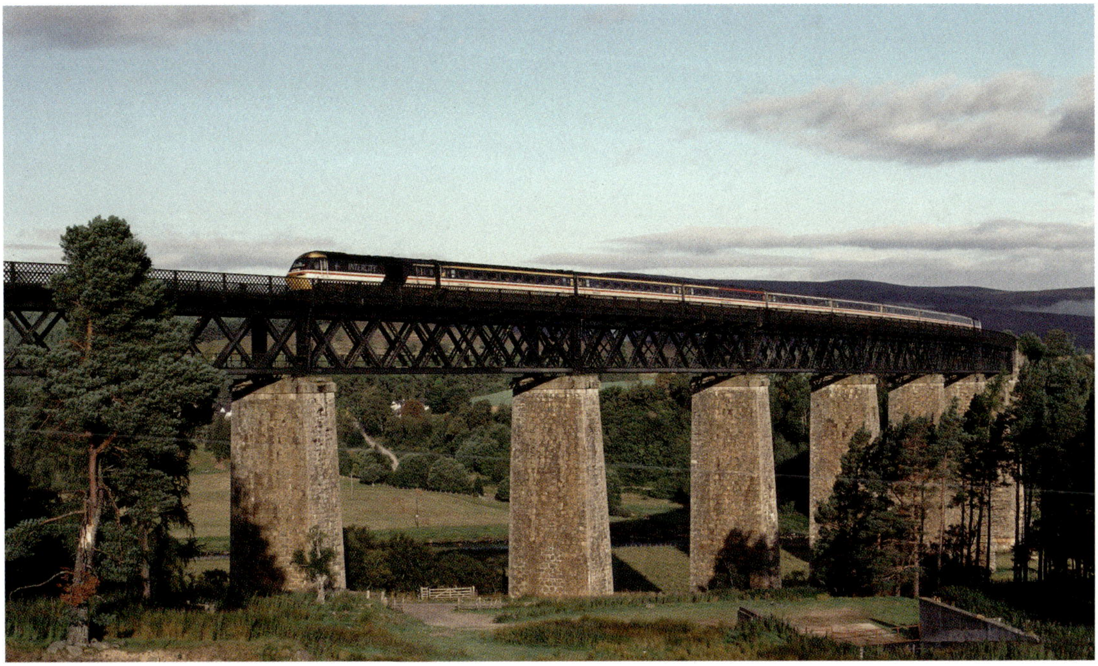

An InterCity-liveried HST works across the Findhorn viaduct with the Inverness to Kings Cross service on 8 September 1989.

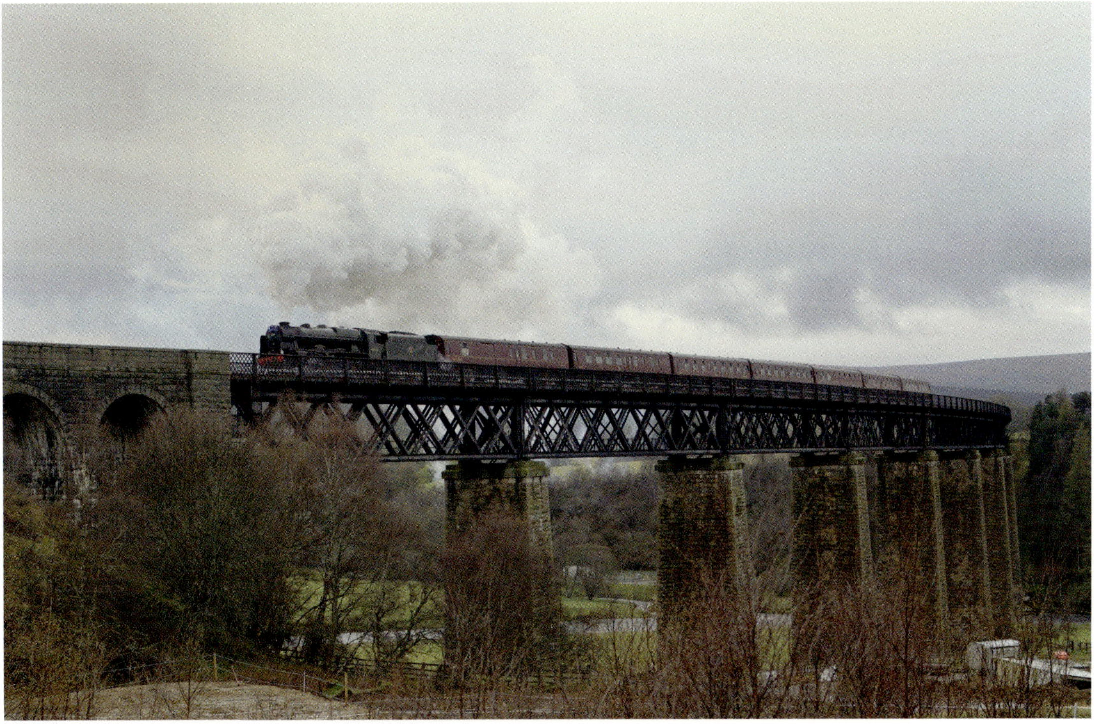

No. 46115 *Scots Guardsman* at the same location on 24 April 2012.

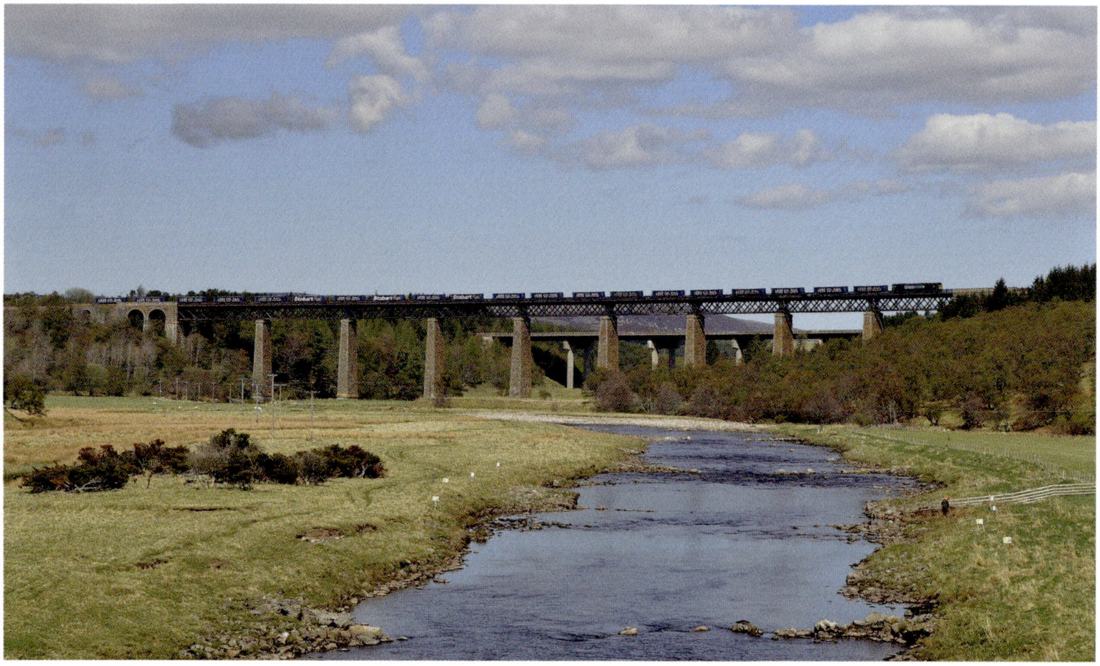

Looking along the river, the full extent of the impressive Findhorn viaduct is seen as No. 66432 crosses with a southbound freight on 2 May 2014. The A9 roadbridge is in the background.

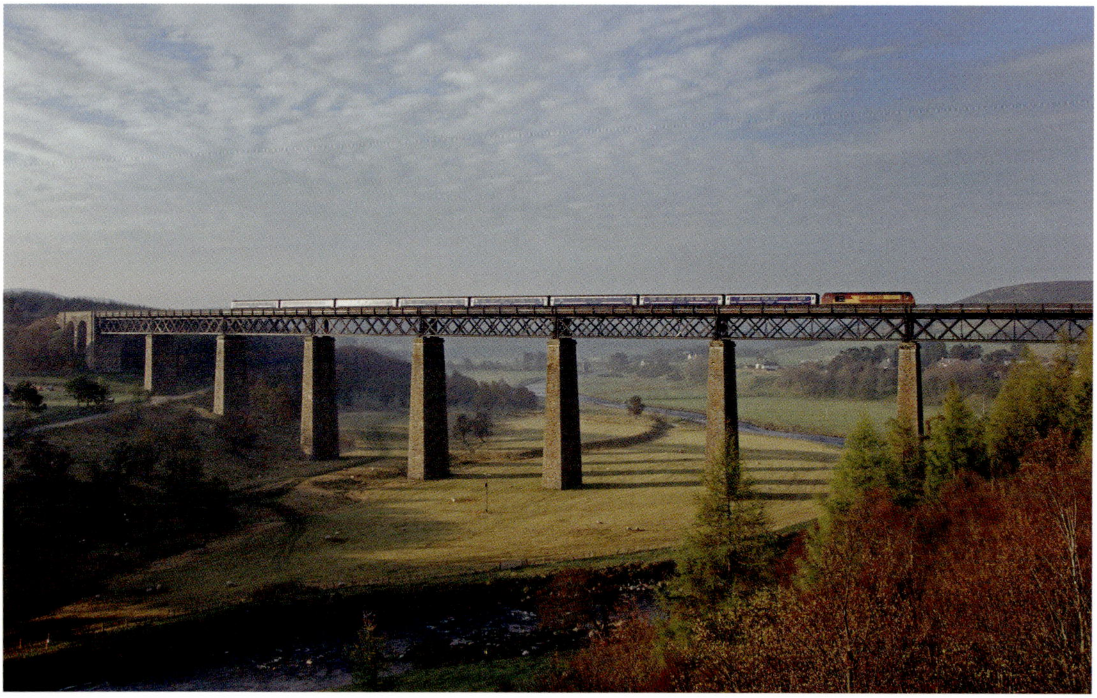

The view from the A9 bridge as Class 67 No. 67030 works the Euston to Inverness sleeper on 20 April 2011.

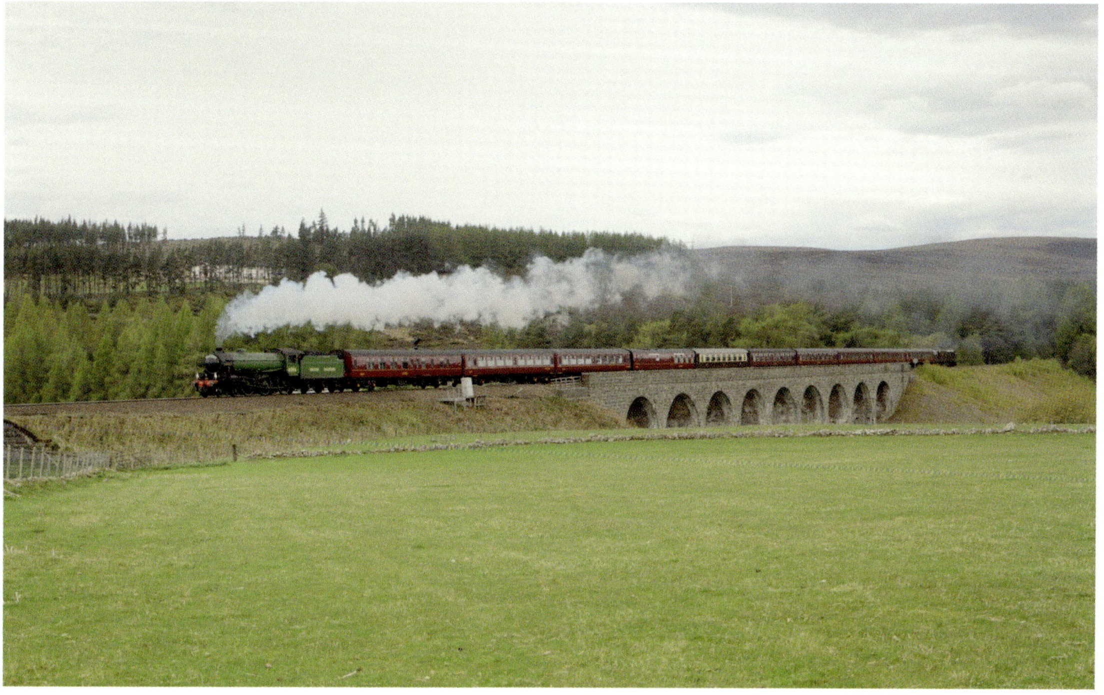

B1 No. 61306 crosses Tomatin viaduct with the southbound Steam Dreams trip on 13 May 2019.

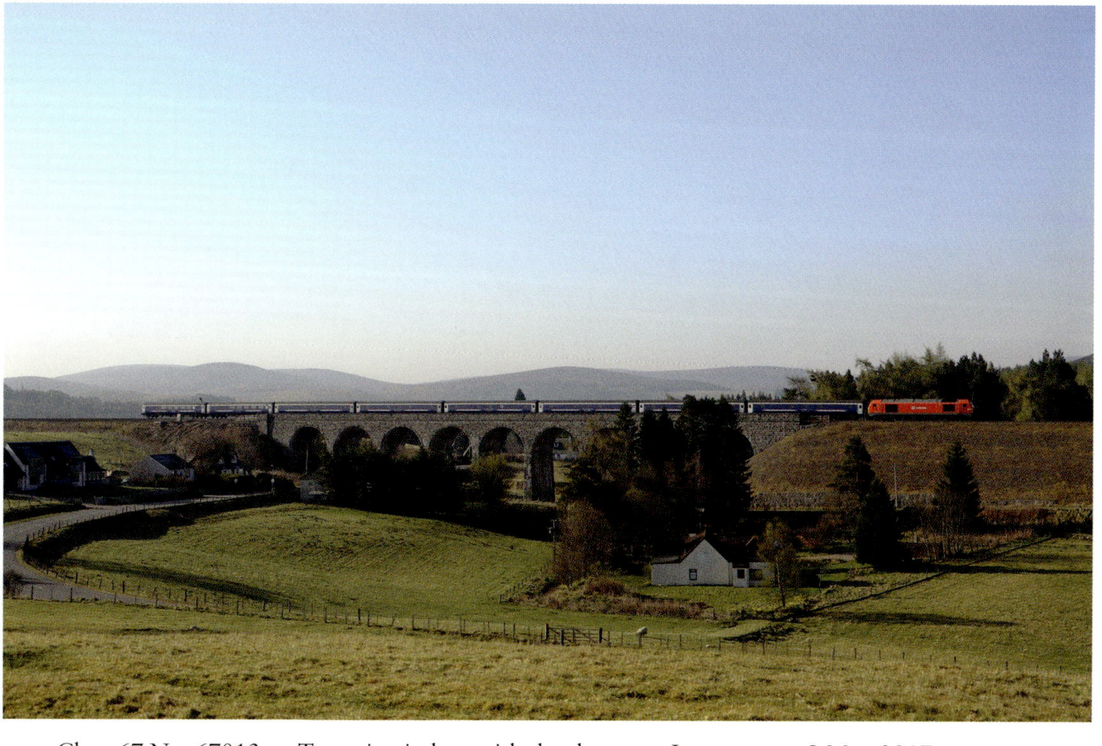

Class 67 No. 67013 on Tomatin viaduct with the sleeper to Inverness on 2 May 2017.

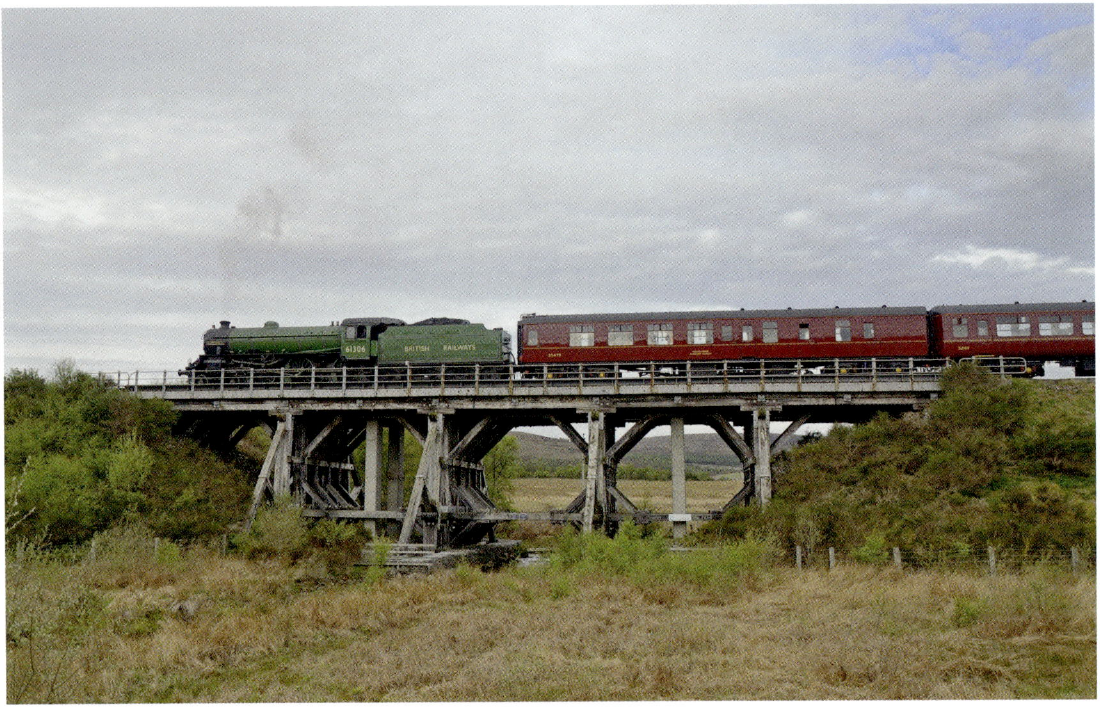

No. 61306 *Mayflower* crosses Allt-na-Slanach viaduct near Moy on the way south on 13 May 2019. This is the last remaining timber viaduct on the Scottish railway system, although it was reinforced with steel in 2002.

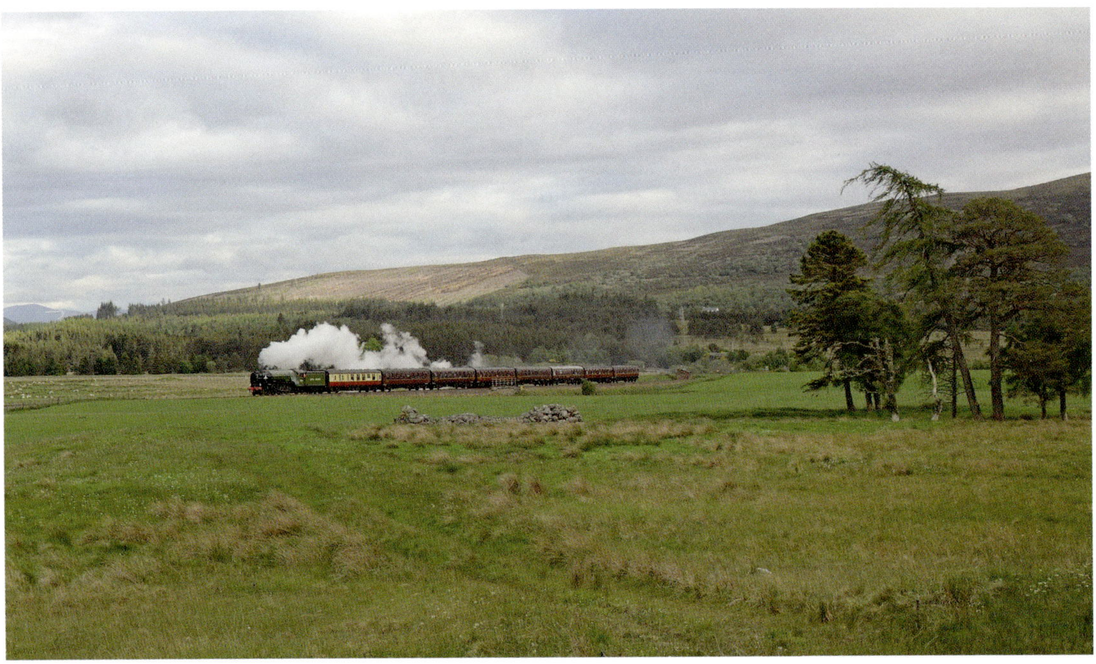

No. 60163 *Tornado* heads north near Moy on 20 June 2015.

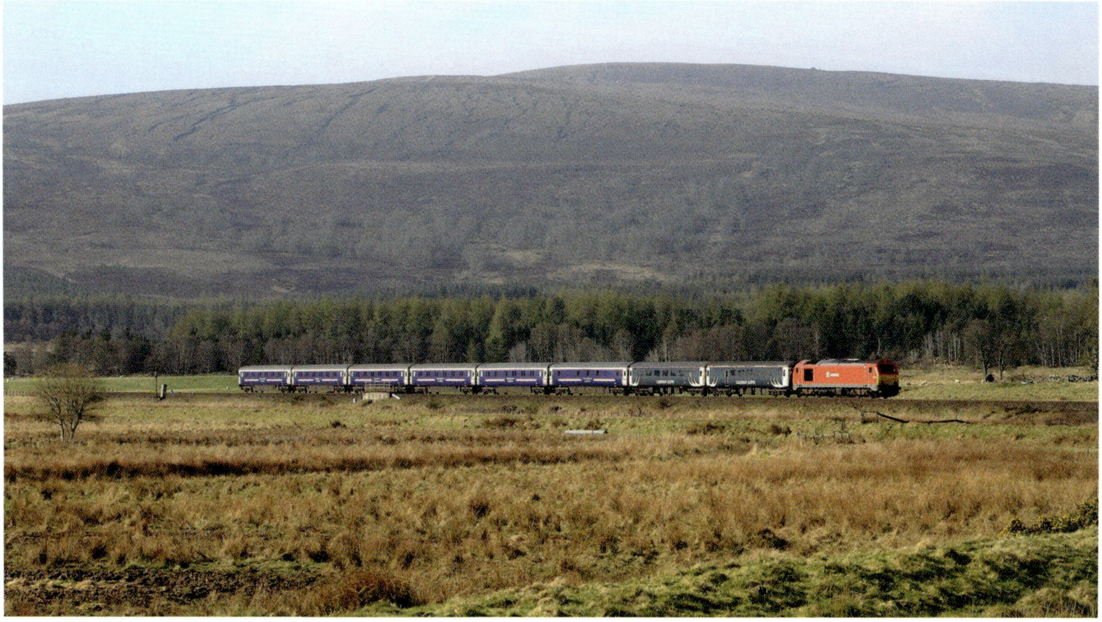

Class 67 No. 67013, north of Moy with the sleeper from Euston on 1 May 2017.

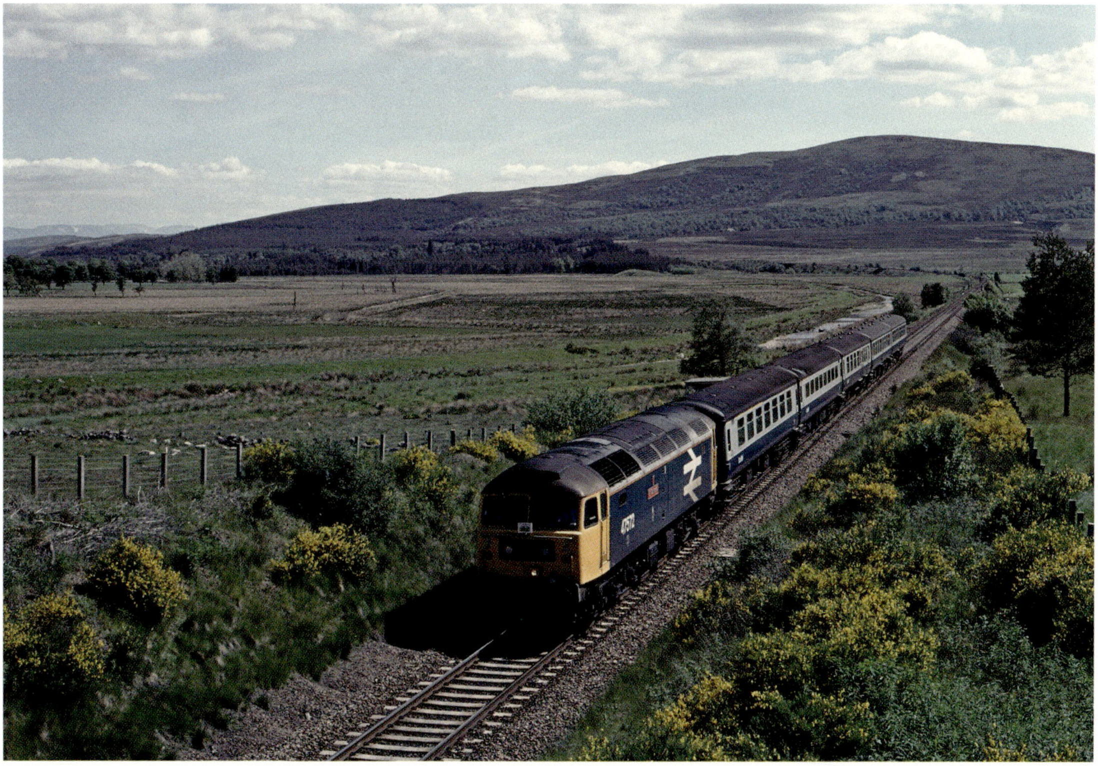

The lineside vegetation adds some colour as No. 47572 heads away from Moy with a northbound service on 17 June 1989.

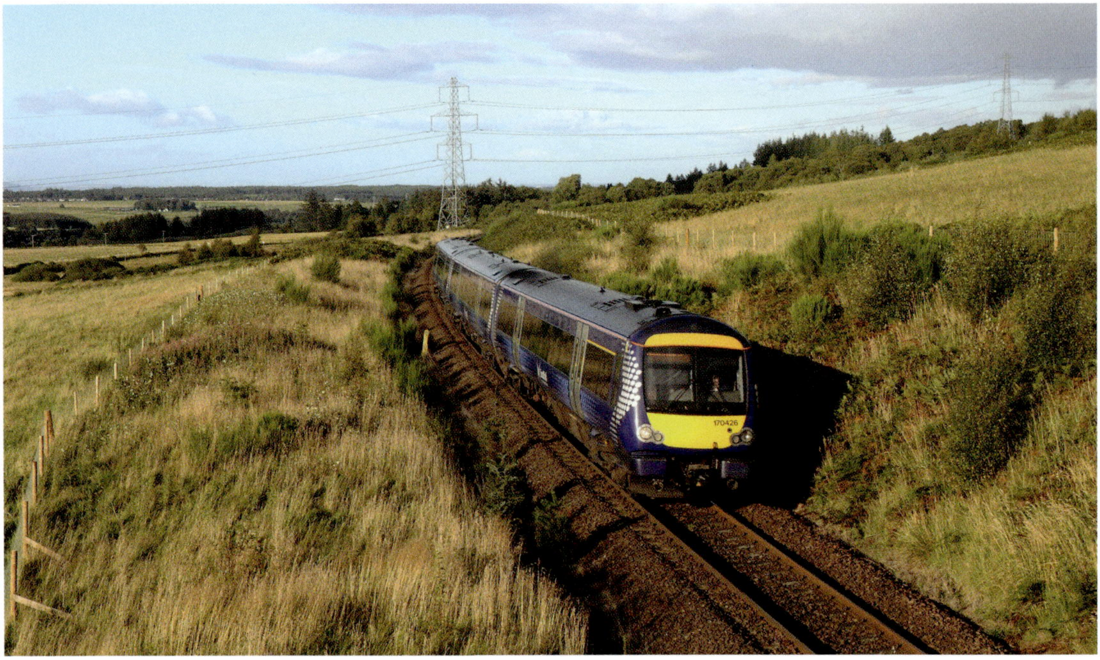

A 170 unit works south at Cottartown on 12 September 2019.

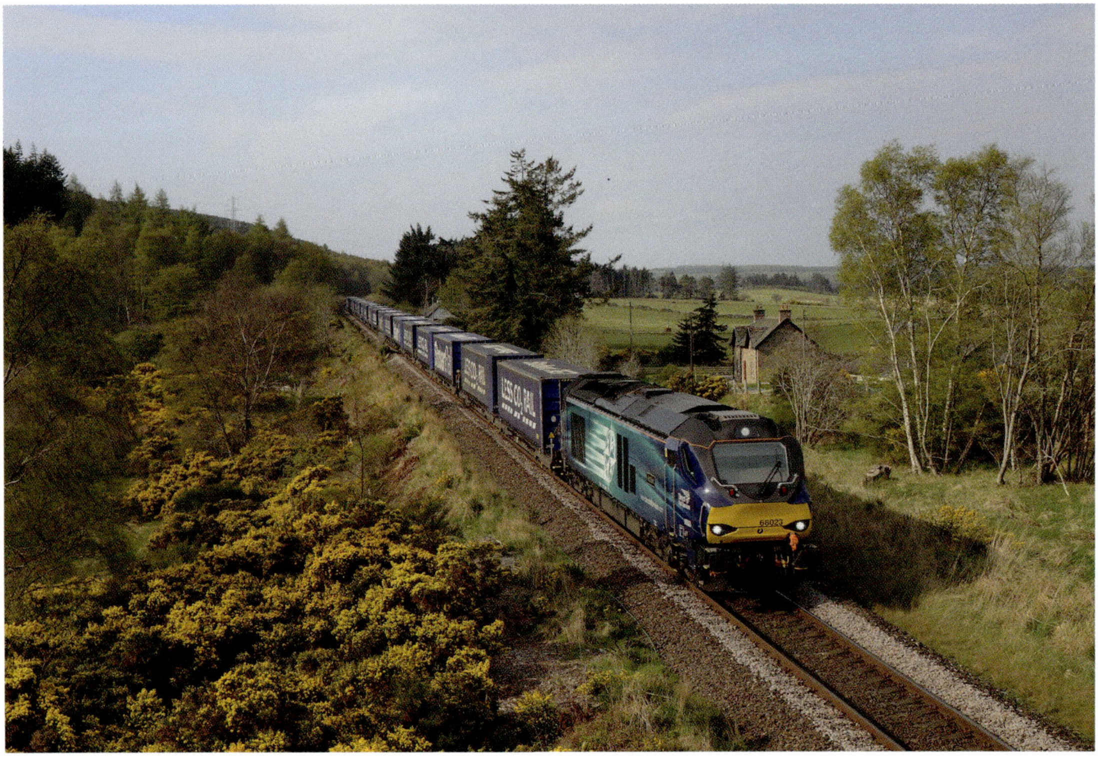

Class 68 No. 68023 passes Castletown with the Mossend to Inverness Tesco freight on 1 May 2017.

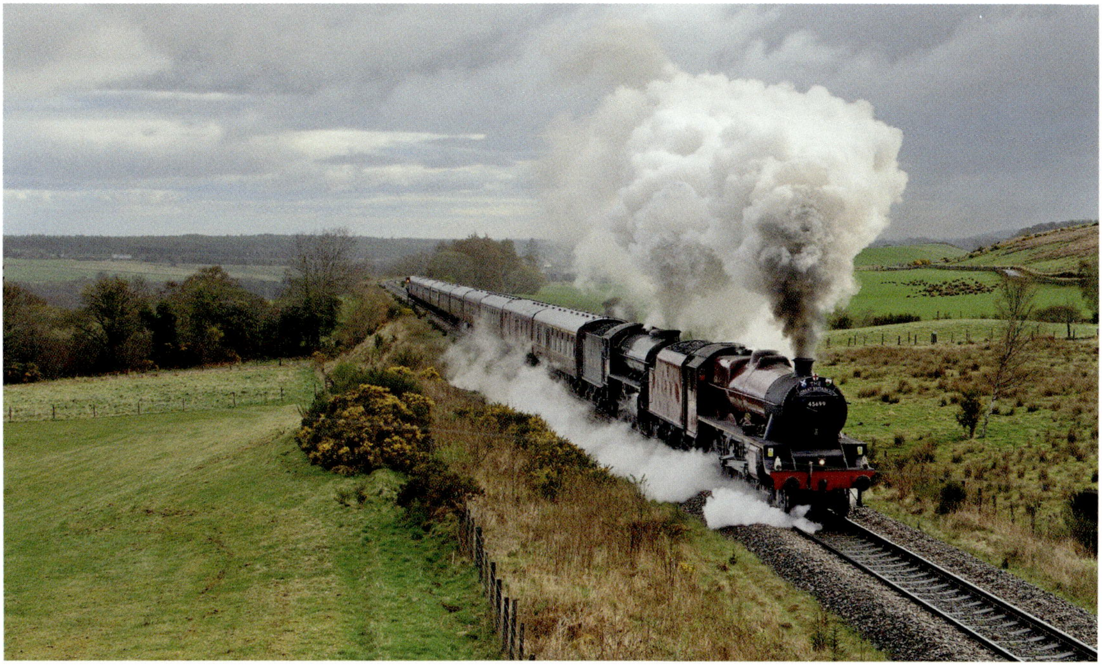

Seen from the overbridge at Castletown, Nos 45699 and 1264 head south with GB XI on 23 April 2018.

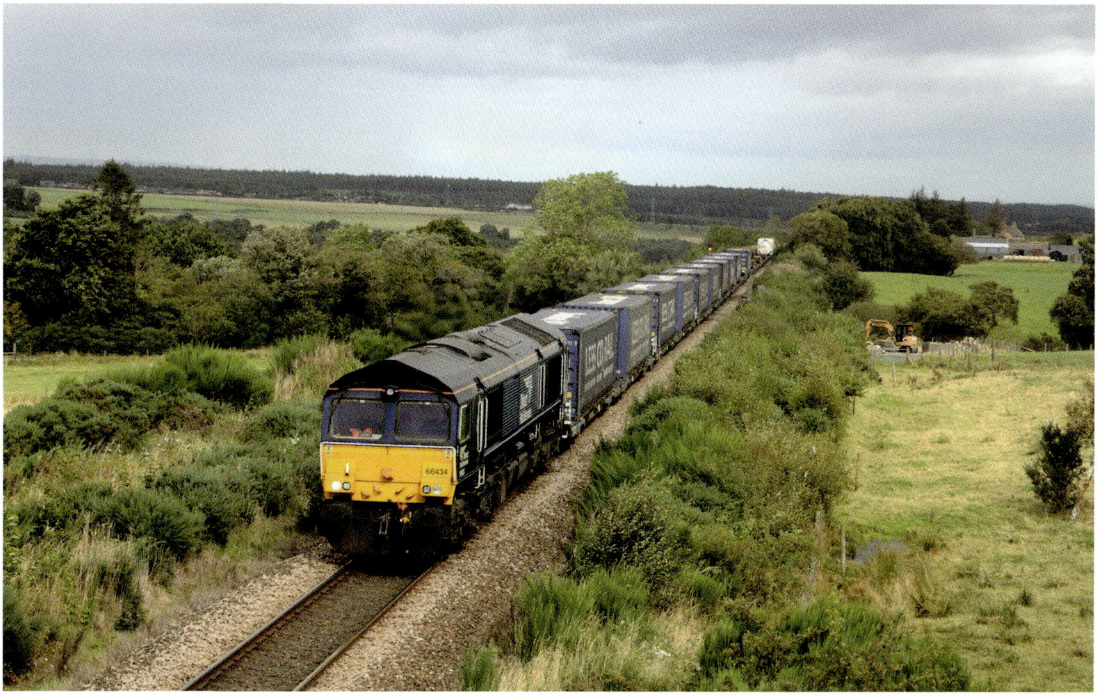

DRS Class 66 No. 66434 works an Inverness to Mossend freight south at Castletown on 11 September 2019.

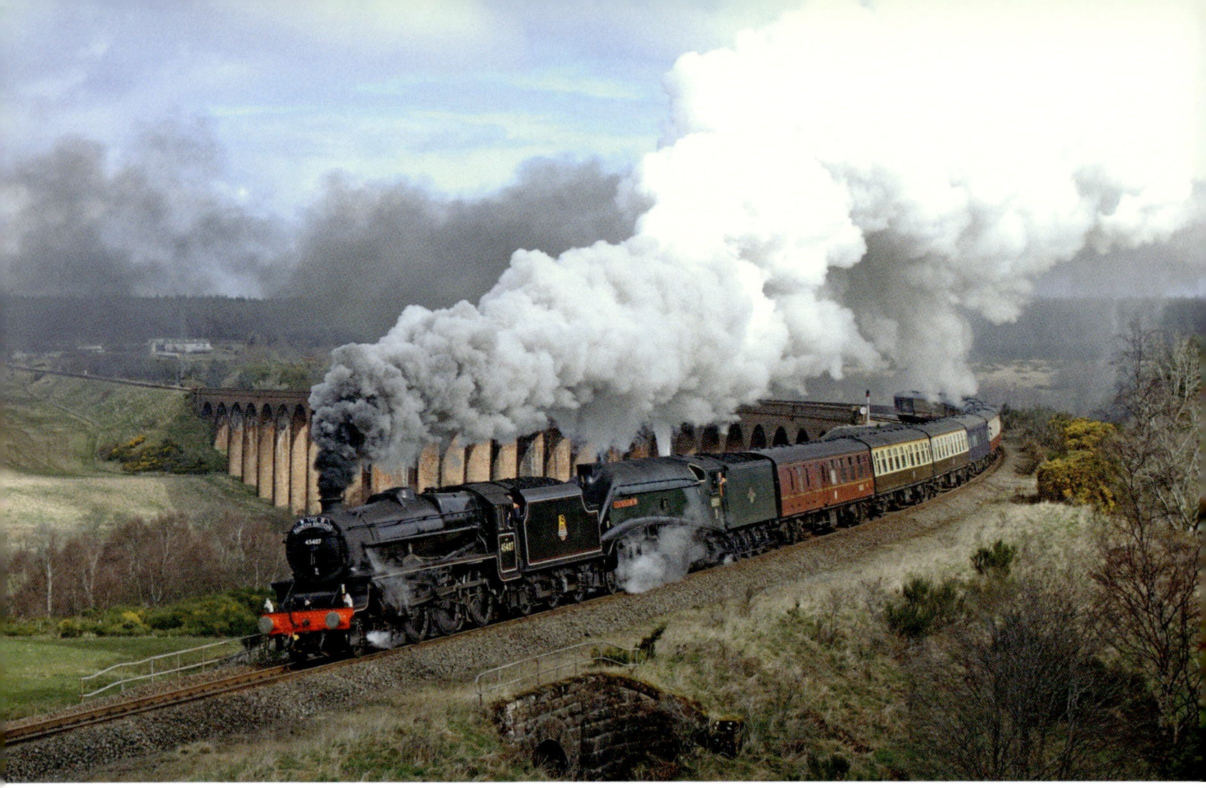

Nos 45407 and 60009 haul the North Briton leg from Inverness to Perth away from Culloden viaduct on 15 April 2008.

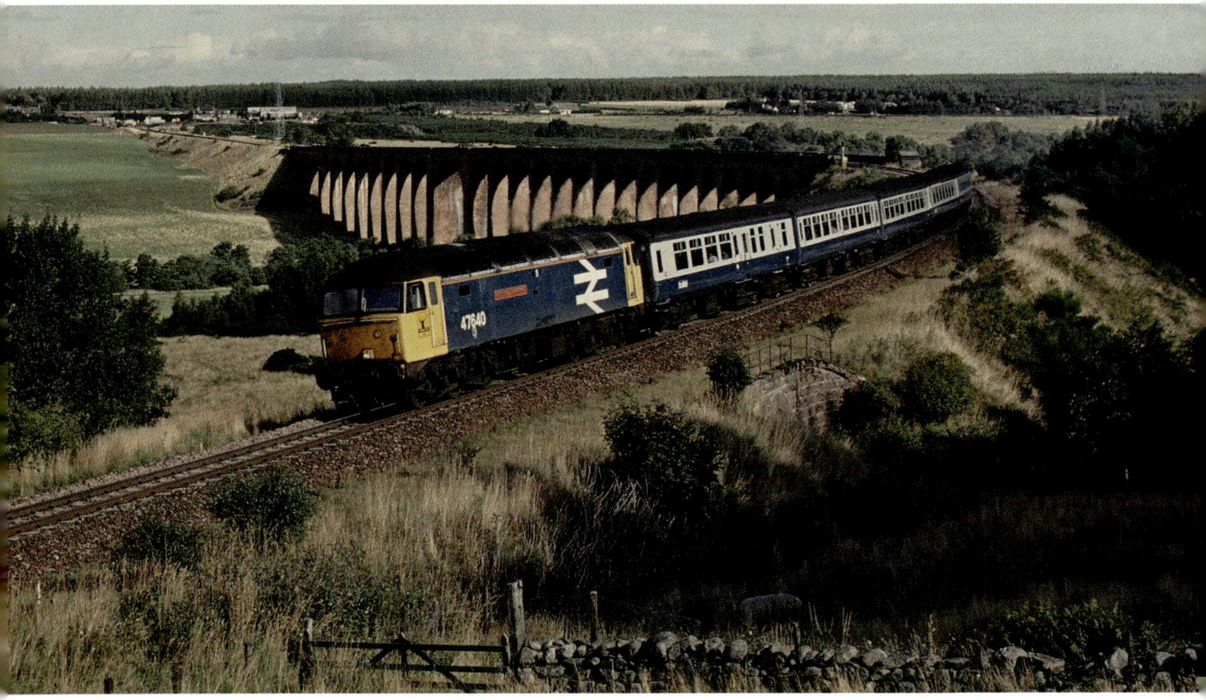

With the impressive Culloden viaduct in the background, Class 47 No. 47640 heads to Glasgow on 8 September 1989.

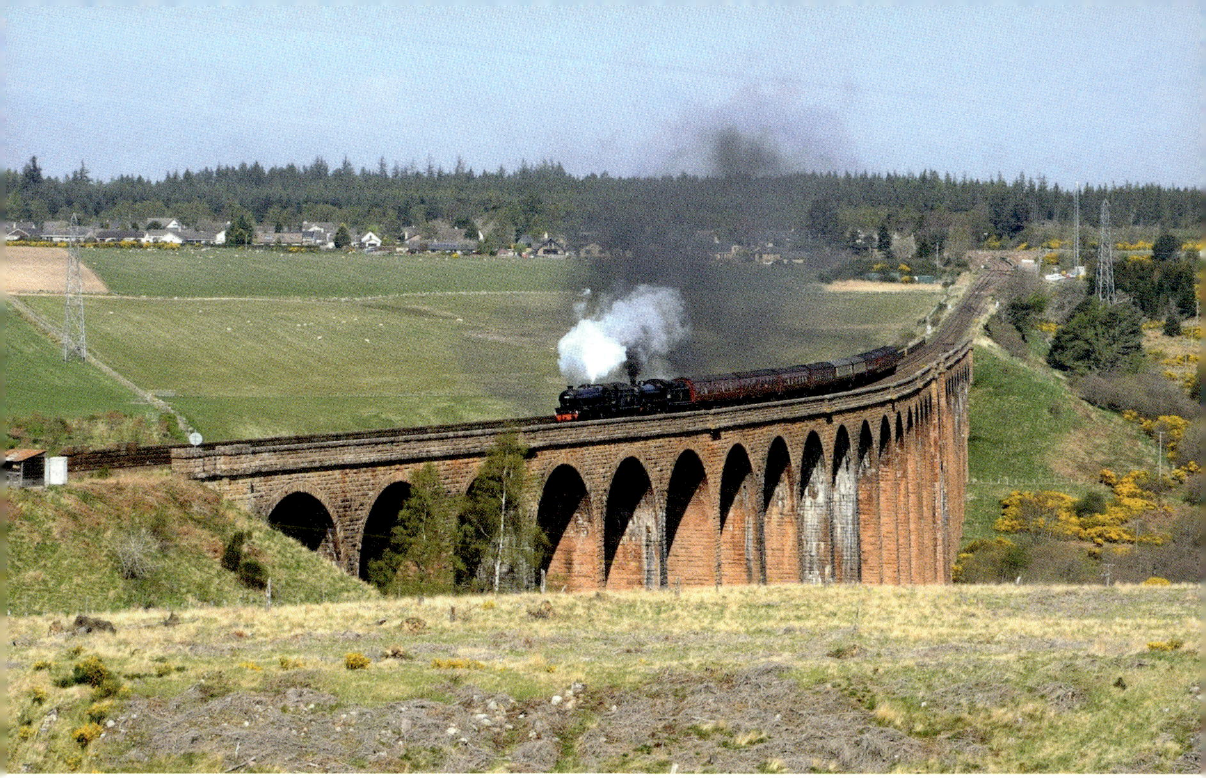

Extensive forestry clearance opened up this view of Culloden viaduct as Nos 45212 and 62005 double-head GB X south on 2 May 2017.

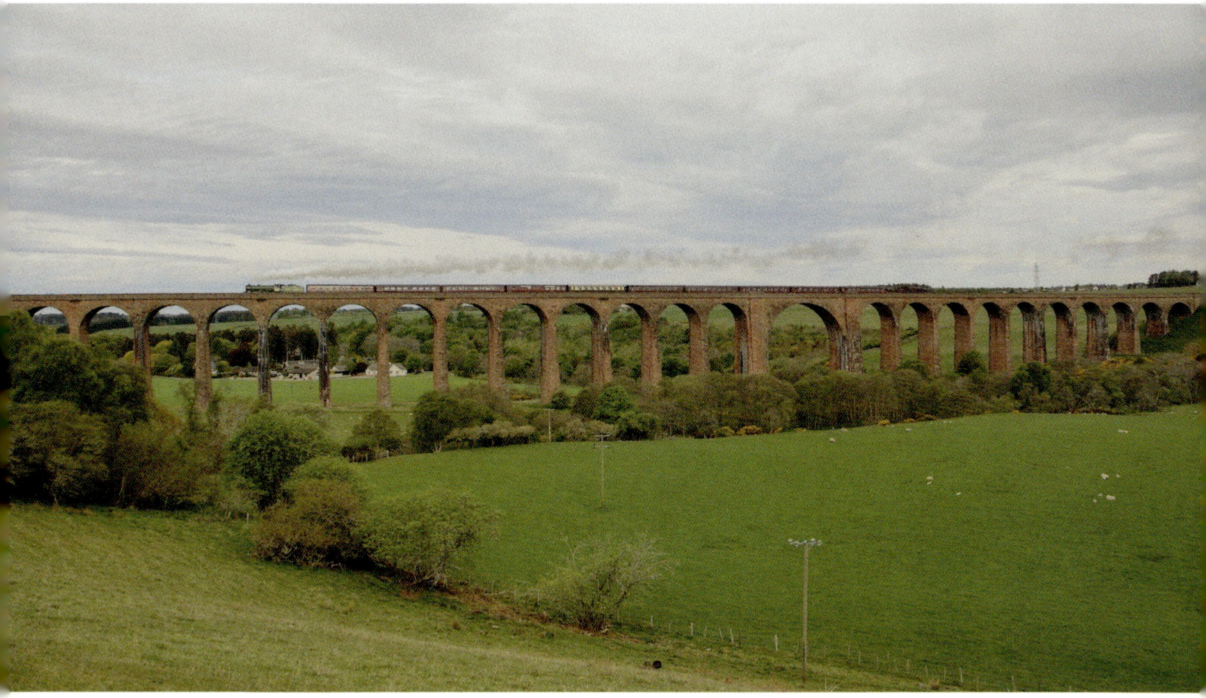

B1 No. 61306 *Mayflower* crosses Culloden viaduct with the Steam Dreams leg to Glasgow on 13 May 2019.

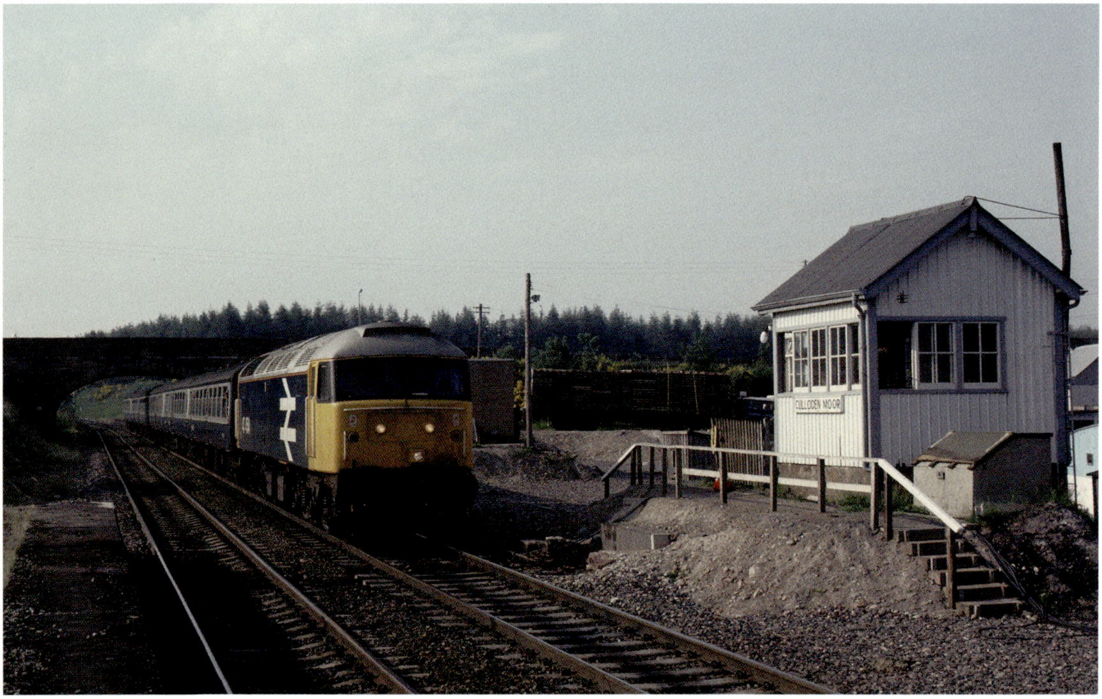

No. 47454 passes Culloden Moor signal cabin with a working to Glasgow on 28 June 1986. The cabin was closed in 1987.

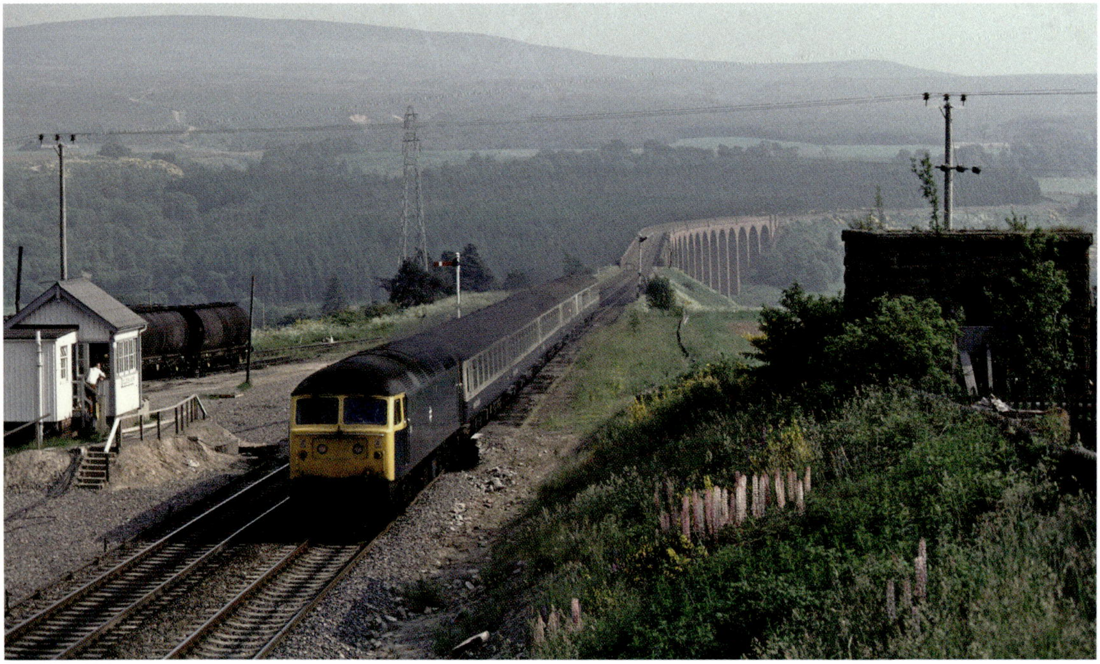

No. 47534 passes Culloden with a service to Inverness on 28 June 1986. The bitumen depot to the left was still in use but traffic ceased in the early 1990s.

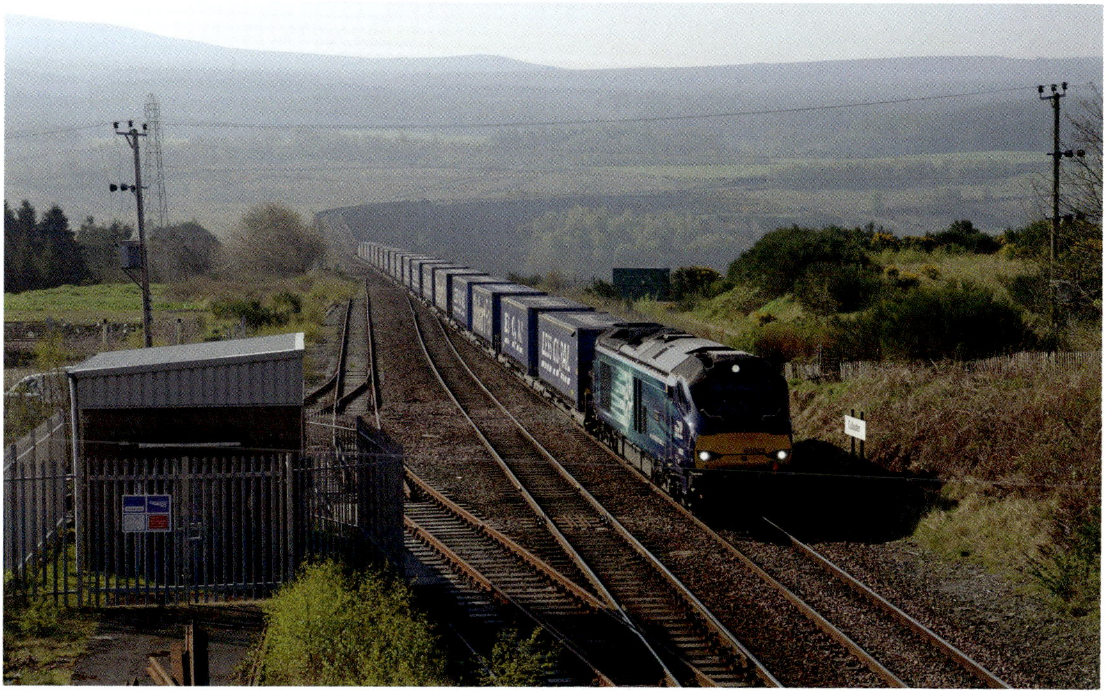

Class 68 No. 68023 works the northbound Tesco freight past Culloden on 2 May 2017.

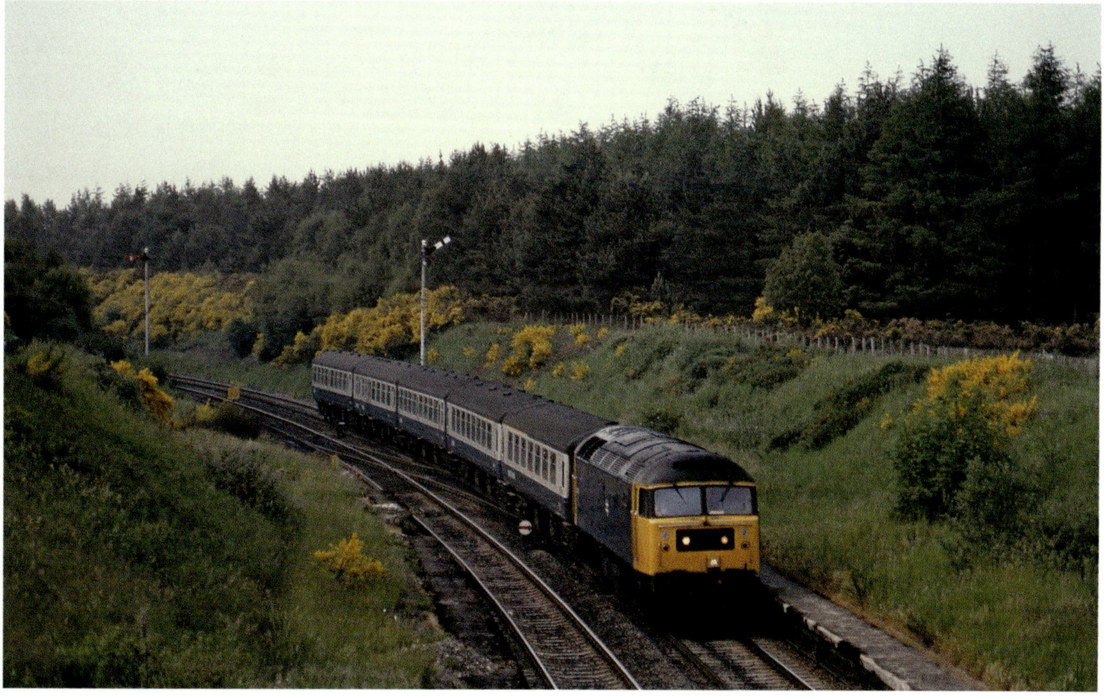

No. 47586 passes the remains of Culloden Station on the way south on 28 June 1986. The station was closed in 1968.

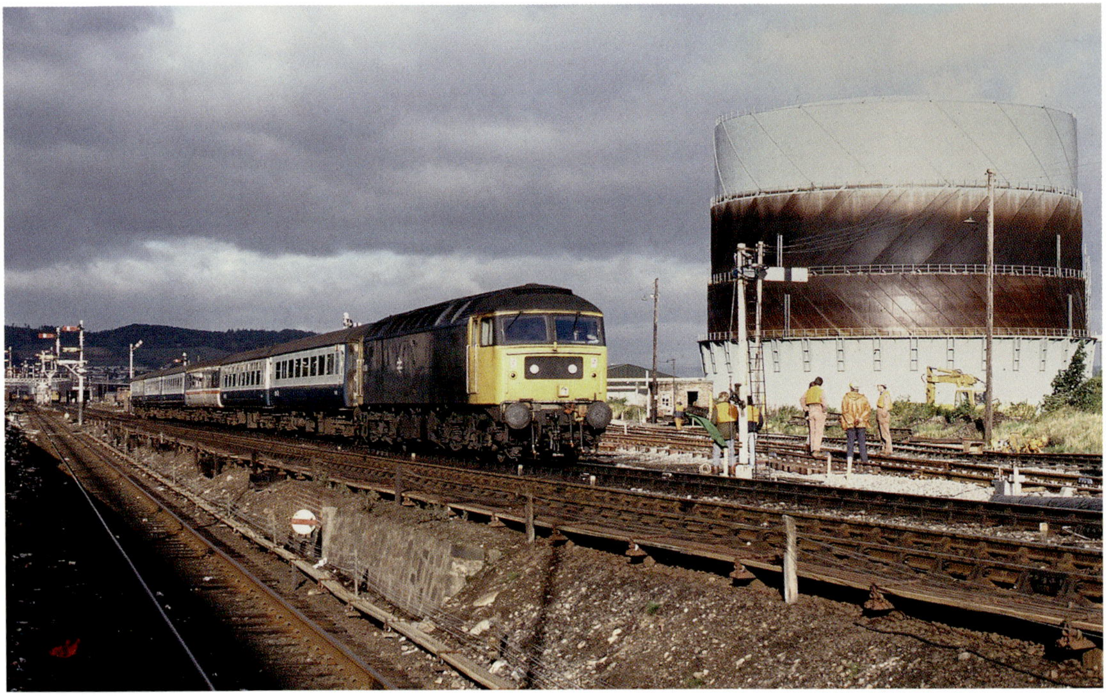

A Class 47 heads south past the yards at Inverness on 1 September 1986.

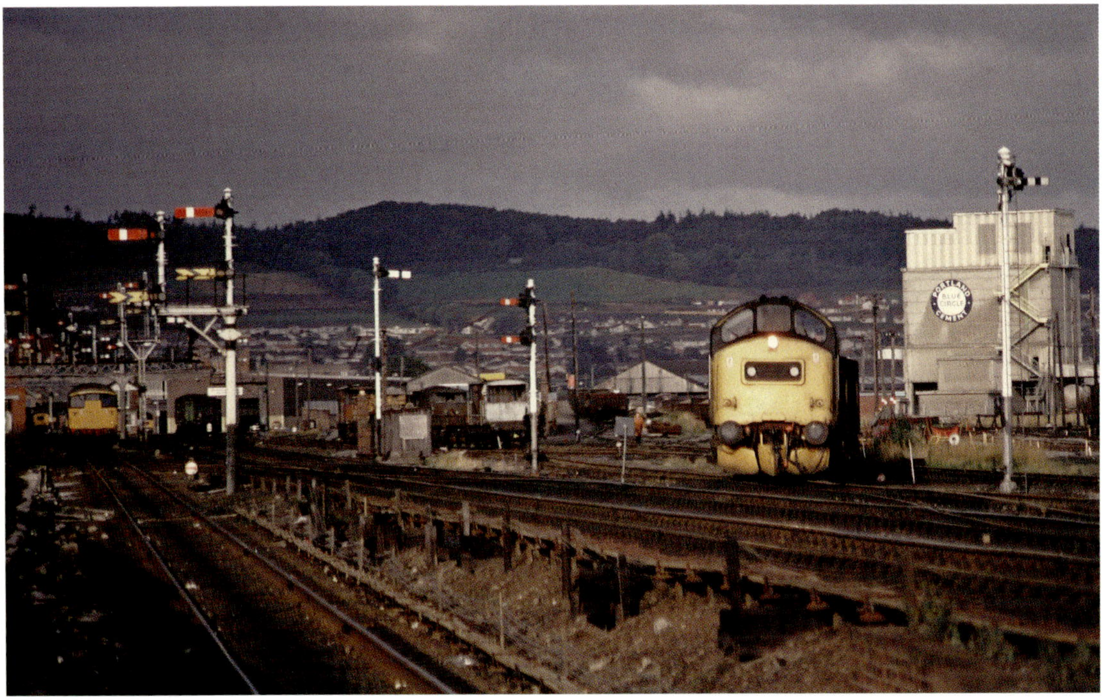

On the same day, a Class 37 shunts the yards. There is a fine array of semaphore signals visible as well as several other locomotives.

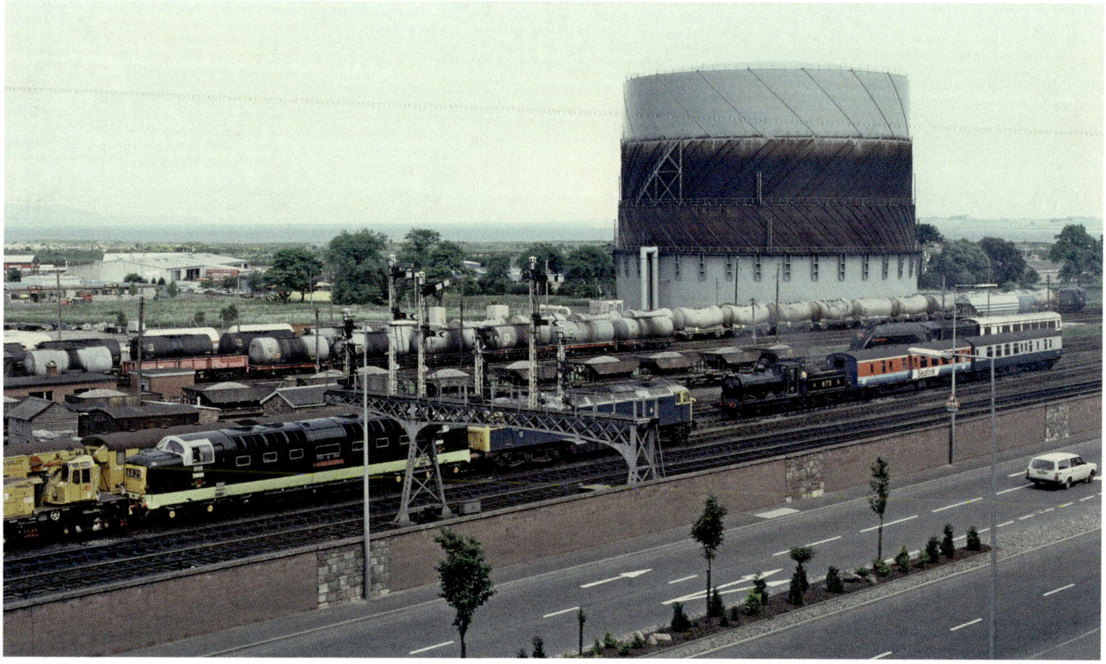

The Inverness yards are busy on 27 June 1986. No. 673 *Maude*, A4 No. 60009 and the Deltic D9000 are attending the Railfair the following day.

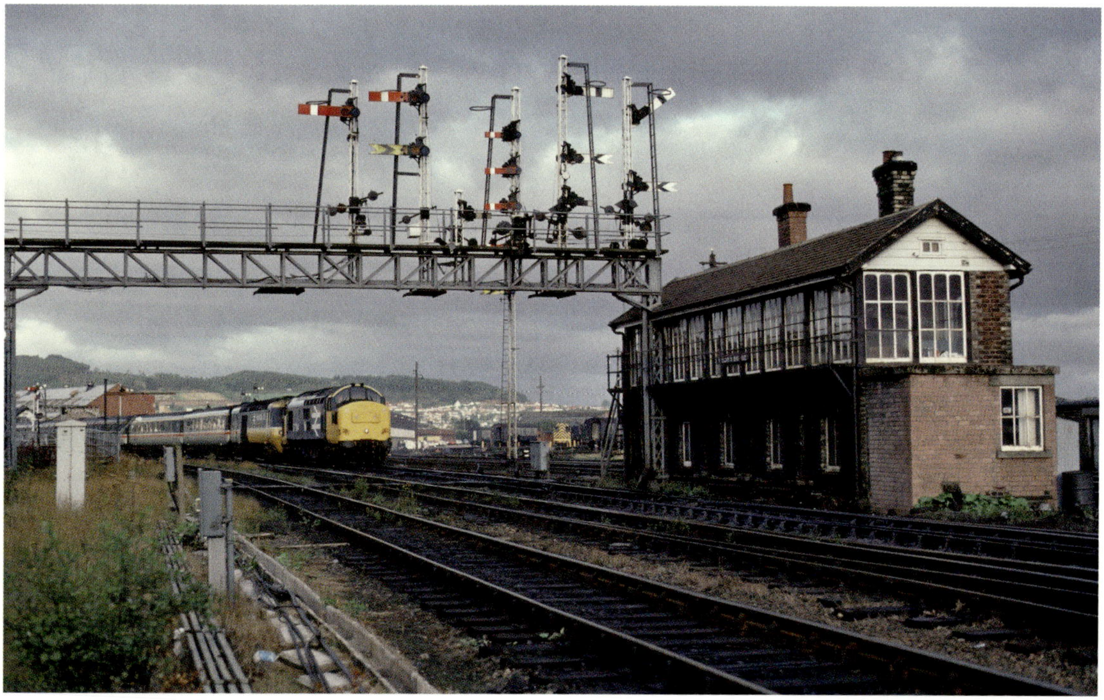

With Welsh's Bridge signal cabin and gantry in the foreground, Class 37 No. 37264 assists the HST to Kings Cross away from Inverness on 1 September 1986.

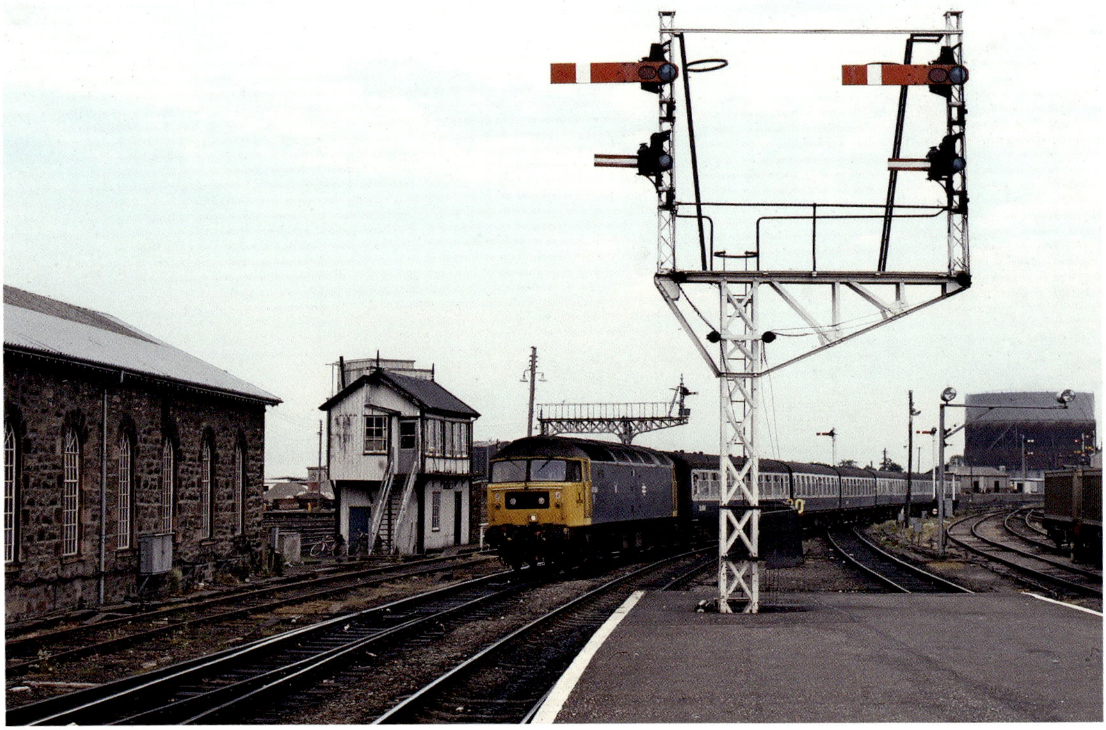

No. 47604 passes the Inverness Loco signal cabin on the approach to the station on 27 June 1986.

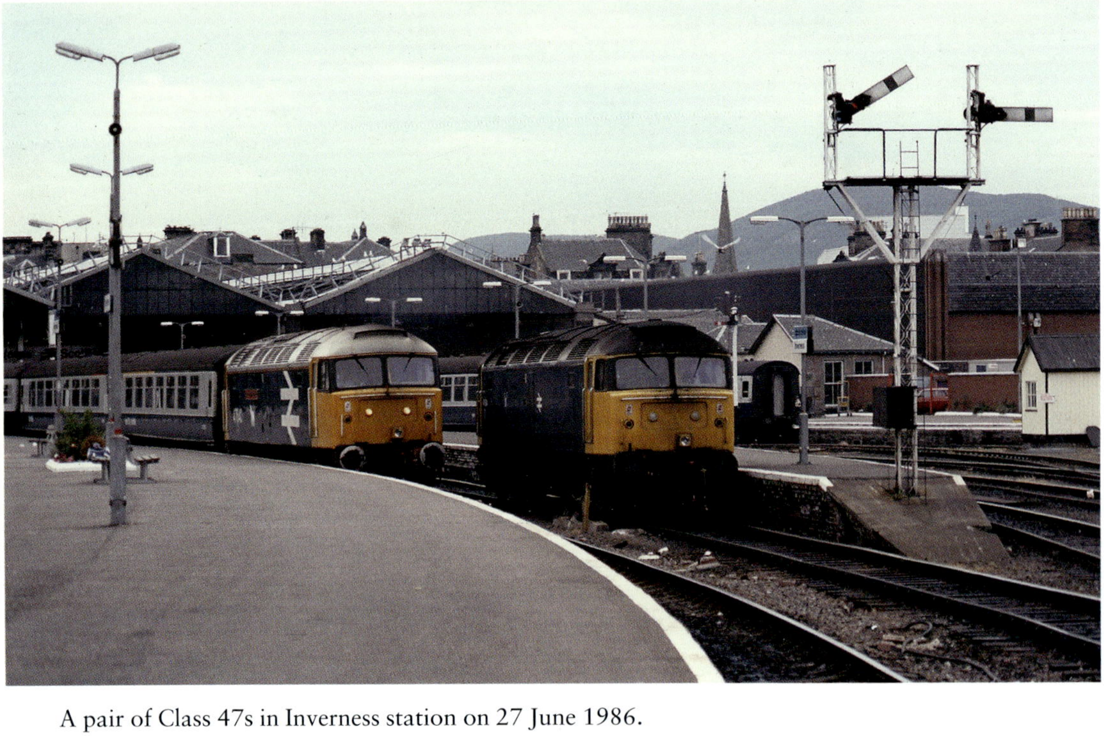

A pair of Class 47s in Inverness station on 27 June 1986.